Forbid Them Not

Involving Children in Sunday Worship

Based on the Revised Common Lectionary, Year C

Forbid
Them
Not

Carolyn C. Brown

Abingdon Press
Nashville

FORBID THEM NOT:
INVOLVING CHILDREN IN SUNDAY WORSHIP
Based on *The Revised Common Lectionary*, Year C

Copyright © 1991, 1994 by Abingdon Press

Where necessary, the materials contained herein based on the Scripture readings in the Common Lectionary have been altered or replaced to reflect the readings in the Revised Common Lectionary.

This book is printed on recycled, acid-free paper.

98 99 00 01 02 03 — 10 9 8 7 6 5

Library of Congress Cataloging-in-Publication Data

(Revised for vol. 3)
Brown, Carolyn C. (Carolyn Carter), 1947–
  Forbid them not.
  Includes indexes.
  Contents: Year A—Year B—Year C.
  1. Children in public worship. 2. Common lectionary (1992) 3. Worship (Religious education)
  I. Title.
BV26.2.B76   1991   264'.0083   90-45012
ISBN 0-687-13255-X (Year A : alk. paper)
ISBN 0-687-13256-8 (Year B : alk. paper)
ISBN 0-687-13265-7 (Year C : alk. paper)

All readings taken from *The Revised Common Lectionary* © 1992 by the Consultation on Common Texts are used by permission.
Quotations from the *Good News Bible*—Old Testament are copyright © American Bible Society 1976; New Testament, copyright © American Bible Society 1966, 1971, 1976. Reprinted by permission.
Those from The New Jerusalem Bible are copyright © 1985 by Darton, Longman & Todd and Doubleday & Co., Inc. Reprinted by permission of the publishers.
Those from the *Holy Bible: New International Version* are copyright © 1973, 1978, 1984 by the International Bible Society. Used by permission of Zondervan Bible Publishers.
Those from the New Revised Standard Version of the Bible, Copyright © 1989 by the Division of Christian Education of the National Council of the Churches of Christ in the USA are used by permission.

MANUFACTURED IN THE UNITED STATES OF AMERICA

CONTENTS

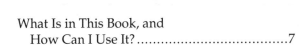

This volume follows the new Revised Common Lectionary. Where necessary, the materials of the 1991 version for Year C (based on the Common Lectionary) have been altered or replaced to reflect the new Scripture readings.

*Because the lections for a few special days in the lectionary are the same in all years, material for these days appears in only one year (A, B, or C), with appropriate cross references in the table of contents.

WHAT IS IN THIS BOOK, AND HOW CAN I USE IT ?

There seem to be two opposing camps when it comes to children's participation in congregational worship. On one side are those who say that worship is really for adults—that children should be taught to behave until they appreciate what is going on, or that they (and their parents) should be relieved by the provision of a children's church or other activity during the worship hour. On the other side are those who say that the congregation's worship should be reworked entirely, to make it appealing to children. Proponents of this side claim that once adults loosen up and begin to worship as children worship, they will not miss the staid old adult-oriented forms.

This series carves out a middle ground, based on the convictions that

• children *do* belong in the sanctuary, worshiping with God's people; that

• worship planners are responsible for creating worship experiences that are meaningful to all who come to the sanctuary, including children, youths, and adults (this does not require that all worshipers find all parts of worship equally meaningful, but that each worshiper has some appreciation for the whole, and special appreciation for certain parts within the whole); and that

• children can worship meaningfully, using traditional forms, *if* they are learning the meaning of those forms, and *if* the forms include content that reflects *their* lives and concerns as well as those of adults.

This book is written for worship leaders who share these views and want to be responsive to the elementary-school-aged children in worship, but who are uncertain about how to do this effectively and do not have large amounts of time to develop their skills in this area. It is written for those whose consciousness has been raised by books which advocate the inclusion of children in congregational worship, but who are at a loss for "what to do this Sunday."

This series offers specific suggestions for prayers, litanies, sermon illustrations, and ways to present Scripture that will include children without offending adults. Although it is based on the texts of the Revised Common Lectionary, those who do not follow that lectionary can use the index to locate suggestions related to any Scripture passages.

This series could be used by the pastor who plans worship alone, by a staff team, by a liturgical team which includes both clergy and laity, or by a worship committee. It is a reference to be used with commentaries and liturgical resources in preparing a service for each Sunday. As you gain confidence and insight into what is meaningful for children in your congregation, the ideas here should become springboards to other ideas and to home-grown prayers, litanies, and so on.

Materials for each Sunday include:

From a Child's Point of View, a commentary on each of the readings for the day. The main ideas of each passage are expressed in children's terms and connected to children's concerns. On Sundays when there is a reading that is best for children, that reading is presented first. When there is no central theme or focal reading, the texts are presented in lectionary order.

Watch Words offers vocabulary helps, warning against words that are beyond the understanding of elementary children or that are easily misunderstood by them; it suggests words that speak clearly to worshipers of all ages.

Let the Children Sing suggests several hymns (chosen from church hymnals) that are related to the Scripture themes, and which children can sing—at least in part. The assumption here is not that every hymn sung in worship ought to be child-accessible, but that one or two each week could be. These hymns have been chosen because they have concrete language, themes to which children respond, or tunes that are easily sung. Some have been included because of the repetition of a word, phrase, or chorus which even a nonreader can sing each time it appears—for instance, the Alleluias in "Christ the Lord Is Risen Today."

The Liturgical Child outlines a variety of ways to use the passages in worship to bring them alive for children (and adults). Specific directions for dramatic readings, litanies, and congregational readings are given for some passages. Children's prayer concerns related to the theme or time of year are listed for inclusion in the congregation's prayers. And possibilities are raised for relating other parts of the worship service to the day's theme for children. No worship planner will use every idea offered for every week, but can select several that will fit the worship experience planned for the congregation.

Sermon Resources are offered in the belief that children do listen to at least parts of sermons and can learn from those parts. These resources are offered to be included in the "real" sermon rather than in a segregated children's sermon. The assumption is that if we communicate to children that the sermon is for them too, they will learn to listen to more and more of it as their attention span for verbal messages grows. So this section includes potential sermon illustrations and stories that will catch the attention of children and also will speak to adults, based on their childhood experience. Occasional sermon-related assignments for children to do during the sermon will be found here as well.

Finally, for each week there will be a one-page **Worship Worksheet**—a sheet of games, puzzles, or questions related to the day's passages. Just as children often work on projects (even homework) while they watch TV, they are often more apt to listen to the sermon if they have something to do with their hands.

When the minister expresses interest in their worksheets as the children leave the sanctuary, posts the sheets on a bulletin board in the narthex, or refers to them during the sermon, children can see that this activity is one way they can participate in worship. Both parents and children will realize that the Worship Worksheets are not just a clever attempt to keep children quiet so that the adults can worship.

The purchase of this book gives you permission to reproduce these Worship Worksheets for your children each week. Look carefully at each worksheet before reproducing it. Some, especially those for Propers in which the readings do not share one central theme, offer two half-page activities, each related to a separate theme. Choose the one that goes with your worship theme and enlarge it to full-page size on a copy machine. Then reproduce that page for the children. Unless they are enlarged, the half-page activities may not provide enough space for children to work.

The Worship Worksheets can be distributed by ushers as children enter the sanctuary, left in a designated place for the children or parents to pick up, or they can be placed in a Worship Kit.

A Worship Kit could be a large paper envelope or sealable plastic bag containing the Sunday bulletin, the Worship Worksheet, a small pencil, and bookmarks for marking the hymns and readings for the morning. Bookmarks can be made of strips of poster board decorated with appropriate stickers. To emphasize the church year, poster board of liturgically correct colors could be used. An older children's class, a group of teenagers, or an adult may be willing to prepare such bookmarks as a contribution to the congregation's worship life. Children can be asked to leave the bookmarks and pencil in the envelope, and the envelopes can be placed on their seats, to be picked up for use the next week.

Note: In some congregations the Worship Worksheets may be difficult to reproduce. Worship leaders in such congregations may focus their efforts on other suggestions.

ADVENT FROM A CHILD'S POINT OF VIEW

The church year officially begins with a very adult season—Advent. During Advent we await and get ready for One who has already come—a rather strange thing to do, from a child's point of view.

As adults we can speak of God's kingdom which came in Christ and is yet to come in its fullness. We can celebrate the coming of the Child in the manger and ask how fully we welcome Jesus and his message into our hearts today. But those who study child development tell us that until the age of eight or nine, children have great difficulty in comprehending time. So to talk about a king who came, who is coming, and who will come is talking nonsense.

It is tempting to avoid such difficulties and have the children simply count down the days until Christmas, make decorations, and prepare gifts. But this passes over the real meaning of the season, some of which can be presented to children.

Children can hear the stories of people who waited for Jesus. They can celebrate Ruth, the outsider who was an ancestor of Jesus. They can hear John's insistence that all people work together to make the world a more loving place while they wait for Jesus. They can bask in the prophetic promises that God will always love and care for them—will even come to live with them. Each of the lections for the season has a message children can appreciate when it is appropriately presented to them.

In addition, the candles, evergreens, flowers, and special music of Advent can speak to children in the language of feelings and senses. These things will speak more clearly if we shape them with the children's presence in mind.

We can include the children actively in lighting an Advent wreath during worship. In more for-mal churches, members of an older children's class can take turns being acolytes (complete with robes) to light the candles, while a teenager or adult reads an appropriate Scripture or meditation. Families can also light the Advent wreath, the entire family coming forward to light the candles and make the statement. (If you use families, be sure to include single-parent families and families of all shapes and sizes.) We can further increase the significance of the Advent wreath by helping families create wreaths to light in their homes. (Many religious bookstores provide orders of family worship for lighting the Advent wreath.)

We can help the children recall the story of biblical waiting and preparation by moving crèche pieces around the sanctuary toward the manger. The pieces can be moved before worship each week, and their movement mentioned in the sermon or Scriptures of the day. Or the pieces can be moved during worship—perhaps as part of a children's sermon.

We can decorate trees with Chrismons. If the congregation already has a Chrismon tree, we can help children learn the meaning of the symbols. We can use the ornaments to make points in sermons, or we can make one ornament the center of attention each week in worship. We can even hang some simple child-made Chrismons on the tree.

We can include the children in the special music of the season. Young instrumentalists can play a carol as the prelude. A children's class can become a one-Sunday choir—even if you do not usually have a children's choir. In a day when religious carols are not taught in many schools, we in the church need to make an extra effort to pass on our musical heritage. The quoting or exploring of verses of carols within the sermon, or the carefully planned introductions to hymns can make congregational singing prime teaching opportunities.

Think about each of the Advent traditions of your church. Which are child-accessible? How could they be more so? The answers to these questions can more often lead to honing what is already being done, than to adding new programming to an already hectic season.

FIRST SUNDAY OF ADVENT

From a Child's Point of View

Old Testament: Jeremiah 33:14-16. The child's cry, "But, it's not fair!" reminds us that justice and fairness are big concerns for children. They yearn for teachers, parents, and playmates who are fair. They want just rules for the groups in which they participate and the games they play. They protest vehemently when they sense injustice—especially when it affects them. Therefore Jeremiah's Advent promise—that when God's kingdom comes fully, there will be justice for everyone and a leader who deals with people fairly—is good news for children.

The words of the promise, however, need to be decoded for children. Before the passage is read, Children need to hear that "house of Judah" and "house of Israel" are names for God's people; and that when God made this promise, God's people, being ruled by cruel foreigners, felt as hopeful as an old dead stump. It also helps them to see, or hear described, the possibility of a fresh branch growing from a stump.

Psalm: 25:1-10. This passage is a personal prayer, asking God that I be treated well by others, that God teach me how to live, and that God not remember all my sins and shortcomings. It is a prayer for people of all ages.

Epistle: I Thessalonians 3:9-13. In this loving message to friends in the church at Thessalonica, Paul prays that God will help them love one another and the people beyond their church as much as Paul and God love them. To love others that much is a good Advent challenge for children.

Gospel: Luke 21:25-36. This apocalyptic passage is filled with images that are not easy for children to understand, and an idea (that we should watch and be prepared) that is hard for children to grasp. It is probably best to read the passage for the older worshipers and present the idea for the children during the sermon.

One interpretation of this passage that speaks to children is that some frightening, horrible things happen in human experience, but that God is still in control and will be there for us even after "the worst." Given this, we are called to avoid both (1) worrying too much about the awful things and (2) ignoring the awful things by partying and being self-centered. Instead, we are to remember that God is in control, and we are to live accordingly.

Warning: Do not underestimate the "horrible things" children worry about. At an early age they see television's graphic pictures of war, famine, natural disasters, and the potential for nuclear annihilation. Many see the devastation of divorce in their own families or in those of their friends. More children than we wish have been mugged by older kids and know the fear of participating in the drug culture. Children need to know that God will see them through even these "horrible things." They also need to hear that such things are the products of our imperfect age and that when God's kingdom comes in its fullness, those things will end.

Watch Words

Avoid *tribulation, affliction,* and other big words that describe suffering. They are obsolete. Instead, use specific, concrete words to describe wars, natural disasters, and personal tragedies.

Be careful about using *righteousness*. If children have heard the word at all, it has probably been used with a negative connotation, such as *self-righteous*. Instead, speak about living by God's rules, or take time to explore what righteousness means today.

Children use the word *fair* before they use *justice*. Using the words interchangeably will help make the connection between them.

Let the Children Sing

"Come, Thou Long Expected Jesus" is filled with difficult, unfamiliar vocabulary. But when it is sung after a sermon about Jeremiah's promise, older children, when encouraged, can find phrases that identify Jesus as the promised "righteous branch."

The words of "O Come, O Come, Emmanuel" are beyond most elementary-school readers. But the sad, "stumpy" feeling of the music of the verses and the happy, hopeful music of the chorus attract them. Invite even young readers to feel the sad sound of the verses, and then sing along on the simple-to-read happy chorus.

"Song of Hope" offers a straightforward message in words that are easy to read and understand. If the Argentine folk melody is unfamiliar, ask a children's choir or class to sing the hymn at the close of the service.

The Liturgical Child

1. For your worship area, ask someone to create a banner picturing a branch growing out of a stump, with the words of Jeremiah. Or replace the usual flowers with a stump from which a branch is growing. (This may be a real stump into which a seedling or leafed branch has been drilled. Or it may be a potted seedling wrapped with brown paper or burlap to look like a stump.) Refer to this display before reading Jeremiah's promise, urging worshipers to listen for the unusual stump in the reading.

2. In the congregation's prayers, pray for fair teachers, coaches, community leaders, and government officials. Also, ask for God's wisdom to see unjust situations at home, at school, on the job, and in the community, and for God's courage to do what we can to change them. Ask the choir to sing "Lead Me, Lord, in Thy Righteousness" (a paraphrase of Psalm 25:4-5) as a choral call to this prayer.

3. Psalm 25 is best understood and claimed when it is read in its original responsive form from a translation such as *Today's English Version*, the Good News Bible. So invite the congregation (or half the congregation) to read verses 1-7, with the understanding that they are "I." A worship leader (or the other half of the congregation) then can assume the priest's part and read verses 8-10 to assure the worshipers that God wants the same things for them.

4. One effective use of the Epistle passage would be to recite verses 12 and 13 from the Good News Bible as the charge and benediction with which worship concludes.

Sermon Resources

1. Even if you do not use the Worship Worksheets, challenge children to draw a picture of an unjust or unfair situation *and* a picture of the same people in the same situation acting justly or fairly. Provide blank space on the worship bulletin or suggest using the back of a pew card. Invite them to share the pictures with you as they leave the sanctuary. Take time to learn what caused the difference in the two pictures.

2. Everyone likes stories in which seemingly hopeless situations come to a happy ending. The beast in *Beauty and the Beast* felt hopelessly trapped by the spell that could be broken only when a woman loved him. Kevin, accidentally left behind by his family in *Home Alone,* had to defend himself and his home from robbers. Jeremiah promises that one day God will bring all the unfair, seemingly hopeless situations in our world to fair, happy solutions. (*Beauty and the Beast* is the richer example because two people must learn to love before the situation is resolved.) Both videos are available in video rental stores and many public libraries.

Color each space that has a dot in it to fill in the missing word.

Today we begin the season of _____.

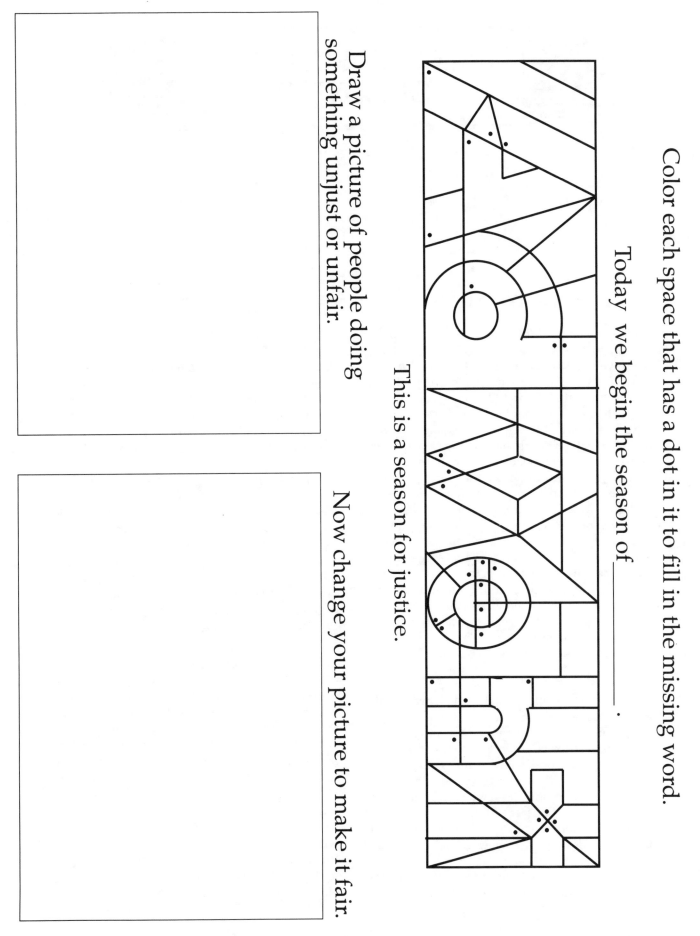

This is a season for justice.

Draw a picture of people doing something unjust or unfair.

Now change your picture to make it fair.

SECOND SUNDAY OF ADVENT

From a Child's Point of View

Old Testament: Malachi 3:1-4. Malachi spoke harshly to people who expected God to endorse whatever they were doing. He warned of the coming of a messenger who would bring "strong soap" and "refiner's fire." Today's soap (except some shampoo) seldom burns, and few children have experience with refiner's fires. But children do know that hurting is sometimes part of healing and that discipline leads to strength. Medicine that stings, painful therapy for a broken bone, and sport disciplines teach them this. Still, Malachi's idea that God may come as a demanding coach or teacher, rather than as a supportive, somewhat indulgent parent, may be new to children. So explain that Malachi's message means that to be fully God's people, they must be disciplined and obedient to God. Point out specific disciplines such as attending worship and church school, obeying God's rules, practicing peacemaking, and seeking justice every day. Challenge the children to choose an Advent discipline.

OR Baruch 5:1-9. While Malachi spoke harshly when he told people to change their ways, this poet called people to change with an offer of hope. The image of changing dresses in verses 1-4 is the easiest for children to understand. They need to hear lots of specific examples of how people feel and act when they are dressed in sorrow and distress, and how those who are wrapped in God's saving justice feel and act. The translation of the New Jerusalem Bible suggests some of these examples (e.g., the names given in verse 4).

Gospel: Luke 3:1-6. Child-development experts have found that children cannot interpret symbolic imagery until late childhood or even early adolescence. This means that calls to fill in the valleys, bring the hills low, and make crooked paths straight can sound like calls to massive construction projects. Even children who sense that these calls are not to be taken literally need help to convert them into sensible calls to repentance. One way to help is to provide parallel examples from everyday life (e.g., straighten out your life, live by God's rules, treat others more kindly).

Epistle: Philippians 1:3-11. While John the Baptist and Malachi speak harshly to people who need to repent, Paul writes to encourage people who are repenting. Paul gives repentance a good name and feel. He indicates that all Christians are always repenting, and he offers those who repent his love and support in their efforts. Use this passage to help children understand repentance as a positive, lifelong activity for Christians, as individuals and as congregations.

Today's Psalm: Luke 1:68-79: Children's interest in this prayer is based more on context than content. They are curious about the old priest who did not believe the angel who promised him and his elderly wife a baby and consequently was struck speechless until the promised child was born. They can imagine his silent excitement as he waited for the birth of the two special babies in his family and appreciate his burst of praise when John was born and his speech returned. They do have trouble following Zechariah's praises, filled with abstract words and Old Testament images. When they know Zechariah's story and are urged to listen for prayers about Jesus and about John, older children can catch occasional phrases.

Watch Words

They key word is *repent*. Be sure the children understand the difference between being sorry about something and repenting. We can be sorry about failing a spelling test because we did not study. But when we repent, we make time to study so we can pass the test next week. It is easy to be sorry we cannot get along with a difficult person at school or at work. But when we repent, we work to improve our relationship with that person.

Let the Children Sing

A good choice is "Lord, I Want to Be a Christian."

"Open My Eyes, That I May See" and "Take My Life and Let It Be Consecrated" have some difficult vocabulary. But their references to "using our bodies to repent" make them understandable to children.

The Liturgical Child

1. Bring these Scriptures to life with very dramatic readings. Let Malachi and John the Baptist thunder in your best street-corner-preacher style. Shake your fist and point your finger for emphasis. Take the role of Zechariah as he praised God and rejoiced over the birth of his son John. (Ask an older man to come in costume, carrying a doll or an infant, to recite Zechariah's prayer.) In reading Paul's letter, imagine yourself in prison writing to friends you love and miss. Let that love show in your voice.

2. To give a personal twist to Paul's message, suggest that worshipers listen as if Paul were speaking to them individually and/or to the congregation.

3. Challenge children (and adults) to write about or draw a picture of some repenting they want to do during Advent. Invite them to place their paper in the offering plate as an Advent commitment to God. Instruct ushers to respect the privacy of those notes and pictures.

4. Lead corporate prayer, with pauses for individual prayer about repenting:

Lord, we hear John and Malachi call us to repent, but we think they must be talking to someone else. We do not often stop to think about the repenting we need to do. Help us to look honestly at ourselves.

We know we need to repent in our families. It is strange but true that we often treat members of our families with less care than we give strangers. We expect others in our family to accept us when we feel cross and tired, but we are not so ready to put up with them when they are fussy. Help us see the changes we need to make in our families. (Pause)

And we know we are not always kind and loving at school or at work. We want things done our way. We become angry when our work or our ideas are criticized or when we get bad grades. There are people we need to forgive, but we do not. Help us make some changes, God. (Pause)

Lord, we are all members of groups. We are Scouts, Jaycees, Women's Leaguers, Virginians, and Americans (adapt to fit your congregation). We enjoy these groups, but we know we are to work in them for your peace and justice. Sometimes it is easier to go along with the others than to stand up for your ways. Help us change the groups to which we belong. (Pause)

God, be with us during Advent as we repent. Help us see the changes we need to make, and give us the courage and power to make them; for we pray in Jesus' name. Amen.

Sermon Resource

The movie *Karate Kid*, which many children and parents have seen, provides a current example of Malachi's "strong soap" or "refiner's fire." After agreeing to teach him karate, the old master puts the boy to work—washing and polishing cars, then sanding and painting a long wooden fence. After a while the boy objects that this is not what he came to do. The wise teacher then demonstrates that the work has strengthened his muscles and made certain crucial moves second nature. If you have not seen this fine movie/video, do so now as sermon preparation—and for a treat!

REPENT means to change our ways.
John the Baptist said, "REPENT! God's Kingdom
   is coming!"
Write REPENT in the box below every time you hear
   it, say it, or sing it in worship today.

You may have to repent many times to find your
   way through this maze to Christmas Joy.

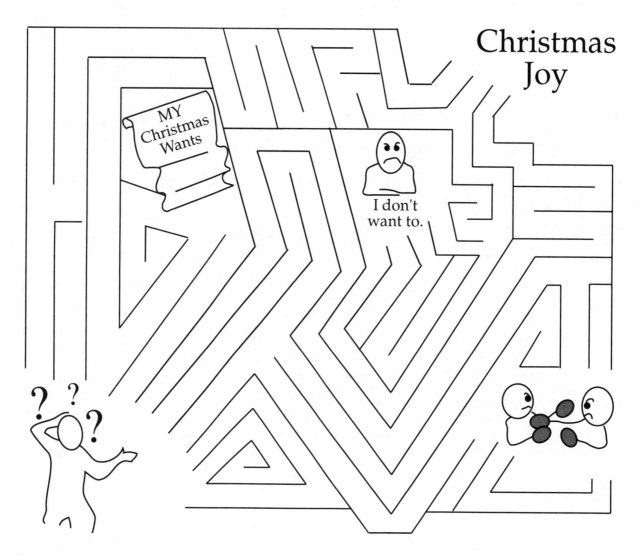

THIRD SUNDAY OF ADVENT

From a Child's Point of View

"God is at work in and through history, reconciling all the world to himself." In children's words, God has a plan that we all will become friends with one another and with God. God is working on this plan every day. God has the power to make this plan work, and God wants us to help.

Old Testament: Zephaniah 3:14-20. To fully understand the word pictures in this poem, the hearer must have detailed knowledge of Old Testament history. Most children do not. However, if they are told that when the prophet spoke of Jerusalem and Zion, he also was speaking of all God's people (even us today), and if they are challenged to listen to the passage as if it were addressed to each of them as one of God's people (which it is), then they can grasp the prophet's message that God's plan has a good ending for them and that God has the power to make this plan a reality.

Psalm: Isaiah 12:2-6. This song of praise was included in today's lections as a response to the messages of Zephaniah, John the Baptist, and Paul. It is full of short, simple phrases praising the strong, active God who saves us.

Gospel: Luke 3:7-18. When reading this passage with the other lections for the day, do not place the emphasis on John's call to repentance, but on his expectation of One who is coming from God; One so great that John is not worthy to tie his shoelaces; One who will baptize us with the Holy Spirit; and, yes, One who will judge us.

John's sense of expectation might be compared to the way an eight-year-old would feel if Michael Jordan were coming to coach her basketball team, or if she were going to study with a New York ballet company. Joy, excitement, fear of higher standards, and hope for what she could become as she works with some of the best instructors in the world, would be all rolled up together. Expectantly, she would practice harder to be ready. With this as a frame of reference, children can sense John's excitement that God is coming to live among us; they can understand John's insistence that we get ready by working harder to live up to God's standards.

Epistle: Philippians 4:4-9. Paul restates John's message to encourage his friends at Philippi. Paul's list (vs. 8) is abstract. Children will need help in identifying which kinds of interests and activities fall in each category (e.g., a backyard club may not be pure and noble if it cuts people out and encourages ridicule). The vocabulary in the New International Version of the Bible is the clearest for children.

Watch Words

Avoid theological generalities like *salvation* and *reconciliation.* Instead, talk about specifics. Praise God for specific saving events in the life of your congregation and community. Cite local examples of people who have become friends with one another and with God.

Let the Children Sing

"Rejoice, the Lord Is King" is a good choice because the chorus can be sung even by nonreading children.

"Now Thank We All Our God" is a praise hymn frequently suggested in church school materials. Its familiarity and concrete language make it another good choice.

The Liturgical Child

1. Plan for two people to read the Gospel—one to read the words of John the Baptist and the other to read the narrative. One reader could stand in the lectern, the other in the pulpit. Or a dramatic "John," perhaps in costume, could memorize his lines, come through a side door, speak from the front of the sanctuary, and leave. In preparation for either approach, practice with "John" answering the questioners in verses 10-14 in a way that would encourage the questioners to prepare for the wonderful One who is coming, rather than berate them.

2. Read Zephaniah 3:14-20 (GNB) responsively to get the happy feel of these promises. Assign half the congregation to read #1 and the other half to read #2. Read "ALL" in unison.

ALL: Sing and shout for joy, people of Israel! Rejoice with all your heart, Jerusalem!
#1: The LORD has stopped your punishment;
#2: he has removed all your enemies.
#1: The LORD, the king of Israel, is with you;
#2: there is no reason now to be afraid.
ALL: The time is coming when they will say to Jerusalem,
#1: "Do not be afraid, city of Zion!
#2: Do not let your hands hang limp!
ALL: The LORD your God is with you; his power gives you victory.
#1: The LORD will take delight in you.
#2: and in his love he will give you new life.
#1: He will sing and be joyful over you,
#2: as joyful as people at a festival."
ALL: The LORD says,
#1: "I have ended the threat of doom
#2: and taken away your disgrace.
ALL: The time is coming!
#1: I will punish your oppressors;
#2: I will rescue all the lame
#1: and bring the exiles home.
#2: I will turn their shame to honor, and all the world will praise them.

ALL: The time is coming!
#1: I will bring your scattered people home;
#2: I will make you famous throughout the world and make you prosperous once again."
ALL: The LORD has spoken.

3. Present (reciting if possible) the Philippians text as a personal charge to worshipers just before the benediction.

Sermon Resources

1. Spin a tale in which children in your town prepare for the arrival of Michael Jordan, who is to coach their basketball team.

2. If you focus on the questions to John about what preparations to make, challenge the children (and other worshipers) to imagine what John would say to them during this Advent season, if they were to ask, "What should I do, John?" To prime their thinking, re-create John's encounter to include people of today. Try a few safely obvious ones, such as:

The sports professionals asked, "What shall we do?" and John replied, "Be content with reasonable salaries. Play fair."

But also tackle students, businessmen, Christmas gift buyers, and so on.

3. If you have a Chrismon tree in your sanctuary, point out and describe the significance of ornaments that relate to today's theme. Consider some of the following:

- Cross Over the World—God has a wonderful plan for the whole world. God's plan will be successful.
- Jerusalem Cross—God's plan began with Jesus in Jerusalem and spread to the four corners of the earth.
- Crowns—Jesus is King!

Draw a picture of God's work in each box.

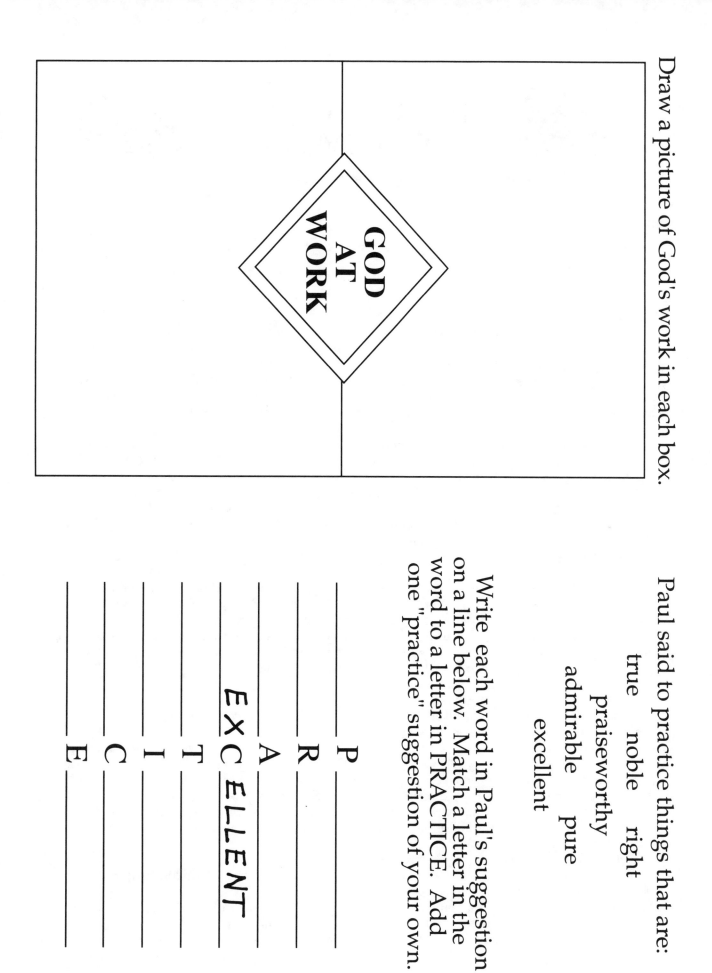

GOD
AT
WORK

Paul said to practice things that are:

true   noble   right

praiseworthy

admirable   pure

excellent

Write each word in Paul's suggestion on a line below. Match a letter in the word to a letter in PRACTICE. Add one "practice" suggestion of your own.

P _____

R _____

A _____

EXCELLENT

T _____

I _____

C _____

E _____

FOURTH SUNDAY OF ADVENT

From a Child's Point of View

Today's Scriptures celebrate God's choice of small, insignificant people and places, for the big, exciting tasks. For children who often feel small, insignificant, and overlooked, this offers hope.

Old Testament: Micah 5:2-5a. Micah announces that God's promised leader will not come from a big, famous city, but from Bethlehem, the littlest town in one of the smallest tribes in the Jewish nation. That's like being born in a small town in the smallest state or province in the country. Comparing Bethlehem to an insignificant town in your area gives it reality.

Gospel: Luke 1:39-45 and Psalm: Luke 1:46b-55. Mary praises God for choosing her, a poor nobody, to be the mother of the Messiah. Although adults may wish she had been a bit more humble, children can identify with her excitement: "From now on people will call me happy, because of the great things the Mighty God has done for me" (48b-49 GNB). Any child who has ever been chosen last for a ball game or a spelling bee can appreciate being chosen first, over much more likely candidates.

Older children can hear Mary celebrate God's preference for the poor and overlooked. For children who do experience poverty and oppression in their daily lives, this is welcome news. For children who know they are among "the proud," "the mighty," and "the rich," it is as disconcerting as it is for their parents. But this message can remind them not to look down on those who wear poorer clothes, have less money, are less gifted, or are less "anything" than they are. It can remind all children that being the biggest, the best, or the most is not God's main goal for their lives.

Alternate Psalm: 80:1-7. To understand this prayer, hearers need to know about the winged figures on the Ark of the Covenant; recognize the names of the tribes of Israel; and understand the situation during the Babylonian exile. This one is definitely for adult Bible students.

Epistle: Hebrews 10:5-10. The technical discussion of atonement theology is beyond children. The one phrase in this passage that can speak to them is Christ's statement, "Here I am, O God, to do your will." It echoes Mary's annunciation response: "I am the Lord's servant. Let it happen to me as you have said" (Luke 1:38 GNB). It calls each of us, no matter what our age, to do whatever God wants us to do. Children, although aware of the loving actions God would have them take (e.g., when a younger sibling wants help or a classmate is teasing unkindly), often choose easier, more self-serving courses. This passage reminds them that, like Jesus, they are to be God's obedient servants.

Watch Words

Fortunately, we have yet to invent a complicated word for God's tendency to work through the insignificant rather than the powerful. So vocabulary holds few traps today.

If you use the term *Magnificat* for Mary's song, explain its Latin origin.

Let the Children Sing

"O Little Town of Bethlehem," although it focuses on tiny Bethlehem, is not a carol children understand or generally choose to sing.

Either "Away in a Manger" or "Once in David's Royal City" stress the humbleness of Jesus' birth in children's language.

"My Soul Gives Glory to My God," based on Mary's song of praise, is a new hymn with simple words and a familiar tune.

The Liturgical Child

1. Invite two women to read the Gospel and Psalm. One (perhaps an older woman) might read the narration in verses 39-46a, and the other (perhaps a teenager) might read Mary's song in 46b-55. Practice with "Mary" to prepare a strong, dramatic reading full of feeling. The Good News Bible provides the clearest translation of Mary's song for children.

2. Create a litany prayer of petition and intercession. The congregation's response to each request is like Jesus statement: HERE WE ARE, O GOD, TO DO YOUR WILL. Include such prayers as:

> God of Christmas, we are filled with plans and hopes for this week. Some of us are excited about special gifts we have ready for those we love. Some of us are dreaming about gifts we might receive. Some of us are looking forward to visits with family or dear friends. Others of us face Christmas with less pleasure. Christmas looks more like a lonely endurance test. So we begin our before-Christmas prayers by asking you to be with us. In our excitement, keep us kind and loving. In our loneliness, keep us aware of the needs of others.
> (RESPONSE)
> God of Mary and Elizabeth, we pray for all the forgotten, unimportant people. We pray for those who are poor, who are sleeping in cars and under bridges. We pray for those who are hungry and do not know when they will have their next meal. We pray for people who are friendless, ignored, and pushed aside. We know that you care about each of these people. Be with us and show us ways to love them.
> (RESPONSE)
> God, who greeted the shepherds with "peace on earth," we pray for your peace on earth today . . . .
> (RESPONSE)

3. Before the offering plates are passed, point out that we can help to do God's will by giving money to support the ministry of the church. Name one or two familiar efforts that are funded by your congregation. Instruct worshipers to say (either silently or aloud), "Here I am, O God, to do your will" as they place their offering in the plate.

Sermon Resources

1. Remember some of the insignificant people God chose, such as Miriam, who advised a princess on the care of her brother; David, the youngest brother who became king; Esther, the pretty teenager who saved her people from a ruthless oppressor; and the scruffy bunch Jesus chose as his friends and disciples.

2. Tell the stories of the insignificant people God uses today, such as Samantha Smith, the Maine schoolgirl who wrote a letter to Mikhail Gorbachev urging peace. When Gorbachev invited Samantha to visit the Soviet Union, she became a goodwill ambassador between the United States and the Soviet Union. The Soviets printed a stamp with her picture on it. Such stories challenge children (and all of us unimportant people) to be God's servants where we are.

3. If there is a Chrismon tree in your sanctuary, point out and describe the significance of ornaments related to today's theme:

- Stars—Consider building a sermon around the stars on the tree, particularly if Christmas Eve is on the fourth Sunday of Advent or falls early in the week. You may have a five-pointed nativity star, the six-pointed star of David, and Creation Stars (these may have seven points, or lots of toothpick rays). Check a Chrismons book for descriptions of other star designs.
- Rose Centered on a Star—The rose is a symbol for both Mary and Jesus. Centered on a star, the rose reminds us that Mary's decision to do God's will made the star of Bethlehem possible.
- The Shepherd's Cross—This may be the one way to present the message of Psalm 80 to children—that the Messiah will lead us as a shepherd leads and cares for the sheep.

In the space below each letter, write the letter that comes before it in the alphabet. One has been done for you.

JESUS SAID...

I F S F   J   B N ,   P   H P E ,

"H ___ ___ ,

U P   E P   Z P V S   X J M M.

___ ___ ___ ___ ___ ___ ___ ."

Hebrews 10:7

Answer: Here I am, O God, to do your will.

Do you have your Christmas gifts ready? What will you give God for Christmas?

Draw or write about your gift for God in the package below.

To: God
From:

CHRISTMAS EVE/DAY
(FIRST PROPER)

From a Child's Point of View

Old Testament: Isaiah 9:2-7. This prophetic poem, with all its imagery, is a passage children can feel, rather than understand. It is best "felt" during a candlelight worship service. The one thing children need to know before hearing the poem is that the ruler it describes is Jesus. Although this is obvious to adults, it is not immediately clear to children.

The text makes more intellectual sense to children when the birth announcement in verses 6-7 is read and explored *before* they hear verses 2-5, which describe our response to that birth.

Psalm: 96. This psalm is a collection of short statements praising God. Most are easily understood by children, and those that are not are quickly followed by some that are. Again, the Good News Bible offers a clear translation in vocabulary children can understand.

Gospel: Luke 2:1-14 (15-20). The story is simple, powerful, and easy to follow. But do remember that even older children are still trying to put the details of this story, which they hear only one month a year, into coherent order. Few children understand why taxes made a trip necessary. Older children appreciate the hardship of the journey if the approximately sixty miles are compared to a similar distance in your area. Younger children are likely to define a manger as "a bed for baby Jesus" unless they are told of its other use as a feed trough for animals. With that background, children are able to make sense of the angels' clue that the shepherds would know they had found the right baby when they found a baby

in a manger. A manger was not a normal place to find a baby. "Glory to God in the highest," although commonly used in carols and on Christmas cards, requires explanation if it is to be more than "what the angels say at Christmas."

Epistle: Titus 2:11-14. Let's face it—on Christmas Eve or Christmas Day, few children will tune in to this theological reflection on the events of Luke's story and Isaiah's poem-prophecy. This passage is for adults.

Watch Words

Wrap Jesus in *soft cloths,* not *swaddling clothes.* Avoid *incarnation* and *salvation.* Instead, describe what God did in this very specific situation and how that affected the people in the story and us today.

Let the Children Sing

"Silent Night" is probably the most familiar carol. It is sung by children (and many adults) with emphasis on the feelings of the music, rather than with appreciation for the meaning of the words.

"There's a Star in the Sky" is less familiar but has simple words and a singable tune.

"Away in a Manger" is well known, but is viewed by many older children as a baby's song. So if you sing it, invite people of all ages to sing together, rather than ask the children to sing it while the adults listen. Older children generally feel exploited by such requests.

The Liturgical Child

1. Begin Christmas Eve worship in a darkened, quiet sanctuary. Read the Isaiah passage as candles around the sanctuary are lighted by one or several acolytes. Then invite the congregation to sing a Christmas praise song.

2. Although it cannot be proved, I think the angel choirs must have sung something like Psalm 96 when Jesus was born. It is easy to imagine groups of angels singing the short praise statements back and forth through the sky. So invite your congregation to join the angel choirs by reading the psalm responsively. Worship leaders and people could alternate, or the right side and left side of the congregation could alternate.

Group 1	Group 2
verse 1a	verse 1b
2a	2b
3a	3b
4	5
6a	6b
7a	7b
8a	8b
9	10
11-12a	12b-13a
13b	13c

Or a Sunday school class (perhaps fourth- through sixth-graders) could prepare in advance to read the psalm responsively during the service.

3. Although there have been other pageants during the season, consider staging a simple pageant of Luke's account during the reading. Ask a couple with a baby to be Mary, Joseph, and Jesus. Find another family with several children to be the shepherds. A third group can be angels—or the angels can be left to the imagination. A manger is the only prop needed. The actors, wearing simple costumes, walk through the story as it is read from Luke. One forty-five minute rehearsal before the service is adequate preparation when adults and children are working in teams.

Note: For families new in town, this can be a very special Christmas Eve experience in their new church.

This pageant could take the place of the sermon at a family service. Or the acts of the story could be interspersed with carols and prayers in a lessons-and-carols format as the outline of the entire service. At the end of the service, invite the congregation to get a closer look as they file quietly out of the sanctuary, or send the actors on their way in accord with the story.

Sermon Resources

1. Children are not ready to listen to sermons on Christmas Eve or Christmas Day. For them, a lively presentation of the Scriptures for the day and a chance to sing and pray in a setting that involves all their senses are most effective.

2. There is no Worship Worksheet for Christmas Eve or Christmas Day. Worship on this day should be so full of feeling and the story that paper and pencils would deter rather than help children enter worship.

FIRST SUNDAY AFTER CHRISTMAS

From a Child's Point of View

All of us, both children and adults, are always growing. To the delight of children, today's readings ask adults to follow the example of two growing children, rather than ask that children follow the example of adults.

Old Testament: I Samuel 2:18-20, 26. This story offers two important messages for children. First, Samuel wore "the sacred linen apron." That is, he had an important job at the Temple. He wasn't just watching the grown-ups work. (What mission and worship work do the children of your congregation do?) Second, while Samuel was growing up, he was respected by people of all ages and by God. Remind the children that their gifts and ideas also are appreciated and respected *now.*

Warning: Even though Samuel was not living with his parents, they continued to love and care for him. They were proud of his special place at the Temple. God did not ask Samuel's parents to abandon Samuel, nor will God ask the children's parents to give them away. It is easy for children to miss this truth.

Psalm: 148. This is a call to praise that children appreciate. Younger children, who still attribute human capabilities to all parts of creation, take the psalm literally and enjoy hearing the poet call on animals, weather, and plants to join in praising God. Older children who realize that inanimate objects cannot praise in the same way humans do, but who do not yet grasp the poetry of mountains or wind praising God, are more comfortable in calling on a variety of groups of people to do the praising. The simple words and familiar vocabulary enable middle-elementary children to read with the congregation.

Epistle: Colossians 3:12-17. These verses can be viewed as Paul's guidelines for growing up as a Christian. Paul informs us that how we do our growing-up work is important. Whether we are learning to ride a bicycle, struggling to learn math at school, or trying to cope with a neighborhood bully, we are to be compassionate, kind, humble, gentle, and so forth. If we do this, we will grow in wisdom and favor with God and with people—just as Samuel and Jesus did.

Gospel: Luke 2:41-52. This story about Jesus at age twelve echoes that of young Samuel. Again, the child is respected in the congregation. In this story, Jesus' questions and ideas are taken seriously. So adults are called to listen to children and talk with them about our faith, and children are called to learn all they can about God and to ask all their questions—even the ones that may sound odd.

Watch Words

Speak simply of the everyday business of growing up.

Let the Children Sing

"O Come, All Ye Faithful" and "Joy to the World!" are appropriate for the Sunday after Christmas and are known by most children. The words to "O Come, All Ye Faithful" are easier for children to understand.

"O Sing a Song of Bethlehem" traces Jesus' growing up with simple words and a singable tune.

"All Creatures of Our God and King" parallels the praises of Psalm 148. Even nonreaders can join in on the Alleluias.

The Liturgical Child

1. See the First Sunday After Christmas of Year A of this series for directions on reading Psalm 148 responsively.

2. Invite a twelve-year-old to read the story of Jesus in the Temple. Practice with the reader in the sanctuary, using microphones if they are used on Sunday, until the child can read the text comfortably, at an appropriate speed, and with good inflection. (The sixth-grade Sunday school teacher can help identify a child who reads well and would be comfortable reading in the sanctuary.)

3. Pray your way through Paul's instructions in Colossians:

> Lord, you have called us your people. You have loved us and chosen us for your own. In return, you have asked us to be compassionate, kind, gentle, and patient. None of that comes easy for us. We try to ignore people who need our help. Hear our confessions about our lack of compassion. (Pause)
>
> We do not say the kind words friends need to hear and avoid doing gentle deeds that would make others happy. Hear our confessions about our failures to be kind and gentle. (Pause)
>
> And we all want to do what we want to do when we want to do it. Having patience with those who are slower than we are or who want to do things another way is not easy. Hear our prayers for patience. (Pause)
>
> Lord, You have asked us to tolerate others. Hear our prayers about the people we need to tolerate at home, at school, and at work. (Pause)
>
> You have asked us to forgive one another. Hear our prayers about people we are trying to forgive. (Pause)
>
> Be with us. Give us your peace and love to guide us; for we pray in Jesus' name. Amen.

4. Remember to include in the day's prayers the week-after-Christmas concerns of children: being tired and bored with nothing to look forward to; broken or disappointing toys; weather that keeps them cooped up indoors.

5. Turn Paul's instructions in Colossians into a pre-benediction charge by pausing after each phrase for the congregation to respond, "With God's help, we will try."

Sermon Resources

1. The text about Samuel is sketchy when it comes to details which children need in order to understand what was going on. "Small Boy Leaves Home," in *The Children's Bible in 365 Stories* by Mary Batchelor, supplies those details in a warm, human way. Use the author's ideas or read her short account in its entirety, either as part of the sermon or as a second reading immediately following the biblical text.

2. Celebrate growing up with lots of everyday examples—going to school for the first time, getting a driver's license, learning to be a good husband or wife, learning how to live alone after a spouse leaves or dies. Share with children and remind older worshipers that we are never "grown-up" but are always facing new tasks that call us to grow even more. Remember that Jesus also grew up just as we do—being a big brother, learning new games from friends, and accepting new responsibilities.

3. Recall Peter Pan and the lost boys who refused to grow up. They preferred to play, be dirty, and do what they wanted to do when they wanted to do it. Wendy and her brothers, on the other hand, enjoyed their childhood stories and games but also knew that growing up is part of life and were unwilling to stay children forever in Never Never Land.

4. Stress the importance of asking questions and talking together about God to keep us growing as God's people. This is a chance to push Christian education for all ages.

5. As children leave the sanctuary, be ready to read alphabet poems about growth and to comment on the children's illustrations on their Worship Worksheets.

6. Find additional Worship Worksheet Activities for Psalm 148 on the First Sunday After Christmas (Years A and B) and the Fifth Sunday of Easter (Year C).

Write an **alphabet psalm** for God about growing up. For each letter below, write a short prayer that begins with that letter. Some have been started for you.

Alleluia! God, I am growing up!

Be with me when _____

C _____

D _____

E _____

Forgive me for _____

G _____

Hurrah for growing up like Jesus!

Draw a picture of Jesus for each verse of "O Sing a Song of Bethlehem."

1.	2.
3.	4.

THE EPIPHANY

Note: When the day of Epiphany falls very close to Sunday, use the Epiphany lessons rather than those for the Second Sunday of Christmas.

From a Child's Point of View

Gospel: Matthew 2:1-12. The details of this story are often missed in children's Christmas pageants, when wise men simply follow the star to the manger. The encounter with Herod is skipped. When the story of the wise men is the focus of the day, it is possible to mine from the story two themes that are important to children.

First, God went to some trouble (by providing the star) to announce Jesus' birth to people of another race and country. In other words, God loves all people everywhere. Jesus came to all people. Thus, as Jesus' followers, we are to be one family with all people everywhere. We are to exclude no one from God's church or from our family. Although this inclusiveness is to be extended to people in our own school and community, Matthew's account of the wise men focuses on God's insistence on racial, national, and cultural inclusiveness.

Elementary children get heavy doses of national and cultural pride in school, Scouts, and similar activities. This is a chance to balance that pride with deep appreciation for other nations and cultures. It is also an opportunity to explore the value of nations working together and of cultures sharing their ways of doing things.

Second, this is a story of palace intrigue in which God and several foreigners outwit an evil ruler. The wise men learn from Herod where to find Jesus, but do not give Herod the information he needs to kill the child. God is at work on the side of the powerless. This is one of the success stories in the struggle of the powerless. Invite children to celebrate the story.

Epistle: Ephesians 3:1-12. Paul's announcement of God's "secret plan" reminds us that all people are members of God's family. Therefore, the wise men, like the Gentiles, are not "foreigners" but "kin." Today most children have contact at school or in their communities with children of other nationalities, races, and cultures. Older children are aware of people in other countries who dress, eat, speak, and act differently from the way we do. Paul's secret is that all these people are part of God's family. We must, therefore, respect them and treat them lovingly.

Note: The compound/complex sentences in this text are hard for children to follow. You will need to put Paul's announcement into simpler statements.

Psalm: 72:1-7, 10-14. This is both a prayer for, and a description of, a ruler who is everything Herod is not. This king is God's ideal—fair, caring, and kind. Christians have interpreted the passage as a description of the king that Jesus would be. But it also can be instructive for team captains, class officers, Scout patrol leaders, and other young leaders.

Old Testament: Isaiah 60:1-6. This Old Testament prophecy is read today to point to the arrival of the wise men. The connection is too obscure for most children.

Watch Words

Our tendency to use the terms *wise men*, *magi*, and *kings* interchangeably can confuse children.

28

Stick with one of the terms, or explain your use of others.

Do not assume that the children recognize the word *Epiphany* and understand its significance.

Let the Children Sing

"We Three Kings of Orient Are" is an obvious choice, but it includes abstract vocabulary that needs detailed explanation before children can sing all the verses with understanding.

"Come, Christians, Join to Sing" praises Christ the King with a repeated chorus of "Alleluia, Amen!"—in which even nonreaders can join (a specific invitation helps!).

"Jesus Loves the Little Children" is a familiar children's song celebrating the worldwide family of God. Perhaps a young children's class could sing it for the congregation, or the entire congregation could sing it as a hymn or in response to a point within the sermon.

The Liturgical Child

1. Light the Christ candle in your Advent wreath once more today. Then use it to light any other candles in your worship center. Explain the significance of the candles as they are lit. For example, many congregations light two candles on the table to recall Jesus' "twin" statements that he is the light of the world and that we also are called to be the light of the world.

2. Psalm 72 is a combination of the good wishes (or prayers) and cheers of a crowd celebrating their good king. So have four readers read the psalm with enthusiasm:

Reader 1: Verse 1	Reader 3: Verse 7
Reader 2: Verse 2	Reader 4: Verse 11
Reader 3: Verse 3	Reader 1: Verse 12a
Reader 4: Verse 4	Reader 2: Verse 12b
Reader 1: Verse 5	Reader 3: Verse 13
Reader 2: Verse 6	Reader 4: Verse 14

After delivering a sermon on leadership, repeat this reading as a prayer for specific leaders in the world today.

3. Use the characteristics of a good king found in Psalm 72:1-4; 12-14 as the basis of a prayer for leaders of the world today—name presidents, governors, and local leaders. Be sure to include leaders of countries other than your own.

4. Include prayers and music from different cultures and branches of Christianity in today's worship to celebrate the worldwide family of God. Perhaps a choir can prepare a hymn from another culture as an anthem. Create a display of hats from around the world in your worship center. (An older children's class might be enlisted to gather such hats.)

5. Pray for people of different nations and cultures. Using weather as a format, note the different kinds of weather in which Christians are gathering to worship on this day; then move to deeper concerns for the worldwide family of God.

For example, in a northern-hemisphere congregation, we might say, "It is hard to remember that for some Christians, today is the middle of summer. We remember our brothers and sisters in South Africa who gather in hot buildings and summer clothes to worship you and to find ways for black and white Christians to live together as your children."

Sermon Resources

1. Many children and adults would like to be "king." Compare the kings in this story: grasping, jealous Herod; the three worshiping kings; and King Jesus, who would be a serving, sacrificing king. Illustrate with stories about leaders of all ages.

2. Build a sermon around the three strange gifts the wise men brought. Consider using the verses of "We Three Kings of Orient Are" as an outline. Ask worshipers to follow along in open hymnbooks. Some religious bookstores sell samples of frankincense and myrrh, which you could display in your worship center.

Artists have drawn many very different pictures of the 3 wise men.

In some they come on camels.
In others they ride horses.

In some they wear crowns like kings.
In others they dress like teachers.
In still others they wear clothes from 3 different countries.

Draw YOUR picture of the 3 wise men.

Herod was a jealous, mean leader.
The wise men worshiped a baby who would be a great leader.
Jesus died for us all.

What kind of leader are you?

Draw a picture of yourself being a leader or write a prayer telling God about the kind of leader you want to be.

From a Child's Point of View

Today's texts focus on the role of the Holy Spirit in baptism, a difficult subject. But for children the basic message is that just as God's Holy Spirit was with Jesus, giving him the power for his work, God's Holy Spirit is also with us and works through us. The presence and power of the Holy Spirit is not something we deserve or earn but is given to us by God at our baptism. God gives the Holy Spirit to every Christian—even those who are different from us or those we do not like much.

Gospel: Luke 3:15-17, 21-22. The focus in this story is not on what happened in the water, but on the coming of the Holy Spirit. Before the Holy Spirit descended at Jesus' baptism, Jesus worked in the carpenter shop, studied the Scriptures at the synagogue, thought deeply, and prayed. After the Holy Spirit descended, he began his work of teaching and healing. Children are interested in the difference the Holy Spirit made in Jesus' life and can make in ours.

Children need help to move past the appearance of the dove and identify other ways we recognize the presence of the Holy Spirit (e.g., a sense of deep peace at times in worship; knowing exactly what God wants us to do and feeling God with us as we do it; taking a brave disciple's stand that we know we would not be brave enough to take on our own; feeling God very close to us; and so forth).

Old Testament: Isaiah 43:1-7. Though Isaiah addressed this message of hope to a people in exile, promising their return to their homeland, in the context of today's lections, it also could have

been addressed to Jesus at his baptism and to us today. Children do not grasp the phrases that include references to Old Testament geography and speak symbolically of fire and water. But they do hear and claim scattered phrases that promise safety: "Do not fear, for I am with you" (vs. 5), and "I have called you by name, you are mine" (vs. 1b). These offer the security children crave and tie in with God's promises to Jesus and to us at baptism.

Epistle: Acts 8:14-17. The Holy Spirit is the mark of all Christians and is given by God—even to Samaritans and today's outsiders. The challenge to children is to follow the example of Peter and John, welcoming all who are baptized and recognizing that God's Holy Spirit lives in them and works through them too.

Psalm: 29. Psalm 29 celebrates the power of God felt in a thunderstorm. The psalm traces the path of a storm as it comes in from the sea, crosses the mountains, and moves into the desert. Children will not appreciate the connection for which this passage is read today (i.e., the connection between the water, wind, and fire of baptism and that of a thunderstorm). However, they will respond to the psalmist's invitation to the fearful child in each of us—not to fear the power of the storm but to let it remind us of God's great strength.

Watch Words

Check your *Holy Spirit* vocabulary. *Holy Ghost* sounds like a friendly sort of Halloween spook. *Holy Spirit* comes closer to the realities of the power that moves us to action. The ways we sense the presence of God's Spirit and respond to it are similar to the ways we sense and act on team spirit or patriotic spirit.

Avoid the harvest imagery (winnowing shovel, threshing grain, burning chaff). Today's nonagricultural children understand harvesting as gathering the good products, rather than as separating the good from the bad.

Let the Children Sing

The inner verses of "How Firm a Foundation" parallel Isaiah's promises. When fifth- and sixth-graders are told that these verses are God's promises to them, they can understand the promises as they sing them.

None of the hymns about Jesus' baptism is particularly attractive for, or make much sense to, children. However, "Open My Eyes, That I May See" is a prayer to be as responsive to God's Spirit as Jesus was. Children understand and share its specific, everyday requests.

"The Lone, Wild Bird" and "I'm Goin'a Sing When the Spirit Says Sing" are simple folk tunes about the Spirit that children enjoy.

The Liturgical Child

1. Highlight regular elements of your worship that mention Spirit: the Gloria Patri, Doxology, etc. Put each one into your own words. For example, in the Gloria Patri we praise God whose Spirit gives us the power to live and work as his people, and we remember that God's Spirit has been at work in God's people since the beginning of time and will be until the end of time. Note in passing that Holy Ghost is an old name for the Holy Spirit. (This might be done as the references come up in worship or during the sermon.)

2. If there are baptisms, invite children forward where they will be able to see. Point out the ways the Spirit is mentioned and involved in promises made and actions taken. Put one of the key traditional phrases into your own words, or tell what we mean when we say it. For example, in infant baptism you could say, "When we pray for God's Spirit to dwell in name, we are praying that name will learn about God and Jesus as he/she grows up and will be a loving, kind person. We

pray that one day name will stand before a congregation to make his/her own profession of faith and become Christ's disciple. None of that is possible without God's Spirit working in him/her."

3. To emphasize the sense of the thunderstorm in Psalm 29, invite the congregation to accompany the reading of the psalm by following a "hand-choir" director. The director stands near the reader and shows the congregation what to do:

verses 1-2	hands folded in lap
verses 3-4	pat lap in strong, slow cadence
verses 5-6	beat the pew seats or pewbacks a little faster
verses 7-9	clap hands still faster
verses 10-11	fold hands in laps again

The reader will need to read with a strong voice to be heard and to emphasize the strength of God's voice in the storm. If you cannot imagine your congregation doing this, ask a children's class to serve as a hand choir to accompany the reader. This group and the reader should practice together.

Sermon Resources

1. Explain the use and purpose of a breath prayer and suggest that worshipers use God's baptismal promise—"I have called you by name, you are mine"—as a breath prayer several times a day this week. Lead worshipers in practicing the prayer with the breathing. Describe what it would mean to pray the prayer in a variety of situations, such as getting up in the morning, when you feel very capable and good about yourself, when you've received a bad grade or someone has made you feel very stupid, and so forth. Encourage members of households to share their experiences with this prayer each day this week.

2. Tell stories about times you have sensed the Holy Spirit's presence in the life and work of this congregation. Include activities such as worship services, retreats, mission projects, and educational moments in which children have participated. Describe what happened, how it felt to be there, and what made you sense that the Holy Spirit was involved.

Find the promise God gives us at baptism.

A	B	C		J	K	L		S	T	U
D	E	F		M	N	O		V	W	X
G	H	I		P	Q	R		Y	Z	

Check the answer in Isaiah 43: 1 c.

Write the letters of your name in the first column.

Beside each letter write a word that contains that letter and describes you or something you do well.

Tell God about each word. As you pray, remember what God says about you: "I have called you by name, you are mine."

First Sunday After the Epiphany / Baptism of the Lord / © 1994 by Abingdon Press.

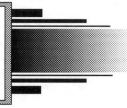

SECOND SUNDAY AFTER THE EPIPHANY

From a Child's Point of View

Today's readings speak of the way God's great power is shown to us—an important subject for children. Children need the security of knowing that God is the strongest power in the universe (Ps. 36). They also need to know that God uses this enormous power to care for us (John 2), to work in history on our behalf (Isa. 62), and to give each of us our own powers to use and enjoy (I Cor. 12). Because the language and images in these passages are often beyond children, worship leaders will need to concentrate on the theme, rather than on the passages.

Old Testament: Isaiah 62:1-5. The message is that God can and will eventually save us from our political and social messes. The specific example is that God will rescue the people of Jerusalem from captivity and reestablish the Jewish nation. To get from the specific example to the general message requires more explanation of Jewish history and Old Testament marriage images than time or the children will allow. This passage is for adult Bible students.

Psalm: 36:5-10. The psalmist praises God by citing attributes such as faithfulness, righteousness, and justice—words that are too abstract for children. References to drinking from the river of God's goodness, finding protection in the shadow of God's wings, and seeing the light of God do not speak clearly to children. Still, if the psalm is read with a sense of happy confidence and joy, the children will feel, rather than understand, these praises.

Epistle: I Corinthians 12:1-11. Verses 4-11 of this passage may be the easiest of today's lections for the children to understand. God has the power to give each of us special gifts or powers. Although each gift or power is different, all are of great value. Paul makes his point clearly in verses 4-7. Unfortunately for children, the examples that follow are difficult to translate from their first-century setting. Rather than explain each example, help the children identify the gifts/powers from God that they see in themselves and in others in the congregation. In citing these gifts, be sure to include "gifts of the spirit," such as patience in dealing with others, as well as talents such as musical ability.

Gospel: John 2:1-11. The writer of John explains who Jesus is by presenting a series of meaning-filled signs that Jesus performed. The first sign of God's power and love is that, through Jesus, God keeps a party going by providing extra high-quality refreshments. John's message is that God has the power to give us more than just what we need; God surprises us with unnecessary abundance. To children, this says that God wants all of them to have more than just enough to get by or to meet their needs. God's plan is that everyone should have all the wonderful, good things of life.

Children are often puzzled by Jesus' conversation with his mother. John includes that conversation to make the point that Jesus acted as he did because he chose to live by God's plan—not because his mother or anyone else told him what to do. Likewise, children today are called to live by God's plan because they choose to do so—not because their parents, teachers, or anyone else tells them to do so.

Watch Words

Watch out for the big power words such as *omnipotence, omniscience,* and *omnipresence.*

Rather than speaking of God's *vindication* of Jerusalem (Isa. 62) or of other oppressed groups, tell specifically what God did or promised.

Instead of *faithfulness* or *steadfastness* (Ps. 36), speak of *loyalty.* God is loyal to us, even when we are not loyal to God.

Let the Children Sing

"I Sing the Almighty Power of God" is first choice.

This is a Sunday for several praise hymns, such as "Now Thank We All Our God," "For the Beauty of the Earth," and "All People That on Earth Do Dwell."

The Liturgical Child

1. Read the psalm responsively, between either leader and people or two halves of the congregation. When introducing the psalm, point out that when we read it, we join the poet in telling God how great we think God is. Challenge worshipers to show how they feel by the way they say the words:

Lord, your constant love reaches the heavens;
  Your faithfulness extends to the skies.
Your righteousness is towering like the mountains;
  Your justice is like the depths of the sea.
People and animals are in your care.
  How precious, O God, is your constant love!
We find protection under the shadow of your wings.
  We feast on the abundant food you provide;
You let us drink from the river of your goodness.
  You are the source of all life,
And because of your light, we see the light.
(All) Continue to love those who know you
  and to do good to those who are righteous.
                    (Based on GNB)

2. Today's Worship Worksheet challenges the children to create a rebus of the hymn "I Sing the Almighty Power of God." To give the children time to work on the rebus, plan to sing the hymn after the sermon. As you begin the sermon, challenge the children to work on the rebus while they listen, so they will be ready to sing the hymn with their own "picture words."

Sermon Resources

1. To start the people thinking about power and the powerful people and groups in our world today, name political leaders and sports figures. If your children are caught up in Super Bowl frenzy, talk about the power claims in the chant "We're Number One!"

2. Name and discuss the power brokers of the cartoon world—Superman or Batman, Spider Woman, and the Ninja Turtles. For children who know themselves to be very unpowerful because of their size and age, such figures often become talismens against all the powers they fear. Children need to hear that God is even more powerful and dependable than any of those heroes and heroines. There is no evil power that God cannot conquer.

3. Compare "grabbing" power with "giving" power. Use the descriptions of God's power in today's lections as examples of giving power. Challenge worshipers to choose giving power by citing examples:

Albert Schweitzer was already becoming a famous concert organist. (This does not sound exciting today, but in his day, an organist was like a rock star.) But he chose to become a missionary doctor. He gave up riches and fame to spend the rest of his life taking care of people deep in the jungles of Africa.

Millard Fuller had made a million dollars by the time he was thirty years old. He had cars, houses, and a fancy boat. But he was not happy. Then he decided to change his goal. His new goal was to build a million homes for people who had no decent place to live. He founded Habitat for Humanity. Now people all around the world are working with him to build thousands of homes every year. He says he is happier now in his small house and building houses for others than he ever was in his fancy house.

Cite examples of people in your congregation who put their giving power to work. Remember to include examples of children who sing in the choir, participate in mission projects, or whatever else your children do.

In your hymnbook, find

I Sing the Almighty Power of God.

Draw pictures in the boxes of the things God made. If you sing this hymn today, use your picture words.

I sing the almighty power of God,

that made the [　　mountains　　] rise,

that spread the [　　flowing seas　　] abroad,

and built the [　　lofty skies　　]

I sing the wisdom that ordained

the [　　sun　　] to rule the day;

the [　　moon　　] shines full at God's command,

and all the [　　stars　　] obey.

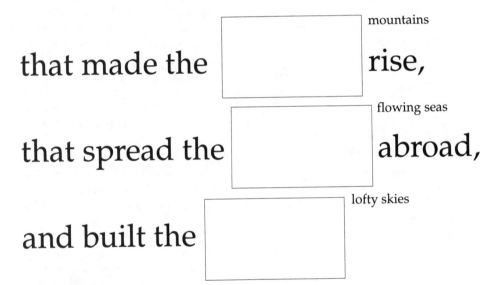
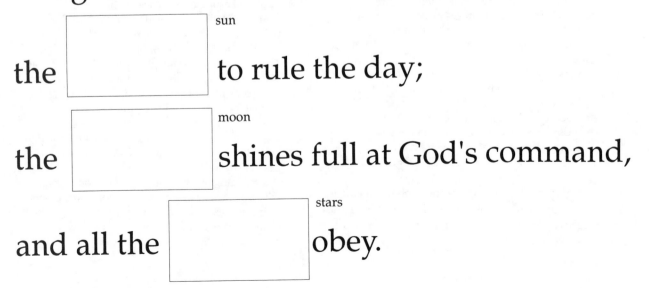

THIRD SUNDAY AFTER THE EPIPHANY

From a Child's Point of View

Old Testament: Nehemiah 8:1-3, 5-6, 8-10. Before children can understand all the excitement and tears in this story, they must know what the Law is. For this passage, the Law is five books of the Bible that include (1) the *stories of what God had done for people*, from Adam and Eve to Noah, to Abraham, to Moses and the people he led out of slavery in Egypt; and (2) *what God expected of people* (including the Ten Commandments). Children also must know that none of these people had heard the Law read for many years. (You might compare the situation to what would happen if the Gospels were read in your congregation for the first time in many years.)

With this background, children follow the story easily and generally are impressed by how long the crowd listened and by their tearful response. The key idea is that the stories and rules in the Law were very important to those people. We are challenged to see the importance of the Law (and the rest of the Bible) for our lives, too.

Psalm: 19. In this context of Nehemiah, the focus of this reading is on verses 7-10. No matter which translation you select, these verses are filled with big words that are synonyms for the Law, or the Bible. Older children are helped by being reminded that Hebrew poets rhyme ideas, rather than sounds. So these verses are a repetitious list of wonderful things about the Bible.

Epistle: I Corinthians 12:12-31a. This passage requires symbolic thinking beyond the ability of younger children, but this is a good opportunity to challenge older children to begin such thinking. The challenge is most effectively presented by working on both sides of Paul's symbol before trying to connect them.

Most children quickly understand the interdependence of the parts of a physical body. With some guidance, they can recognize that people within the congregation doing different kinds of work need one another and their differing gifts. The similarity between these two truths, however, will be a hard connection to make. It requires that children see themselves as parts of Christ's body. This vision often begins when an older adult thanks an errand-running child for "being my feet." Once children can see themselves as Grandma's feet, they can understand that they also can be Christ's feet. Many everyday examples of being Christ's hands, eyes, and so on will clarify this possibility. As this vision becomes clear, children will finally understand Paul's symbolic connection and, thus, his point. This is a job to chip away at over several years—not to complete in one sermon.

Gospel: Luke 4:14-21. In this passage Jesus introduces the goals for his life and ministry. His goals are ones children can understand, especially if they are given some help with difficult words. Children can be challenged to see Jesus' goals as goals for their congregation and to accept some or all of them as goals for their own lives.

Watch Words

Define *Law,* and be careful about the synonyms you use. "Anointed me to" means "chose me to." To "proclaim liberty to the captives" means "to free prisoners." To "proclaim the acceptable year of the Lord" is to promise that God (through me) is acting to save you now!

Let the Children Sing

About the Law (Bible): "Wonderful Words of Life" has an easy chorus and repeats the title in each verse, making it easy for nonreaders.

"Tell Me the Stories of Jesus" does not celebrate the whole of the Bible, but only the stories about Jesus. It is one of the few hymns about the Bible that children can sing with understanding.

About Jesus' Commitment, and Ours: "Be Thou My Vision" is a hymn of commitment that many children love. Because it has some difficult words, use this hymn only if it is familiar. Try "Lord, Speak to Me That I May Speak."

The Liturgical Child

1. Ask six older children, or six readers of a variety of ages, to present the following reading of Psalm 19:7-14 (GNB). (This reading preserves the sense of parallel or rhyming ideas about God's Law.) In the sanctuary, practice reading loudly and clearly, with happy, proud voices.

Reader One:	The law of the Lord is perfect; it gives new strength.
Reader Two:	The commands of the Lord are trustworthy, giving wisdom to those who lack it.
Reader Three:	The laws of the Lord are right, and those who obey them are happy.
Reader Four:	The commands of the Lord are just and give understanding to the mind.
Reader Five:	Reverence for the Lord is good; it will continue forever.
Reader Six:	The judgments of the Lord are just; they are always fair.
Reader One:	They are more desirable than the finest gold;
Reader Two:	they are sweeter than the purest honey.
Reader Three:	They give knowledge to me, your servant;
Reader Four:	I am rewarded for obeying them.
Reader One:	No one can see his own errors;
Reader Two:	deliver me, Lord, from hidden faults!
Reader Three:	Keep me safe, also, from willful sins;
Reader Four:	don't let them rule over me.
Reader Five:	Then I shall be perfect
Reader Six:	and free from the evil of sin.
All:	May my words and my thoughts be acceptable to you, O Lord, my refuge and my redeemer!

2. To emphasize what Jesus read from Isaiah, begin reading the narrative in Luke from the Bible at the lectern. Then, from a large scroll, read the Isaiah passage in verses 18 and 19. If possible, step out of the lectern to read this passage. Then lay the scroll aside, step back to the center of the lectern, and continue Luke's narrative.

3. At the end of the service, change the pronouns in the Isaiah passage from first person to second person to charge the congregation: "The Spirit of the Lord is upon *you*, because God has chosen *you*." In the benediction, remind worshipers that just as Jesus sent out his disciples with the promise that he would be with them always, so he also sends us out with the same promise.

4. If you focus on the Law, pray for the church school classes and teachers. If you focus on work and goals, pray for the specific gifts and ministries of your congregation.

Sermon Resources

1. If you focus on the Law, challenge all listeners to participate in the congregation's study classes; also offer other specific suggestions for reading the Bible.

Pockets, a monthly magazine published by The Upper Room, offers daily Bible readings with prayer suggestions (as well as stories and games) for elementary children. Give a copy to each child to introduce them and their families to this fine resource. Order from: *Pockets,* 1908 Grand Ave., P.O. Box 189, Nashville, TN 37202-9929.

2. If you link the New Testament lessons, write a paraphrase of Paul's message, using groups in your congregation. For example, the choir cannot say to the church school teachers, "We do not need you." Nor can the youth group say to the women's circle, "God has no use for you anymore."

Depending on the Scriptures you choose, use the worksheet as it is, or enlarge the appropriate half to a full page.

Unscramble each group of letters to find the psalmist's prayer.

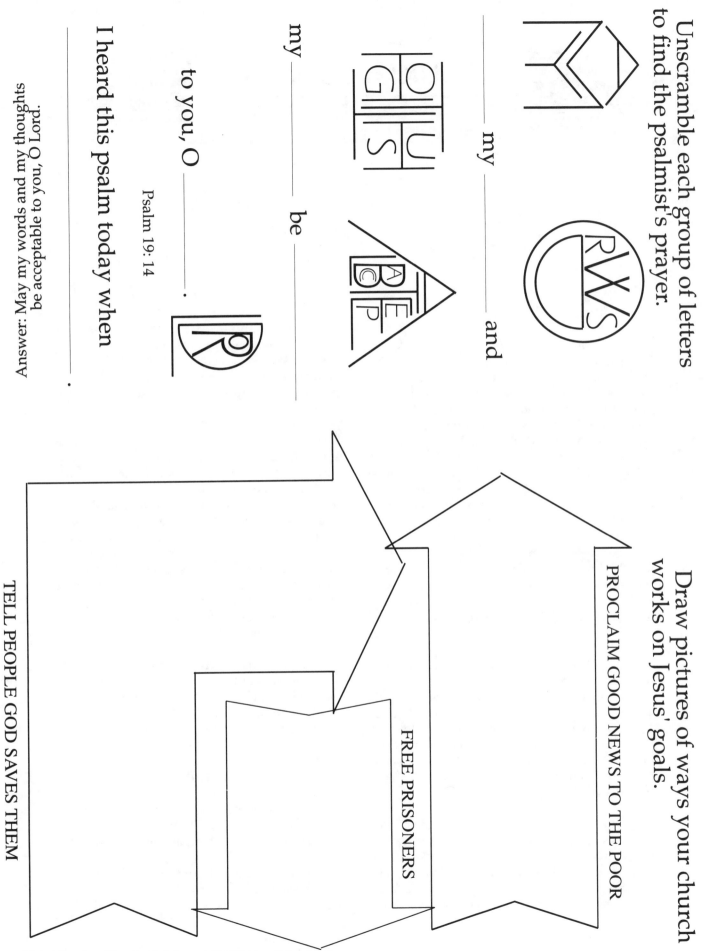

_____ my _____ and

my _____ be

to you, O _____ .

Psalm 19:14

I heard this psalm today when

_____ .

Answer: May my words and my thoughts be acceptable to you, O Lord.

Draw pictures of ways your church works on Jesus' goals.

PROCLAIM GOOD NEWS TO THE POOR

FREE PRISONERS

TELL PEOPLE GOD SAVES THEM

Third Sunday After the Epiphany / © 1994 by Abingdon Press.

FOURTH SUNDAY
AFTER THE EPIPHANY

From a Child's Point of View

Old Testament: Jeremiah 1:4-10. God knew Jeremiah before he was born and had a plan for him. God assured Jeremiah that he was capable of following the plan, and God promised to be with him all the way. Although it is possible for children to hear Jeremiah's story as if it were a special case involving someone very unlike themselves, with direction, they can hear in it the truth about themselves. That is, God also knew them before they were born, God has a plan for each of their lives, God has given them everything they need to follow those plans, and God will be with them each step of the way. Each person is important to God. As one poster puts it, "God don't make no junk." (This is a great text for encouraging Christian self-esteem!) The fact that Jeremiah was young when God called him challenges children to begin doing God's work *now* instead of waiting until they grow up.

Psalm: 71:1-6. This is the prayer of an old poet who knows from experience that God does indeed care for those who do God's work. Now in a tight corner, the poet calls on God for help (vss. 1-3) and remembers that God has helped in the past (vss. 4-6). Once children understand this, they will "catch" a few of the short phrases as the text is read, but probably will not follow the passage as a whole.

Epistle: I Corinthians 13:1-13. The most relevant message here for children is that the way to grow up is not to grow smarter, more skillful, or more articulate, but to grow more loving. Few children, however, will hear this message from the text on their own. You will need to point it out

to them, and then work through verses 4-7, which explore grown-up love. Consult several translations to gather the adjectives that will most clearly describe love to these particular children. To help younger children understand these verses, paraphrase them: "A loving person is . . . ," rather than "Love is . . . ."

Gospel: Luke 4:21-30. The message of this passage—God comes not only to us and to our friends, but also to some people we think are not worthy of God's attention—is one children need to hear and can respond to. But they (and many adults) will have difficulty pulling the message from the text. It helps to review or reread the beginning of the story in verses 16-20. Even so, most people will hear Jesus' point in the sermon, rather than in the lesson reading. Though youths and adults will benefit from explanations of Jesus' Old Testament examples, few children will follow them. Count on getting the children's attention when you summarize the message and explore its meaning for today. Identify some of the people in your community to whom God and Jesus come: the homeless, troublemakers at school, kids who are slow academically, "wimps," people with handicaps, people of other races, and so on.

Watch Words

Try *friendship* or *a loving friend*, rather than *love*, for the sake of boys for whom love is a sweet, sissy term used by mothers and in sexual relationships.

In Jeremiah 1 and Psalm 71, the Good News Bible speaks of *before I was born*, rather than *from the womb*, which bypasses the giggles of children who know what a womb is and speaks clearly to those who do not.

Let the Children Sing

Try "I Sing a Song of the Saints of God," a singable new hymn that is becoming a favorite.

Children can begin learning "God of Grace and God of Glory," a more traditional hymn of commitment, by joining in on "grant us wisdom, grant us courage."

"Lord, I Want to Be a Christian," with its verses about being more loving, joins the commitment theme in Jeremiah's call with the "love chapter."

The Liturgical Child

1. Assign two readers or two halves of the congregation to read the psalm. Name one reader "Help Me, God" (vss. 1-3) and the other "I Can Trust God" (vss. 4-6), to reflect the message of these two sections of the psalm.

2. Use I Corinthians 13:4-7 as an outline for a prayer of confession. A leader prays each line, leaving a time of silence for individual confessions (e.g., "Love is patient and kind . . ." [Pause] "Love is not jealous or conceited or proud . . ." [Pause], etc.). Or the leader and congregation can read a responsive confession:

Love is patient and kind;

Lord, it is hard to be patient when there is so much we need to do and want to do. When other people slow us down, it is easy to forget to be kind.

Love is not jealous or conceited or proud;

But we are, God. We look at some people and think we are better than they are. We look at others and feel jealous of what they have and can do. Forgive us.

Love is not ill-mannered or selfish or irritable;

But we often blurt out rude, hurting names and accusations, almost before we know what we are saying. Help us learn to think before we speak.

Love does not keep a record of wrongs;

But we remember even those wrongs we have really tried to forgive. We remember them and bring them up when we are angry or when we want our own way. We use them to hurt even the people we love. Help us to forgive and forget.

Love is not happy with evil; love is happy with truth;

But it is hard not to take secret delight when people get what they had coming to them. Teach us compassion, God.

Love never gives up; and its faith, hope, and patience never fail.

But we give up easily. We give up on other people. We give up on ourselves. We give up on making a difference. We lose hope that anything will ever be any different. Forgive us, for we pray in Jesus' name. Amen.

Assurance of Pardon: Hear this about God's great love! God is patient and kind. God does not keep a record of our wrongs. God does not remember our failings at loving, but is happy about every one of our successes. God never gives up on us because God's love is forever!

3. For the charge and benediction, paraphrase God's call to Jeremiah as a call to each worshiper: "I chose you before I gave you life. . . . Do not be afraid, but go to the people to whom I send you. . . . I will protect you and give you the words you need."

Sermon Resources

1. To explore Luke's lesson, tell a story in which Jesus comes to visit a playground, skating rink, or other place where children gather in your area. In your story, have all the children recognize Jesus and try to get his attention so he will talk and play with them and their friends. Describe some of the groups vying for Jesus' attention and their tactics. Then describe Jesus choosing to reach out to some children who are usually overlooked or looked down on. Tailor the story to fit your community.

2. To explore Paul's message about being a Christian grown-up, create a parable in which four "children" try to be grown-ups in different

ways: One tries to act like a grown-up by wearing make-up, insisting on staying up late, even drinking or smoking; another tries to act grown up by bossing everyone around (pretending to know everything); a third tries to make it with grown-ups by doing everything they want (becoming teacher's pet); and a fourth person tries to love and take care of other people. Challenge your hearers to decide which one was grown up, according to Paul's definition.

3. At the beginning of the sermon, mention the "opposites" activity on the Worship Worksheet and challenge the children to listen for opposites in the sermon. At the end of the sermon, or as children leave the sanctuary, hear and respond to some of their opposites.

"I chose you before I gave you life."

Draw a picture of yourself doing something God chose to make you able to do.

Day and **night** are opposites.
Pretty and **ugly** are opposites.
Good and **bad** are opposites.

In the first column are words Paul used to tell us about love.

In the second column, write a word that means the opposite of each of Paul's words.

Love is . . .
patient _____
kind _____

Love is not . . . .
conceited _____
boastful _____
selfish _____
jealous _____
irritable _____
arrogant _____

Some words to try: humble, generous, pleasant, friendly, helpful, gentle, giving, content.

Listen for love words in our worship.

Write a prayer about the way God made you.

_____
_____
_____
_____
_____
_____

Fourth Sunday After the Epiphany / © 1994 by Abingdon Press.

FIFTH SUNDAY
AFTER THE EPIPHANY

From a Child's Point of View

Today's texts include three accounts in which a person encounters the greatness of God, feels unable to face God, and then feels called by God. All three stories say to children, who are aware of their vulnerability and insignificance, that the God of the Universe cares about them and needs their help.

Old Testament: Isaiah 6:1-8 (9-13). This poetic description of the power of God is tough to present to literal-minded children. They tend to see it as a photographic peek at God. One approach is simply to read the passage, letting the children respond to the power scene literally. Such a scene makes Isaiah's response very understandable.

Another approach is to compare the passage to a poetic line, such as "my love is like a red, red rose"; then, to help older children analyze the seraphim, who had two wings to cover their eyes (because they were afraid to see God's great power and purity), two wings to cover their bodies (because they were afraid for God to see how unpure they were), and two wings to fly about to do God's will. With some direction, these older children can begin to understand the seraphim as pictures of the way we feel when we sense God's great power and holiness and do God's will.

Children will need help to interpret the burning coal as cleansing, rather than as punishment or torture. The examples of washing dishes in steamy hot water or burning a stick in a campfire before putting a hot dog on it may help children understand the cleansing function of the coal.

Psalm: 138. This psalm, which praises God, is simple enough to understand, but it does not speak of things that are particularly important to children. It is a good psalm to read, but not one to explore in any depth.

Epistle: I Corinthians 15:1-11. This passage offers two key ideas to children. First, while Isaiah felt God's power and presence in the Temple, Paul encountered it in the life, death, and resurrection of Jesus. Though Paul did not meet Jesus while he lived on the earth, Paul knew Jesus' story and, based on that story, believed that God loves us, cares for us, and forgives us more than we can imagine. Paul knew Jesus in the same way children today know Jesus.

Second, God called Paul to discipleship, even though he had been a leader in killing Christians. As he wrote this passage, years after his Damascus road experience, Paul was still surprised that God called him instead of punishing him. To children, this says that if God could want Paul as a disciple after what Paul had done, God must surely want us as disciples, no matter what we have done or how little we think we have to offer.

Gospel: Luke 5:1-11. To understand Peter's response in this story, children need to know that he was responding to more than the marvelous catch of fish. Luke tells us that Peter had heard Jesus teach and had watched Jesus in action for a while before this event took place. So on this day, Peter sensed God's presence in all he had seen of Jesus—his loving healing, his demanding teachings, his control of nature. Peter realized, even before Jesus told him, that being Jesus' friend and disciple would not be safe and comfortable, but demanding and life changing. Children are challenged to realize that for them to be Jesus' disciples (as Peter was) also will be exciting, demanding, and life changing.

Watch Words

Take this opportunity to help children define the word *holy*—used only in religion and profanity today, and one of those words defined by words that are even less definable. *Holy* describes the separateness and perfection of God. Some child-sized words that describe *holiness* include *pure, awesome, respected, perfect,* and *unique* (as in a class by itself). If the Revised Standard Version or King James Version of the Bible are used often in your congregation, discuss what it means to "fear" God because God is *holy.* Remember—one sign of God's holiness that is important in today's text is that God does not flaunt (is not "stuck up" about) being *holy* when dealing with us, who are so *unholy.*

Let the Children Sing

Hymns of Praise and Adoration: "Holy! Holy! Holy!" reflects Isaiah's vision and is first choice. With a little coaching, even nonreaders can sing the repeated "Holy! Holy! Holy!" If possible, describe the seraphim before singing this hymn and alert the children to their presence in the hymn. Also consider "For the Beauty of the Earth," "Now Thank We All Our God," or "How Great Thou Art" (if it is familiar to the children).

Hymns of Commitment or Discipleship: "Jesus Calls Us," a hymn based on Jesus' call to the fishing disciples, includes some difficult vocabulary. But children can pick up the short, simple phrases at the beginning and end of the verses.

The Liturgical Child

1. In the major prayer of the day, invite people to pray following the stories from the readings. Use the outline below as introductory prayers for silent or spoken bidding prayers, or as the first lines of leader-stated prayers.

Holy, holy, holy, God! Your power and greatness are more than we can imagine. But like Isaiah and Paul and Peter, we do sense your presence in many ways. Hear each of us as we give thanks for the ways we meet you.

When we think of you, God, we are embarrassed about ourselves. Like Isaiah, we remember our unclean words. Like Paul, we remember our sins. Like Peter, we know how unholy we are. Hear each of us as we confess our sins and unworthiness.

We are grateful that you did not punish Isaiah or Paul or Peter, but called them to serve you. So we offer ourselves to do your will. Hear our prayers about the work we are doing in your name and the work you want us to do.

2. *Charge and Benediction:* When God asked, "Whom shall I send?" Isaiah replied, "Here am I. Send me." When Peter said, "I am unworthy," Jesus replied, "Follow me and you will catch people." And when God stopped Paul on his way to kill Christians, it was to send him to tell the Good News to foreigners. They went and did God's work.

Today, I charge you, in Jesus' name, to go into your schools, neighborhoods, and workplaces, to love people as God has loved you and to tell the Good News. As you go, remember God's promises that you will know what to say and do and that God will be with you always.

Sermon Resources

1. Challenge the children to listen carefully to the Isaiah reading and then draw a picture of what Isaiah saw. Describe the seraphim in the beginning of the sermon to give the children input. Be ready to respond to their drawings as the children leave the church.

2. Talk about how we feel God's presence and power. Isaiah felt it in the Temple. Paul felt it in Jesus' death and resurrection. Peter felt it in Jesus' teachings and power over nature. Invite the children to draw pictures of the places and ways they sense God's presence and power. Respond to the drawings as the children leave the sanctuary.

3. Compare the flow from adoration to confession, to commitment, in each of today's three stories, to the flow of your morning worship service. Direct worshipers to the parts of worship in your printed order of worship, challenging them to see in every Sunday's worship the possibility of experiences like those of Isaiah, Paul, and Peter.

Use the decoder to find
out what Isaiah said to God.

" 8 5 18 5   1 13 9 .

___ ___ ___ ___ .

19 5 14 4   13 5 .

___ ___ ___ ___ . "

Isaiah 6:8

Decoder:

A=1 G=7   M=13 S=19 Y=25
B=2 H=8   N=14 T=20 Z=26
C=3 I=9   O=15 U=21
D=4 J=10 P=16 V=22
E=5 K=11 Q=17 W=23
F=6 L=12 R=18 X=24

Answer: Here am I. Send me.

Draw a picture or write a prayer about
what God is sending you to do this week.

Whom shall
I send ?

Here am I.
Send me.

Fifth Sunday After the Epiphany / © 1994 by Abingdon Press.

SIXTH SUNDAY AFTER THE EPIPHANY
PROPER ONE

From a Child's Point of View

Old Testament: Jeremiah 17:5-10 and Psalm 1. These passages give us one simple message: It is better, and even more rewarding, to be good than it is to be bad. Adults immediately sense problems with this simplification. But studies of the moral development of children indicate that the passages are on target for them. Young children accept rules as the unquestionable mandate of the always-correct all-powerful adults. Children make their earliest moral decisions—to obey or to disobey the rules—to avoid punishment. Growing beyond that, they obey in order to gain reward and pleasure. As older children realize that rules are not irrefutable but can be negotiated, they begin to obey in order to gain the respect and rewards of the group—to be thought of as a "good" boy or girl. Therefore, the clear delineation of the behavior of and rewards for "the good" and "the bad" in these passages speaks to children where they are in their development and forcefully challenges them to act like God's *good* people, thus reaping rewards and/or gaining the prestige of being known as one of God's people.

Second, although their mental development keeps them from fully appreciating the images in these passages, children can respond to the question, "Would you rather be a big leafy pear tree beside a cool river, or a dry leafless bush in a desert?" and accept the two examples as appropriate signs (like national flags) for the "good" people and the "bad" people.

Gospel: Luke 6:17-26. Verses 20-26 parallel the two Old Testament readings but add this insight: Sometimes it does not look as if it is better to be good than to be bad. The promise in these verses is that though this may seem to be true at the moment, eventually God will see that the good prosper. So children are challenged to put up with being called names or laughed at for doing what they know is right on the playground, in the classroom, or even with brothers and sisters at home.

Note: Working with these passages on the children's level provides the opportunity to challenge adults to cut through all the complications of modern ethical decision-making in order to remember that we are called simply to be God's good people.

Epistle: I Corinthians 15:12-20. This is the first of three consecutive readings in I Corinthians 15 related to the resurrection. Each reading offers a slightly different message for children. None of the readings is closely connected to the other readings of the day.

Although the complex sentences and involved logic of this passage are hard for children to follow, the message—that Christ has risen and that we will rise—is simple. Children will be less interested in Paul's insistence that Christ's resurrection and ours are linked than in the truth that God's love and care go beyond death. God did not allow death to be the end of Jesus, and God will not let death be the end of us. We can trust God to love us and care for us *always*—even after we die.

Watch Words

Choose words that emphasize the value of being among the good, rather than heaping judgment and curses upon the bad.

Avoid obsolete words such as *scoffers* and *mockers* to describe the wicked. The Good News Bible offers some good alternatives in Psalm 1.

Resurrection is a long word and a difficult concept. Devote the sermon to defining the word, using it again and again. Or talk instead about how God cares for us even after we die and does not let death be the end of us.

Let the Children Sing

Sing "God of Grace and God of Glory" to celebrate being God's good people and ask for help to serve God well. Encourage younger children to join in on the line "Grant us wisdom, grant us courage" in each verse.

"I Sing a Song of the Saints of God" also celebrates God's good people and calls us to commit ourselves to be among the good people.

Both "The Lord's My Shepherd, I'll Not Want," which will be recognized by most children as Psalm 23 set to music, and "God Will Take Care of You," which repeats the simple phrase of its title, celebrating God's love, which continues even beyond death.

The Liturgical Child

1. At the front of the sanctuary, place a lush, leafy, flowering plant and a dead branch stuck in a flower pot of sand. The person who provides flowers might enjoy the challenge of creating this display.

2. Have Jeremiah's sayings, Psalm 1, and the blessings and woes in Luke read by a pair (or three pair) of readers, standing in opposite lecterns or on opposite sides of the chancel (to emphasize the difference between the good and the bad people). Consider asking some fifth- or sixth-graders to prepare these readings.

Jeremiah 17: Reader 1: verses 5-6
Reader 2: verses 7-8
Readers 1 and 2 (in unison)
or Reader 3: verses 9-10

Psalm 1: Reader 1: verses 1-3
Reader 2: verses 4-5
Reader 1: verse 6*a*
Reader 2: verse 6*b*
Luke 6: Reader 1: verses 20-23
Reader 2: verses 24-26

To highlight the similarity in these passages, read them continuously rather than interspacing them with songs and prayers.

Sermon Resources

1. The key issue in the three related texts is that we all have choices to make and that God wants us to make good, loving choices. Tell stories about children who make choices about doing or not doing what they have been told to do, about families that decide how to work and play together, and about people of all ages who make decisions about helping or not helping others (e.g., deciding who to sit with in the lunchroom or on the bus, how to reach out to a child who is cut out by the others, etc.).

2. To explore I Corinthians 15:12-20, tell stories of people who seemed to be beyond God's help or care, but found they were not. Tell of the Hebrew slaves trapped between the Egyptian army and the sea; of Noah in the ark, floating on the destroying flood; of people today who have found hope in the face of death and new life in hopeless situations. Be sure to include the story of Jesus' arrest, trial, torture, and death, followed by resurrection.

Worship Worksheet

Three of our lections call us to take a stand with God's good people. The fourth is a statement of faith about the resurrection. Therefore the Worship Worksheet focuses on creeds, one way we take a stand in worship. Consider using the Apostles' Creed this week. Be sure to note the location in your hymnbook of any creed you use, so that children and their parents can find it easily.

One way to worship God is to say a creed.

I Believe!

Creed means . . .
I believe.
I think.
This is what I know.

Look in your bulletin for a creed or affirmation of faith (a fancy way to say creed). If the creed is in your hymnbook, look it up.

Now you are ready to say "I believe" with everyone in your church.

Be proud. Stand tall. Say the words clearly.

The **Apostles' Creed** has been said by Christians for hundreds of years. Find it in your hymnbook. (Hint: Look in the Contents.)

Hidden below are 7 things we say that we believe when we say the Apostles' Creed. Can you find all of them?

```
J E S U S C H R I S T Q
X V A B Q C T E N P T Q
L E O L H P T S B X T Q
Z R A G O D Q U B C T Q
K L K N L P D R M H T Q
G A T H Y B N R Q U T Q
Z S S B G R S E P R T Q
S T B R H M N C K C T Q
B I A C O C B T T H T Q
F N Z X S G L I M N T Q
R G S T T V W O Z B T Q
C L D F G H J N K Q T Q
X I R Q K N M R T S T Q
P F O R G I V E N E S S
D E D C R I O E P Z T Q
```

Answers: We believe in God, Jesus Christ, Holy Ghost, church, forgiveness, resurrection, and everlasting life.

SEVENTH SUNDAY AFTER THE EPIPHANY
PROPER TWO

From a Child's Point of View

Old Testament: Genesis 45:3-11, 15. Children with brothers or sisters are fascinated by the story of Joseph and his brothers. Few have considered selling their siblings (but most can enjoy daydreaming about life without them). Although many children believe their siblings are mean and obnoxious, few would expect them to go to the lengths that Joseph's brothers did. One message for children, especially those whose parents are pressuring them to get along better with brothers and sisters, is simply that sibling rivalry is real. It is comforting to know that at least one biblical family was meaner than we are.

Thus reassured, children can hear the amazing fact that Joseph actually forgave his brothers and saved their lives. Joseph could forgive them because he was sure that God loved him and had a plan for his life. He knew that no problem—not even being sold by his brothers—could stop God's love or get in the way of God's plan. In psychological terms, Joseph had such good self-esteem that he could endure vicious attacks by friends and family as passing setbacks, rather than as the final word on his worth.

The challenge to preachers is not to bully children into following Joseph's example, but to instill in them such a sense of God's love that they will be able to see the frustrating events and people of their lives in the way Joseph saw such things in his life.

Psalm: 37:1-11, 39-40. This is a psalm Joseph could have sung. It is a psalm for those days when everything is going wrong and it seems that everyone is out to get you. Because each short statement in the psalm makes sense on its own,

children can hear and respond to one phrase, or to the whole psalm. If your children recognize Yahweh as a name for God, read the strong translation in The New Jerusalem Bible.

Gospel: Luke 6:27-38. If verses 37-39 are read first, the opening verses of this passage make more sense. If you do not judge or condemn and are ready to forgive, you limit the number of people you consider your enemies. That is what Joseph did. He refused to judge his brothers. As one poster summarizes it, "The best way to get rid of an enemy is to make a friend." The challenge to children is to identify ways to think about and then treat their "enemies" as friends.

Epistle: I Corinthians 15:35-38, 42-50. This passage might be titled, "What will happen when I die?" For children, the question is, "What happened to (*name of loved person or pet*) when she or he died?" Because few children understand the reality of their own death, their concern is more for the loved person or pet they have lost than for their own future.

Paul's picture of a seed and the plant that grows from it stretches children's mental abilities, but it can make sense to them—especially if parallel examples of things that grow and change in predictable ways are cited. The bottom line is that after death, we will be as different as a plant is different from a seed, but we will maintain our uniqueness, just as one kind of plant always grows from the same kind of seed. For children, this means that Grandpa is OK. God is still taking care of Grandpa, and Grandpa is experiencing a wonderful new kind of life. The interpretation also leaves room for us to miss (grieve for) those we love who have died.

Watch Words

There are few word traps in Joseph's story.

Beware of comparing *mortal* to *immortal* and *physical* bodies to *spiritual* bodies. Ghosts, fairies, and other magical creatures in children's literature and television inhabit a confusingly separate, yet present territory for children. Therefore, it is easier to communicate Paul's point through the seed images than through these adjectives.

Let the Children Sing

Sing of Trusting God's Care and Plan: "God Will Take Care of You" has a chorus children may know from church school. "The King of Love My Shepherd Is" is a good choice *if* the children know Psalm 23 well. Explain *balm* before singing "There Is a Balm in Gilead." Nonreading children often hear "There is a *bomb* in Gilead."

The Liturgical Child

1. Introduce Psalm 37 as an alphabet psalm (an acrostic) for the days when everything is going wrong. Prepared readers (possibly older children) then flip up the appropriate Hebrew letter card before reading one stanza each.

Aleph	(א)	verses 1-2
Beth	(ב)	verses 3-4
Gimel	(ג)	verses 5-6
Daleth	(ד)	verses 7
He	(ה)	verses 8-9
Waw	(ו)	verses 10-11
Taw	(ת)	verses 39-40

2. The vocabulary with which Jesus' question is posed in Luke 6 is different in various translations. Choose the one that will make most sense to your children.

3. Pray about family relationships today. Offer worshipers a chance to pray silently for each member of their family—especially brothers and sisters. Or pray about the changes that happen in our lives as we are born, grow up, and die. Provide opportunities to pray for people at different stages of life and for those facing changes as they grow.

Sermon Resources

1. Today's texts assume that worshipers know the whole story of Joseph. Since many children (and adults) do not know the complete story, devote sermon time to telling the story of Joseph, placing emphasis on Joseph's self-understanding. Then use the related texts to explore the story's significance.

Try telling the story in sections. Conclude each section by saying a Refrain or inviting the congregation to do so. Consider the outline below:

Tell about the "braggy" boy who was sold into slavery. As he trudges off in slave chains, he thinks of his brothers and says,

(Refrain) I know God loves me and has a plan for me. It was not you who sent me here, but God.

Tell about Joseph the good slave, who was framed by his owner's wife and sent to prison. As the prison doors close, he thinks of his owners and says,

(Refrain) I know God loves me and has a plan for me. It was not you who sent me here, but God.

Tell about Joseph the dream-explaining friend, who was forgotten in prison. As he sits alone, he thinks of the released friend and says,

(Refrain) I know God loves me and has a plan for me. It was not you who sent me here, but God.

Tell about Joseph the powerful brother, who welcomed and cared for the brothers who had sold him. Paralleling today's text, he tells his brothers,

(Refrain) I know God loves me and has a plan for me. It was not you who sent me here, but God.

2. Joseph's dreams and special clothes made his brothers angry. Some of the things that cause sibling fights today are (1) messing with each other's room or possessions; (2) embarrassing each other in front of friends; (3) sensing that another child is getting better treatment from parents (older children see the younger ones as pampered pets, while younger children complain that the older ones get to do all the "good stuff" they are not allowed to do); (4) squabbling over goodies, from cookies to gifts to clothes. Tell stories about such situations to bring Joseph's situation home today.

3. To illustrate Paul's image, bring a seed and a plant (perhaps an acorn from an oak tree in the churchyard) and a picture of yourself as a baby, to compare to yourself as an adult.

Draw a picture of your family or write the name of each person in your family.

Talk to God in prayer about each person in your family.

The hymn "There Is a Balm in Gilead" promises that one day God will heal all our frustrations. Write a verse or draw a picture about one of your frustrations.

Idea: The writer of this hymn wished he could preach like Peter or pray like Paul. Write a verse or draw a picture of something you wish you could do as well as someone else does.

EIGHTH SUNDAY AFTER THE EPIPHANY
PROPER THREE

From a Child's Point of View

Today's texts can be related to one another in a variety of ways. One way that has significant potential for children is that each text expresses confidence in the power, care, and love of God. The psalm celebrates being able to sing praises to God. Isaiah notes the trustworthiness of God's Word. Paul rejoices that God's love and power go beyond death. Luke 6 provides the "therefore," with several suggestions about obeying God and God's Word.

Old Testament: Sirach 27:4-7 or Isaiah 55:10-13. The New Jerusalem Bible offers a beautiful translation of the Sirach passage, which explains that what we say shows us for what we are. However, even in this clear translation, the only comparison easily grasped by children is that of the orchard. Still, if explanations of the function of sieves and kilns are included, children can explore the need to discipline our speech.

Isaiah's personification of God's Word is also hard for children to understand. The best use of this passage is to compare what God's Word tells about God (in this text) to what our human words tell about us (in Sirach and Luke 6:43-45).

Psalm: 92:1-4, 12-15. Verses 1-4 of this sabbath psalm of praise celebrate the joy of singing praises to God. Children can follow easily and share in the praising. If you explored the bush symbols two weeks ago, children will enjoy recognizing the repeat of the image in verses 12-15.

Gospel: Luke 6:39-49. Each of these teachings of Jesus involves a vivid image which must be understood in order to get Jesus' point.

Of all the sayings, the one about the fruits of the bush is plainest to children. In the polarized language of Psalm 1, good bushes bear good fruit and good people do and say good things. Bad bushes bear bad fruit and bad people do and say bad things. This standard is not to be used to evaluate others, but to encourage us to say and do the good things that will number us among God's good people.

Using the same language, children can see that it is better to live in a strong, flood-resistant house than in a flimsy one. The houses will become "flags" (like the healthy and barren bushes) for the good and bad people. The understanding of faith as a kind of dwelling place will come in later years.

Be careful about the splinter/log comparison. The mental picture of a person with a log in her eye trying to get a splinter out of someone else's eye amuses children. But at this point in their mental development, few children can move beyond the funny picture to Jesus' point about judgment.

Epistle: I Corinthians 15:51-58. This summary of chapter 15 is filled with too many strange symbols, abstract words, and detailed theological concepts to be understood by children as it is read. What children can hear and respond to is the mood of happy conviction that we do not need to fear death or worry about loved ones who have died. The powerful and loving God is in control of our deaths and will carry us through. If this message is presented simply to children before they can interpret the details of the passage, as their mental abilities grow, they will find in the passage a confirmation of what they already know.

Watch Words

Vocabulary should not present any problems today—unless you focus on resurrection. If you do, remember that *resurrection* needs to be used with several short, simple words and phrases such as "after we die" and "a new kind of life."

Let the Children Sing

"Come Christians Join to Sing" and "All Creatures of Our God and King" reflect both the psalm and Epistle readings, and offer every worshiper a chance to sing—at least the Alleluias.

The Liturgical Child

1. If the flowering plant and dead branch are still available from the sixth Sunday After Epiphany, display them again. Refer to the display to:

- Illustrate Psalm 92. Point to the display, recalling its significance before reading the psalm.
- Recall the comparison of the bushes to set the stage for a discussion of Luke 6:43-45.
- Remind children of the bush "flags" two weeks ago in order to introduce today's "flags," the two houses.

2. Use Psalm 92:1-4 as a Call to Worship, followed immediately by "Come Christians, Join to Sing" as a parallel hymn of praise.

3. Invite five readers of a variety of ages to read one of the wise sayings of Jesus from the Gospel lesson. Each reader begins by saying, "Hear what Jesus said . . .":

Reader 1: verse 39
Reader 2: verse 40
Reader 3: verses 41-42
Reader 4: verses 43-45
Reader 5: verses 46-49

Sermon Resources

1. In the children's classic *Charlotte's Web*, Charlotte, the spider, faces her life and death with an attitude that Paul would recognize and approve. Cite Charlotte as an example or tell part of her story. Chapters 21 and 22 include a conversation between Wilbur, the pig, and Charlotte about her death and the account of her death.

2. To help children sense the security Paul feels in facing death, tell stories about doing new, rather scary things with a trusted friend who has already done these things. Talk about going down a steep hill on a sled, riding a roller coaster, or going away to camp. Having an experienced friend along does not erase all the fears, but it helps. Similarly, dying with Jesus, our experienced, resurrected friend, is not so scary. We can trust him as we go into a new, unknown experience.

3. At the beginning of the sermon, challenge older children to work the puzzle on the worksheet and to listen for each of the words in the sermon. Then be sure to use the words when speaking about our confidence in God.

4. Be an artist. Use the praise-poem outline on the Worship Worksheet as the format for your sermon. Make it a six-point sermon. Introduce each point in a sentence that begins with one of the letters of PRAISE, then expound on it. At the end of the sermon, summarize your points by reading the entire poem. As the children leave the sanctuary, take a moment to respond to any poems they have written.

PRAISE GOD!

Write a praise psalm. For each letter in the word **praise**, write one sentence praising God.

P _____

R _____

A _____

I _____

S ing to God because _____

E _____

God loves us always.
God takes care of us always.
Nothing is more powerful than God.

Follow the word trails to find 5 words we use in worship to talk about God. Shade the letters as you find them.

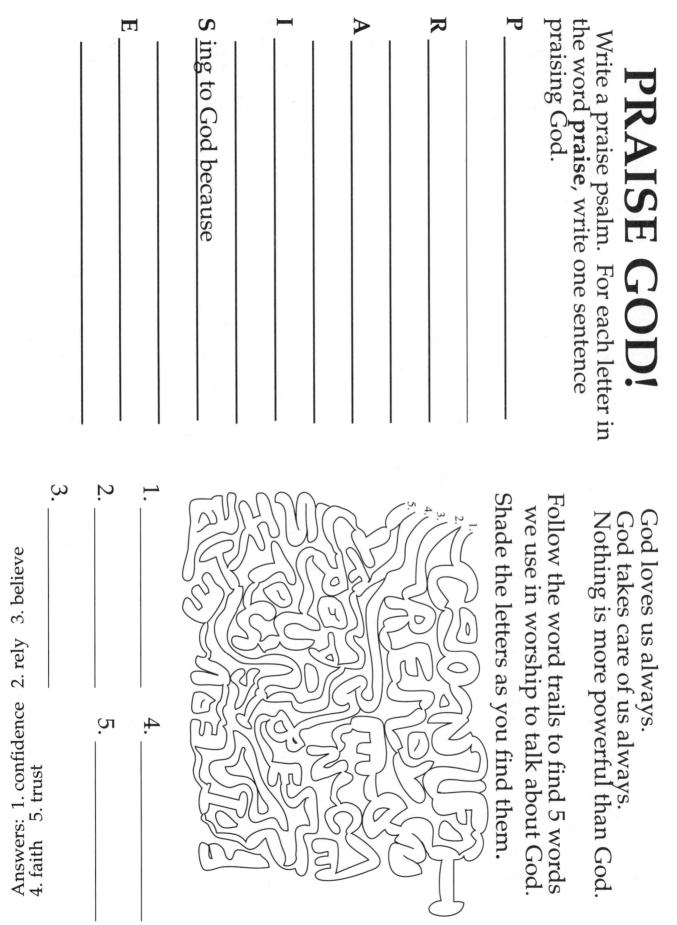

1. _____

2. _____

3. _____

4. _____

5. _____

Answers: 1. confidence 2. rely 3. believe 4. faith 5. trust

LAST SUNDAY AFTER THE EPIPHANY
TRANSFIGURATION OF THE LORD

From a Child's Point of View

We seldom choose to tell children the two stories that are the focal point of today's texts because they lead children to ask uncomfortably unanswerable questions:

Why did God speak to Moses and not to the others? Was God playing favorites?

If I were really in the presence of God, would my face shine? I love God, so how come my face doesn't shine?

Why doesn't the face of anyone in our church shine? Is it because we are not good enough, or was this a special magic trick God did for Moses and Jesus? Did it really happen that way?

Few answers to such questions will satisfy literal-minded children. Children can, however, become familiar with these strange, interesting stories and explore a few key ideas that may seem unrelated to the stories now but will prove related as the children grow older.

Old Testament: Exodus 34:29-35. Children are better able to follow the Transfiguration story if they know that Moses had been on the mountain talking with God for forty days and was bringing back the Ten Commandments written on stone. (The Good News Bible translation is clearest about what Moses was carrying.)

The unstated message of this story is that if you live in God's presence, it will make a difference that others will notice. Moses' shiny face can be seen by adults as a symbol of his attitude toward life and his behavior. While children cannot make

this connection, they can understand that knowing God will make a noticeable difference in their lives. Because they know God loves them, they will love others. Their actions will reflect God's love. As their symbol-making powers grow, they will see a natural connection between this truth and Moses' shiny face.

Epistle: II Corinthians 3:12–4:2. Paul uses Moses' veil as a symbol of all the things we let come between us and God. Paul's argument requires more knowledge of Jews and the Law than children have. But if you restate Paul's message without the first-century details, children can hear Paul's warning not to let anything come between us and knowing God. For children, this means making time to be at church with God's people (because that is one good place to meet God), learning more about God by reading the Bible, and praying (sharing with God) with others and alone.

Gospel: Luke 9:28-36 (37-43). On their first hearing, this story simply says to children that Jesus was special. God showed this with the light and the spoken message. That understanding is a fine place to start living with this story. Older children, if they know who Elijah and Moses were, can learn from this story that God was present with Jesus when he faced a hard task—going to Jerusalem to die. Knowing that God was present to comfort and encourage Jesus, children can be led to expect that God will be present to comfort and encourage them when they face difficult tasks. It would be helpful, however, to point out some phenomena in which we sense God's presence, other than light and voice messages (e.g., God comforting us through the words and presence of other people; a feeling deep inside that God is with us; remembering a Bible verse or singing a song about God).

Psalm: 99. This psalm celebrates the God who shines around Moses and Jesus. To really understand the psalm, one needs to be familiar with Old Testament enthronement language and practices, and to know who Moses, Aaron, Samuel, and Jacob were. Few children do.

However, if children hear this passage introduced as a psalm that praises God, the King of the whole universe, and then are urged to listen carefully to hear what kind of king God is, they can share in the confident mood of the psalm and probably can understand some of the phrases.

Watch Words

Transfiguration has become so obsolete that its dictionary definition refers only to this story about Jesus. It is easy and advisable to explore all the passages without using that word at all. If your tradition names this day of the church year Transfiguration of the Lord, let the term stand as the name of a specific day, rather than try to explain it as a description of what happened to Jesus.

Let the Children Sing

"O Wondrous Sight! O Vision Fair" retells the story of the Transfiguration in fairly simple concrete language.

"Take Time to Be Holy" allows us to sing in short phrases about everyday ways to be close to God.

The Liturgical Child

1. Read the Old Testament and Gospel lessons back to back. Invite the congregation to hear two stories that are very similar. Then read the Old Testament and Gospel stories in your best storyteller style. If you spend "time on the steps" with the children, take the lectern Bible with you and read both lessons there.

2. After introducing it as an enthronement psalm and inviting the congregation to imagine they are in a huge crowd, greeting "God, the King of the Universe," read Psalm 99 responsively. Arrange verses 1-4 and 6-8 in short phrases for responsive reading by alternate halves of the congregation. Plan to read verses 5 and 9 in unison. If there are two worship leaders, have one read with each half of the congregation to keep the pace upbeat and make the readings sound like crowd shouts.

3. Base the prayer of confession for the day on the ways we put a veil between ourselves and God. Children and adults "keep the veil up" when we (1) keep too busy with sports, homework, and television to participate in activities in which we might meet God; (2) avoid activities in which we might meet God, for fear our friends, or even our families might think we are weird and laugh at us; and (3) not even try to meet God because we are not sure how to do it and do not know what it would be like (i.e., we are scared).

Note: Children need to hear the lessons for the day before they can join in this prayer with understanding.

Sermon Resources

1. When two-year-old Jessica McClure was trapped in a well for hours, rescue teams heard her singing Sunday school songs over the microphone they had dropped down the well to monitor her. No one knows for sure what was going on in her mind, but a legitimate case can be made that she sang those songs to comfort herself by remembering times she felt safe and loved—by others and even by God.

2. Invite worshipers to think about times they have sensed God's presence. Share some of your own stories. Be sure to include at least one story from your childhood. For example, I remember sitting on my mother's bed with my brother and sisters to learn the Lord's Prayer. When I peeked at Mother as we were praying together, I felt that she loved God very much and I knew deeply that God loved all of us.

3. Early in the sermon, encourage children to draw pictures of times they have sensed God's presence with them. Be ready to respond to these pictures as the children leave the sanctuary.

Listen carefully when Luke 9:28-36 is read. Draw a picture of what happened in this story.

You may want to read the story again in your Bible to remember the details.

Write a story or draw a picture about a time you felt God very close to you.

FIRST SUNDAY IN LENT

The Revised Common Lectionary provides one set of readings for Ash Wednesday. Year A of this series provides ideas for Ash Wednesday.

 From a Child's Point of View

Gospel: Luke 4:1-13. Each of the three temptations Jesus faced invites a rich variety of interpretations. To children, the first temptation is the temptation to use our power to get what we want. Jesus' temptation, and that of many poor children today, is to be sure to get enough. For other children the temptation is to go for the biggest cookie, the lion's share of the fries, the prettiest dresses on the rack, and the best toys on the block. Jesus' response to this temptation is to remind himself that a life centered on being sure that we get the things we want and need is not much of a life (or will be a lonely, unhappy life, even if we do get most of the goodies).

The second temptation is to be "king of the world"—to get one's own way. In responding to this temptation, Jesus completely ignores the fact that he would have made the very best king of the world ever. Instead, he insists that he is not king of the world—God is. Therefore he will obey God's rules and do God's will. We are called to do the same when we are tempted to make everyone play the game we want to play, go to our favorite restaurant to eat, or watch the television show or video we want to see.

The third temptation for children is the temptation to use our skills and powers to be the center of attention—to show off. Jesus could have used his power to do showy miracles and great feats. Instead, he used it to heal and take care of others. We can use our brains to get the best grades in the class and win all the awards. Or we can use our brains to learn about God's world and find ways to be friends with others. Similarly, we can use our athletic abilities or musical talents to impress others, or we can use them to help everyone have a good time together. Whatever our talents or power may be, we are to use them with as much love and concern for others as Jesus did.

Old Testament: Deuteronomy 26:1-11. Children will not quickly understand this passage. The contradictory repetition of the ritual action is hard to follow, and the story recited in the creed probably will not be recognized without help—even by those who are familiar with the Exodus saga. But this is one case in which providing the needed help is well worth the effort—especially for older children.

Ten- to twelve-year-olds are very interested in the groups to which they belong. Many of them define themselves in terms of these groups: I am an American, one of the Jones family, a Scout—even one of God's people. Being part of a significant group that is "bigger than me" is appealing to these children. They appreciate the possibility of claiming the story of the group as "my" story and letting that story influence the way they act and the things they value. This passage invites children to claim the story of God's people as their story and to let it shape their lives.

Epistle: Romans 10:8b-13. The message of this passage for the children is that God saves and protects all who believe and will say so. The only way to be cut out of God's love is to say we do not want it. Conversely, if we do not stand up for God in what we say every day, we cut ourselves off from God. You will need to present these truths in your own words; Paul's words are too complicated for the children.

Psalm: 91:1-2, 9-16. Many children, especially those who have had fortunate lives thus far, hear this psalm simply as praise for God's care. But other alert, literal-minded children will question the relationship between this psalm and reality as they know it. There are no satisfying answers for these children. Explaining the text's probable source as a psalm for a king going into battle, or its use by Satan to tempt Jesus, may help adults, but it will not answer the children's questions. So it may be best to read the passage and let it stand as is until the children are older.

Watch Words

Confess, to most children, means to admit wrong. In today's creedal lessons, it means to state one's beliefs. Since the word is used in every translation of the Epistle, it would be helpful to redefine *confess* before reading.

Let the Children Sing

"Lord, Who Throughout These Forty Days," a natural choice for adults, is filled with Elizabethan *didsts,* sin jargon like *penitence,* and concepts such as Passiontide, which are strange to children.

"I Love to Tell the Story" celebrates the way we confess our faith. "For the Beauty of the Earth" confesses God's care in everyday terms. It also might be a good Sunday to sing the profoundly simple confession, "Jesus Loves Me." (No less than Karl Barth quoted this song when asked to summarize his faith and theology.)

The Liturgical Child

1. Present the Deuteronomy passage dramatically. As a narrator begins reading the passage from a lectern, a person (possibly wearing a simple tunic) walks forward to the worship center carrying a basket of fruit and vegetables, and places the basket on or in front of the table. At the appropriate time, he or she faces the congregation to recite verses 5b-10, and leaves as the narrator completes the reading.

2. To parallel the Deuteronomy passage and to link our stewardship to our confessions of faith, plan for the congregation to say a creed (perhaps the storytelling Apostle's Creed) at the time the offering for the day is brought forward to be dedicated.

3. Lead the people in praying silently about their temptations. Give instructions such as those below, leaving silence between each one.

> As we come before God, let each of us pray. We each have long lists of things we want and think we need. Let us tell God about these things and ask God to help us avoid the temptations in them. (Pause)
> We all want our own way. We act as though we are king or queen of the world. Let us tell God the truth about how we try to get our own way at home and work and school. (Pause)
> Each of us has talents and abilities and gifts. Thank God for yours, and talk with God about the way you use those gifts to care for others, rather than to make yourselves look good. (Pause, then invite the congregation to join in the Lord's Prayer.)

Sermon Resources

1. To recall the Exodus story, the base of the Deuteronomic creed, show a series of large teaching pictures that illustrate the story. (Look for these in church school closets.) Take the pictures into the congregation one at a time as you review the story during the sermon. In an informal congregation, the worshipers might tell the stories of some of the pictures. In formal congregations, the worshipers will enjoy a close look at the pictures as the preacher tells the stories.

During the rest of the sermon, challenge the children to draw pictures of events in their own faith stories—something that has happened at church, or a time when they felt God was taking care of them. Or they could draw their own version of one of the pictures you showed. Respond to the children's pictures as they leave the sanctuary at the end of worship.

2. Bring three props: a credit card (gold, if possible)—for wealth; a crown (check the Christmas costumes)—for power; and a foil-covered star—for fame. Display each prop on the pulpit as you preach about that temptation, to help the children tune in, at least briefly, on each of the three main points of the sermon.

Draw a picture or
write a prayer
about one
way you
act like
King or Queen of
the world.

Draw one thing you want.

Write a prayer or
draw a picture about
one way you show off.

SECOND SUNDAY IN LENT

From a Child's Point of View

During Lent we wait for God's Easter promises to come true. Today's texts provide an opportunity for children to explore one of God's other promises—the covenant with Abram—to think about what it means to live according to God's promises (Psalm 27, the Transfiguration story, and Paul's challenge to the Philippians), and to look ahead to the Easter promises (Luke 13).

Old Testament: Genesis 15:1-12, 17-18. This is a complicated passage for children, but a part of the familiar story of God's promises to Abram. Recalling some of the rest of this story (Abram's moves and Isaac's birth) will help children understand the promises God made in this chapter.

To help children follow God's conversation with Abram, read from the Good News Bible and take time to explain Abram's concern about not having a son.

If children hear nothing else in this reading, most of them will tune in to the details of the gory covenant-making ritual. The idea that God passed between the split animals in the form of a flaming pot and torch—which, in effect, said to Abram, "May I be split open and left to die if I do not keep the promises I have made to you today"—has great appeal to children. (Remember, this is the age of "blood-brother" rituals and tree-house rites.) The message to children is that God is serious about this and other promises. God's promises can be trusted.

Psalm: 27. This psalm falls neatly into two related halves. Verses 1-6 could be titled "trusting God when everything is going well." Verses 7-14 follow with "trusting God when everything is going wrong." Heard together, the halves remind us that God's promises do not guarantee that everything will always go as we wish it would; but no matter how things are going for us, we can and must trust God's promises. This is a point that older children understand and appreciate, but it is too subtle for them to grasp on their own. They depend on the worship leaders to make the point in introducing the psalm or while exploring the psalm in the sermon.

The Good News Bible offers the easiest translation for children to understand. But if the psalm is read with great passion (see Liturgical Child 2), children can hear past the more difficult vocabulary of other translations to the feelings expressed.

Gospel: Luke 13:31-35 or Luke 9:28-36. Both these passages look forward to Jesus' coming death and resurrection, and both are difficult for children to understand.

In Luke 13, Jesus responds to Herod's threat with the resolve to continue his ministry and go to Jerusalem to fulfill God's promises by dying on the cross. The focus of this passage, however, is less on Jesus' understanding of God's promises than on Luke's readers' (that's us!) anticipation of the promise fulfillment that is to come. Given the poetic "three-day" language, the mother-hen images, and the references to prophetic history, this anticipation can be communicated to the children best by talking in your own words about the coming of Easter and the importance of Jesus' death and resurrection.

The Transfiguration story in Luke 9 promises that God supports those who live by God's promises. In this case, God gives Jesus support to face his coming death so that he may fulfill God's promises. If you read this passage, review the material for Last Sunday After the Epiphany (Transfiguration Sunday).

Epistle: Philippians 3:17–4:1. This passage is also hard for children to understand when they hear it read, but with adult help, they can understand its message—that we are to live as if we believe God's promises. If we believe that God is building a kingdom of love, we should live loving lives, rather than selfish lives focused on getting whatever we want at the moment. Good examples of living according to God's promises can be seen in Paul, Jesus, and Abram.

Watch Words

Promises, especially God's promises to Abram, often lead us to speak of *covenants.* For children, covenant terminology may or may not be familiar. So if you use it, take care to provide definitions as you go. Or avoid misunderstandings by staying with the language of *promises.*

Let the Children Sing

"God Will Take Care of You," which may be listed as "Be Not Dismayed Whate'er Betide," celebrates trust in God's promises. Although many children will not grasp all the language of the verses, the phrase repeated in both the verses and the chorus contains the heart of the message and enables even nonreaders to join in the singing.

"O Wondrous Sight! O Vision Fair" retells the Transfiguration story in song.

The Liturgical Child

Your presentation of these rather complex passages is crucial to how well children will be able to "hear" them.

1. Before reading the Genesis passage, challenge worshipers (especially the children) to listen for the two promises God made to Abram. Either right after the Scripture reading or during the sermon, identify the promises and their source in the text so that children can check for themselves.

2. Emphasize the difference in the two halves of Psalm 27. Ask two people to recite the psalm. As the psalm is introduced, they take their positions, standing back to back at the center of the chancel. They may simply stand without expression, or they may assume positions that reflect their parts of the psalm. The first turns to face the congregation, recites verses 1-6 with happy exuberance, and returns to place. The second then faces the congregation to present verses 7-14, with appropriate expression, and returns to place.

If one person reads the whole psalm, that person can emphasize the difference in the two halves by pausing between verses 6 and 7, turning slightly, and assuming an appropriately different expression and tone for the second half.

3. When reading Luke 13, imagine that you are an actor portraying the scene in the role of Jesus. Read the narrative lines in a matter-of-fact stage-director voice. Read Jesus' lines with great force to portray the humor when he called Herod an old fox and to communicate Jesus' pain in thinking about Jerusalem.

Sermon Resources

1. To pave the way for talking about God's promises, cite some of the promises that are crucial to our relationships with one another. Teachers promise to teach their students what is true and important. When we join a sports team, we promise to attend practices and follow the set disciplines so the team has a chance to win. When two people marry, they promise to love and take care of each other and to be a family. Scouts, Indian Guides, and other clubs require that members make promises when they join.

Describe what it feels like to live according to one of these promises on a good day and on a bad day. For example, it is easy to live by the promises made to teammates when you are playing with friends and the team is winning. It is harder, but just as important, to live by the promises when the team is losing and you feel as if all your work is getting no results. (You might want to tell about a team that goes through both experiences in the same season.)

2. Tell stories of several of God's Promises, such as the promise of the rainbow, the promise of the Messiah, and the promise of the fulfillment of the kingdom of God's love on earth.

Shade each shape with a * in it to find 3 words you will hear, say, and sing in worship today.

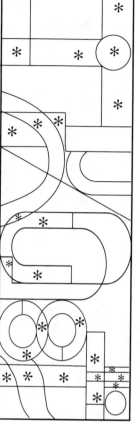

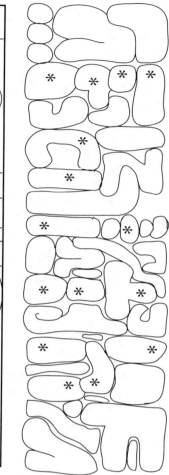

Answers: faith, trust, promises

Pick the words from **Psalm 27** that fit you today. Write those words on the lines below as the beginning of a prayer. Add your own words telling God how you feel.

" I will sing to the Lord."

" Hear, O Lord, when I cry."

"Teach me your way, O Lord."

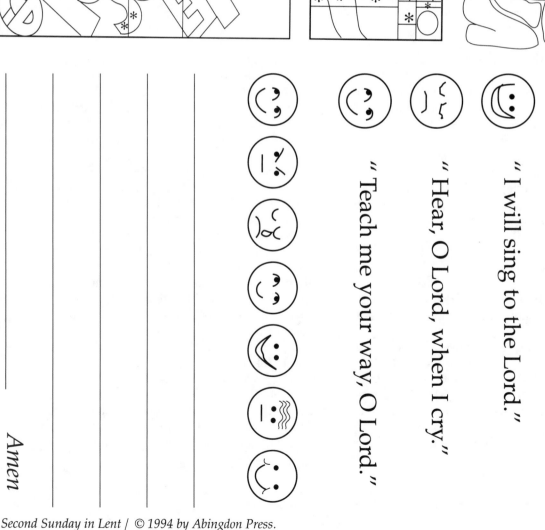

_____

_____

_____

_____

_____

_____

_____

Amen

Second Sunday in Lent / © 1994 by Abingdon Press.

THIRD SUNDAY IN LENT

From a Child's Point of View

Epistle: I Corinthians 10:1-13. This passage, a call to repentance, is the centerpiece of today's lections. The message to children is that all of us are to obey God's rules. We all face temptations. God understands that we are not perfect, but God also expects us to try—and try hard—to do what is right. Verse 13 summarizes these points well.

Unfortunately for children (and for many other worshipers), verses 1-11 assume that readers know the complete story of the Exodus and wilderness wanderings. To understand Paul's points in verse 13, children will need to hear these stories in greater detail.

Gospel: Luke 13:1-9. Few children give death much general thought. Instead, they respond to specific experiences when their pets and people they know die. Therefore, although few children have considered the possibility that terrible deaths are repayment for terrible sins, many older children will be interested in the examples of death that Jesus cites and the problem they present. (They will, however, need help in fleshing out the sketchy biblical references.) The text also provides an opportunity to speak to the common childhood fear that "I have caused the death of (someone I love) by (something terrible I said or did.)"

It is hard for children to find the point in the parable of the fig tree without some help. In children's words, the parable says that God sets high standards for us but is willing to give us many second chances. The parable can be helpfully recast with coaches, as they decide whether to cut a player from the team.

Old Testament: Isaiah 55:1-9. This text offers a truth that is critical to today's discussion of repentance. The truth is that we can trust God to always forgive us when we repent. Without that assurance, even young children know that confession is a risky business. Telling a friend that you told a secret, or telling a parent that you did something forbidden, may meet understanding forgiveness, or it may meet anger and punishment. Even with good friends and loving parents, it can be hard to predict what will happen. Isaiah, however, insists that when we confess to God, we know for sure that we will be forgiven. God is more loving and forgiving than we can imagine.

Unfortunately, children have trouble finding this truth buried in Isaiah's poetic images (verses 1-5 are especially difficult). They are more likely to get the message from the preacher's sermon than from Isaiah's poetic promise.

Psalm: 63:1-8. If this psalm is introduced as a prayer that David prayed while he was hiding in the desert from his enemies, older children will follow and catch the meaning of the first verse. Beyond that, they quickly get lost in the multiple images, even in the Good News Bible's translation. They will grasp the meaning of the psalm more from its happy, confident tone (when it is read well) than from explanations of its content.

Watch Words

Be attentive to the words used to talk, sing, and pray about sin and forgiveness. Many of the traditional words are no longer part of everyday conversation. This means that children need both explanations of and practice in hearing and saying these words in your worship setting.

When speaking of *sin*, use with care the words *transgressions*, *trespasses* (even if your congregation uses the word regularly in the Lord's Prayer), *immorality*, *iniquity*, and *evil*. Remember that for most boys, *offence* is the team with the football and that today's definition of *trespass* is to go uninvited on private land. *Sins* and *wrongs* are just about the only words that require no explanation.

Avoid, when possible, *chide*, *rebuke*, and *requite* to speak of God's judgment of sin. *Punish*, *repay*, and *scold* are actions children recognize.

Mercy and *vindication* are not everyday words. The *redemption* of coupons, the only redemption with which most children are familiar, is not a good parallel to God's activity, *grace* is a girl's name or a reference to moving in a pleasing manner. *Forgiveness* and *pardon* are better words.

Let the Children Sing

Read hymns about repentance carefully. They are so filled with "sin" jargon that none can be suggested for children without reservation. To help children claim a favorite repentance hymn of your congregation, explore it in the sermon or in a children's time before singing it.

"Let My People Go" is a familiar spiritual that retells the Exodus story. Some of the vocabulary in the verses is obsolete, but the familiar chorus is appealing to children.

"Lord, I Want to Be a Christian" is one song in which all of us can sing our commitment to do better. "O Jesus, I Have Promised" is more complex, but it can be sung by older children with a little encouragement.

The Liturgical Child

1. Pay special attention to the usual prayers of confession and pardon in your worship today. Point them out in the bulletin. Explain the movement—from praise, to confession, to thanksgiving. Describe the feeling behind such acts as rising to our feet to sing the "Gloria Patri," after hearing that God forgives us. If there are statements made or responses sung each week, paraphrase them for children before using them. For example, "Kyrie Eleison" means "God forgive me for the unloving things I have said and done."

2. If you celebrate communion today, highlight the fact that when we eat and drink at this table, we remember that God forgives us. Tell stories about Jesus' forgiving the thief who died with him, his frightened friend Peter who pretended not to know him, and even those who killed him. Instruct worshipers to say to the person to whom they pass the elements, *"Name*, God loves us" and *"Name*, we are forgiven."

3. Recite I Corinthians 10:13 as a charge to the congregation before the benediction.

Sermon Resources

1. Set up a rhetorical form in which to tell the Exodus stories cited in I Corinthians 10:1-13. For example:

God gave the Hebrew slaves freedom . . . (tell about crossing the Sea of Reeds). But did the people trust God and live as God's people after this? No . . . (tell about the grumbling about food). We are not to do as they did.

God gave the Hebrew slaves food in the desert . . . (tell the story of the quail). But did the people trust God and live as God's people after this? No . . . (tell about the grumbling about eating only meat). We are not to do as they did.

(Repeat this format with stories of manna, water, God's presence in the pillar of fire and the cloud, and the giving of the Ten Commandments.)

Break out of this format to explore Paul's call to repentance in verses 12 and 13.

2. Talk about sins of which children are capable: cheating; taking what does not belong to them (especially "borrowing" from brothers and sisters); calling names, teasing, or "cutting someone out"; telling lies (or improving upon the truth) to keep out of trouble or to impress friends; breaking promises; and so on.

Find 8 words about sin and
forgiveness. Find 3 people of the
Bible named in worship today.

```
C L F Z C H C
O U O B E Y O
N K R L S Y M
F E G G A K M
E S I N V P A
S K V S E A N
S P E Q Z R D
M A N N A D M
Q U E B Z O E
L L S D R N N
M O S E S R T
```

Draw a picture or write a prayer
to show God one change you want
to make this week. You may want
to change the way you act. Or
you may want to do something to
make life better for another person.

God, I want to change . . .

Amen

Third Sunday in Lent / © 1994 by Abingdon Press.

FOURTH SUNDAY IN LENT

From a Child's Point of View

Gospel: Luke 15:1-3, 11b-32. Most church children will be familiar with this story since it is included in much church school curriculum. The message of the story is that God is like a father who keeps on loving his child no matter what the child has done. The promise to children is that nothing they can do is so bad that God will give up on them. Children who feel they never meet their parents' high standards, children who are constantly in trouble with parents and teachers at home and school, and children who do not have loving parents draw special security from this promise-story.

Be careful about using "father" language. Remember that the parable says God is *like* a father, not *is* a father. God is also like a loving mother, an always-there-for-you grandparent, or a special aunt or uncle. To help children stretch their understanding that God is more than any of our images, and to protect those children who do not have loving fathers, avoid phrases which imply that God *is* a father.

Any child who has a brother or sister can appreciate the older brother's position. It always seems that the other one is getting away with murder. Older children feel that younger siblings go to bed later than they did at the same age, are given less demanding chores and rules, and are "let off" more easily when the rules are broken. Frequently, they are right. Parents often learn as they raise a first child that they need not "sweat the small stuff." Expectations of the younger children are relaxed. Family schedules change as the shape and age of the family as a whole change. And of course, different children have different needs. All this is hard for children to see and to interpret as fair, loving behavior. It is so easy to decide that "they love her more than they do

me" and to cry "Unfair!" with the older brother.

The challenge to the preacher is not to convince children that they are equally loved (some are not), but to urge them to be friends with their siblings—even if they are spoiled and petted. Children are not to judge their siblings harshly, but to judge them with love.

Epistle: II Corinthians 5:16-21. This is what happens when a trained preacher (Paul) puts the meaning of Jesus' parable into his own words: The simple is made beautifully profound in ten-letter words. Although Paul's big words and complex sentence structure are intimidating at first glance, all that children need in order to understand Paul's message is a good definition of *reconciliation*. The Good News Bible provides the best definition: "God . . . changed us from enemies into his friends and gave us the task of making others his friends also." In other words, God (1) has treated each of us with all the forgiving love the father bestowed on the lost son; and (2) asks us to reach out to other "lost sons" as the father asked the older brother to welcome the returned brother.

Old Testament: Joshua 5:9-12. Before reading this passage, remind worshipers of the story and purpose of manna. With this background, children can hear that God kept the promise. God fed the people until they were able to eat the food of the Promised Land.

Psalm: 32. The sin vocabulary of this psalm makes it difficult for children to understand as it is read. But it includes a description of a situation that is familiar to them and parallels that of the runaway son in Jesus' parable. The psalmist, like children, knows what it is like to hide after having done something wrong. It feels awful! It can make you feel sick. Fortunately, the psalmist also knows how good it feels to admit what you have done and be forgiven. Then you feel happy enough to shout for joy (verse 11).

Watch Words

Reconcile, reconciliation, and *reconciling* are key words in these texts, especially in II Corinthians. This word group is worth introducing, defining, and using again and again to build familiarity. The Good News Bible translates these words as phrases about "making enemies into friends." *Peacemaking* and *peacemaker* are good parallel words.

Let the Children Sing

"For the Beauty of the Earth" and "Now Thank We All Our God" praise the God who is Lord of a world united by love.

"Let There Be Peace on Earth, and Let It Begin with Me" gives us the opportunity to commit ourselves to the ministry of reconciliation.

The words of "In Christ There Is No East or West" and "Blest Be the Tie That Binds" are difficult for children. Make the message of either song visual by asking everyone in the congregation to hold hands or to put a hand on the shoulder of the person holding the hymnbook.

The Liturgical Child

1. To create a responsive prayer of confession, the worship leader offers a series of brief prayers about our stubborn sins (greed, wanting our own way, etc.). To each, the congregation responds: "Lord, forgive us when we act like stubborn mules." For example:

> Lord, we admit that even when we know what you would have us do, when we know your will, when we know what the loving thing is, we ignore it. Instead, we do what we want.
> (RESPONSE)

2. As the parable is read, have three actors pantomime the action. Although it is possible for children to do pantomiming with some practice, teenage or adult actors can express feelings with their faces and bodies more forcefully and with more insight.

The richness of their performances will add to the understanding of worshipers of all ages.

Begin with all three actors at the front of the church. The younger son can "run away" down the middle aisle (perhaps throwing party confetti), "eat with the pigs" near the back of the church, then walk "home to meet his father" in the chancel.

3. If you sing "In Christ There Is No East or West" or "Blest Be the Tie That Binds" as a closing hymn, begin the charge and benediction before hands can be dropped. Say something like this:

> God in Christ has changed us from enemies into friends. We are God's friends, and we are friends to one another. Now go out into the world, supported by God's love and the love of your friends in this congregation. Make friends with other people. Reach out in love to draw others into God's worldwide family. Let there be peace on earth, and let it begin with us. Amen.

4. Remember to pray about spring vacations (from school) the week before they occur. Pray for safety, a good time, a chance to be outside, and so on. Remember as you pray that not all children will leave town on exciting trips.

Sermon Resources

1. Tell stories in which children take the lead in peacemaking. School children in Illinois welcomed AIDS victim Ryan White after another community had forced him and his mother to move. Every summer, Catholic and Protestant children, who would not speak to one another at home in Ireland, visit America together. In the process they form friendships they can use to build understanding between warring groups back home.

2. List some of the sinners God loved and used: tricky Jacob, braggy Joseph, hate-filled Jonah, Saul/Paul, and Jesus' disciples (a temperamental fisherman, a fiery troublemaker, a cheating tax-collector). The stories of these people are further proof of God's love. They challenge us to befriend the "impossible" people we live with at home, at school, and in the community.

3. One verse of "Jesus Loves Me" particularly fits the story of the loving father:

> Jesus loves me when I'm good,
> When I do the things I should.
> Jesus loves me when I'm bad,
> Even though it makes him sad.

Paul's message is printed backward. Reverse the order of the letters and the words to find out what Paul said.

"OSLA SDNEIRF SIH SREHTO

GNIKAM FO KSAT EHT SU EVAG

DNA SDNEIRF SIH OTNI

SEIMENE MORF SU

DEGNAHC TSIRHC "

" CHRIST _____

II Corinthians 5:18

Write a prayer about someone who is hard for you to love.

OR

Draw a picture of yourself making friends with a person it is hard to love.

Remember this person as you pray, "Forgive us . . . as we forgive others," when you pray the Lord's Prayer.

FIFTH SUNDAY IN LENT

From a Child's Point of View

Old Testament: Isaiah 43:16-21. Knowing the historical context of the passage is essential to understanding Isaiah's message. Isaiah was speaking to people who were being carried into exile, to assure them that God would not forget them, that this was part of God's plan, and that a wonderful new deed was going to happen. To fully understand Isaiah's message, listeners must know both the Exodus story and the Exile story. This means that few children will grasp what is going on by simply listening to the reading.

However, if the situation is presented as a leader speaking to people who are being carried away from their homes by a conquering army, the child can understand Isaiah's message of hope. Two dimensions of this message speak particularly to children.

First, children can explore the fact that God is working even in unhappy, awful events. The people suffered as slaves in Egypt before they could go into the Promised Land. The Jews had to go into exile before they could rebuild. Jesus had to die on the cross before there could be a resurrection. This reality is good preparation for walking through the dark events of Holy Week.

Second, children can be alerted to look for signs of God at work around them. If God can be at work among people being led away to exile, certainly God can be at work in classrooms, on playgrounds, and in families.

Psalm: 126. All the references to the return from exile and the foreign wilderness images make this psalm hard for children to understand. If the psalm is presented using the reading plan in "The Liturgical Child," some of the older children

will catch the flow of the poem—from "God, you rescued us in the past!" to "God, we need your rescue again," to "We know you can do it, God." Otherwise, this is a psalm for older Bible students.

Gospel: John 12:1-8. Most children like both giving and receiving gifts. They will work for hours crafting a birthday or Christmas gift for a special friend or loved relative, so naturally they are sensitive about how their gifts are received. This is the story of an exquisite gift of love given by Mary to Jesus, who accepted it and protected her and her gift from Judas' mockery. To children, it says that God accepts and values their gifts, just as Jesus accepted and valued Mary's gift.

Although pouring expensive perfume on a person's feet sounds strange to us today, children can follow the story with little explanation. It will, however, help the younger ones if, before the reading, they hear that this Mary was not Jesus' mother but a good friend who also was named Mary.

Epistle: Philippians 3:4b-14. This is difficult reading even for adults. Few children will be able to follow Paul's complex sentences and thoughts. Plan to present Paul's message in the sermon. Themes to develop for the children include the following:

1. Paul knew what was important and what was not. Read verses 4-7 for Paul's list of "garbage." For Paul, being Jesus' disciple was the most important thing. He spent his whole life living as Jesus lived—telling others about God, even when that got him into trouble.

2. Paul did not become a missionary evangelist

to earn God's love or to impress God. Instead, Paul traveled and started churches as a gift to God. Just as Mary gave her gift of nard to Jesus because she loved him, Paul showed his love for God by preaching and starting churches.

Watch Words

The vocabulary in today's readings and themes is fairly simple. Be careful in selecting "exile" and "refugee" vocabulary. *Exile,* especially, may be a new term for the children. Help them decode all the poetic images in Isaiah and Psalm 126. Beware of the temptation to speak about Paul's message in big theological terms such as *sanctification.* If you must use these terms, take care to explain them in everyday-living terms.

Let the Children Sing

To sing about giving God our gifts, choose "Take My Life and Let It Be Consecrated." (Before singing, define *consecrated* as "a way of saying that we are giving ourselves to God.")

If spring is beginning, sing a hymn of praise to the God of creation—"I Sing the Almighty Power of God" or "All Things Bright and Beautiful."

"Tell Me the Stories of Jesus" is a familiar hymn that is good for the Fifth Sunday in Lent.

The Liturgical Child

1. Present Psalm 126 in three sections, with each being read by a different reader or group within the congregation. Identify the sections by the titles below to help worshipers follow the thinking of the poet:

> Remember (verses 1-3)
> Help! (verses 4-5)
> Hope (verse 6)

2. To set the Isaiah passage in context without going into great historical detail, invite the worshipers to imagine that they are refugees living in a foreign country, wishing they could return home. Then read the passage. (The Jerusalem Bible offers a particularly straightforward translation.)

3. If your worship will be focused on gift giving, place on the worship center a large beautifully wrapped gift box with a slot cut in the top. During the offering or at the end of the service, invite the children to put in the box pictures of what they want to give God. Youths and adults also may be invited to put in the box slips of paper on which they have written about gifts they intend to give God.

Sermon Resources

1. Devote the sermon to telling the story of the Isaiah passage—perhaps from the view of a Jewish family watching as the nation is being destroyed and the family is taken into exile in a foreign country with new food and new ways. Talk about what different members of the family would miss most. Then read Isaiah's message. Imagine how this message might have been received by the refugees. What comfort could they find in believing their exile was part of a plan that would end in good? Identify and challenge worshipers to identify dead-end places where God could be at work today.

2. Challenge worshipers to think about the best gift they ever received. Tell about one special gift you have received. Who gave it to you? What made it special? (Note: The best gifts draw giver and receiver closer together.) Mary's gift was her way of showing Jesus how much she loved him. Paul showed his love for Christ by preaching, teaching, and even suffering in prison for talking about Jesus. Challenge worshipers to identify the gifts they give and could give to God.

3. Use Eric Liddell's story (Liddell was the hero in the movie *Chariots of Fire*) to illustrate the effect of knowing what is important. Liddell, after training for months to race in the Olympics, refused to run, even when the king insisted, because the race was to be held on Sunday. He believed that racing on Sunday was disrespectful to God. He loved to run, but he knew God was more important than any race.

God said,

Watch for the new thing I am going to do. It is happening already – you can see it now!

(Isaiah 43:19)

Draw or write about something you think God is doing now in your world, your town, or your church. Listen to the sermon for ideas.

Mary gave Jesus perfume. Paul became a missionary as his gift to God and Jesus.

Draw or write about a gift you want to give God.

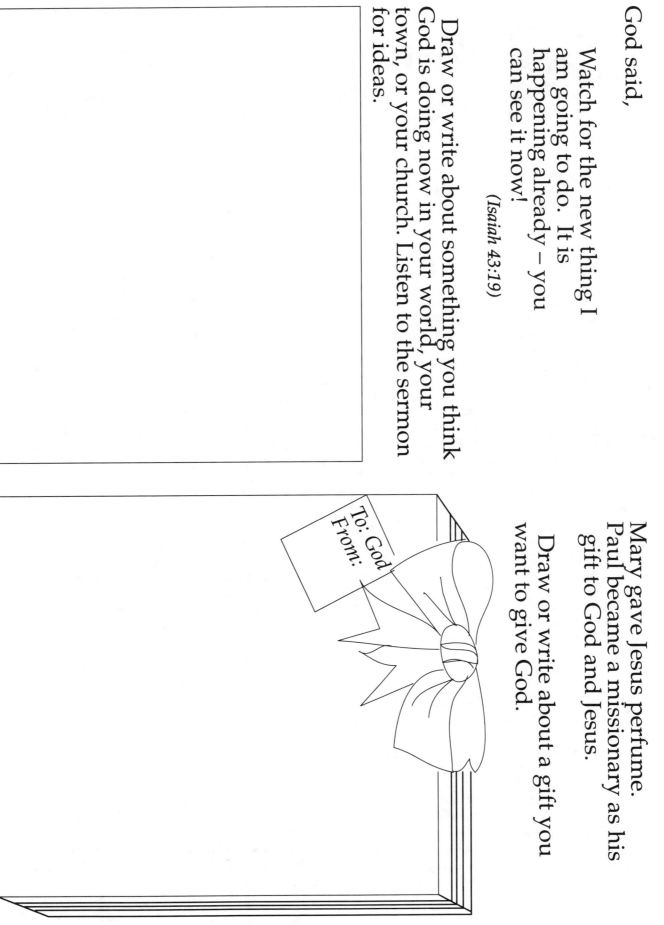

To: God
From:

PALM / PASSION SUNDAY

Note: Read all the materials for Holy Week and Easter Sunday now, even those for days on which your congregation does not gather for worship. Find Resources for Holy Thursday in Year B; those for Good Friday in Year C (this book). Material in each section may be useful in preparing for other sections.

In choosing whether to celebrate Palm or Passion Sunday, give special consideration to children. Often children are rushed from the palm processional to the Easter sunrise. Adults hesitate to explore with them the violent Passion events. Many congregations neither expect nor plan for children to participate in Holy Thursday or Good Friday worship. Consequently, because they have not shared in the pain of the betrayals and the crucifixion, children are unable to experience fully the Easter joy. Instead of protecting children from the darkness of the Passion, we diminish the joy of resurrection. So if children will not worship with the Passion story during the week, you would do well to celebrate Passion rather than Palm Sunday.

From a Child's Point of View

Gospel (Palm): Luke 19:28-40. Luke's account of the triumphal entry mentions neither children, palm branches, nor the word *Hosanna*. The differences in this account and the other Gospel accounts are instructive for careful Bible students. Unfortunately, traditional Palm Sunday hymns include what Luke does not mention, and most worshipers, whether young or old, will "hear" these things in Luke's account anyway. Since there

is little for children to gain in recognizing these differences, it is probably best to celebrate the story of the "combined account" of the Gospels.

The key theme in both Luke's account and the "combined account" is that Jesus is King. Many recent theologians, especially feminists and those in the third world, rightly point to problems in this authoritarian picture of our relationship with Jesus. But children live in a world in which people constantly, and of necessity, tell them what to do and how to do it. A king or teacher or parent is needed for the present. In fairy tales and other children's literature, the king (or queen) is the one who has the right to give the orders, to tell everyone else what to do. This person, like a parent or teacher, is judged bad or good only by the way he or she chooses to use that power.

So the key point of this set of texts is that Jesus, who could have demanded his right to be served by his subjects because he was and is King, chose instead to die for the people he ruled. It is a powerful description of God's love, and a challenging description of how we should treat those we lead when we are the oldest in the group, the patrol leader, the team captain, the class president, and so on.

Gospel (Passion): Luke 22:14–23:56 or 23:1-49. Older elementary school children need basic facts about crucifixion. One fifth-grader, after a very detailed discussion of Roman whips and nails, observed, "The movie I see every year at Aunt Ruth's kind of jumps from Jesus carrying his cross up the hill to the tomb on Easter. I always figured that Jesus was so weak that carrying that cross up the hill had killed him. But he was quite a man to stand all that stuff, wasn't he?" So the gory details do make an important difference.

The betrayal by Judas, Peter's three denials, and the flight of the other disciples are personal injuries that all children can appreciate. The loyalty of friends, especially best friends like Peter, is highly valued. Most children have experienced painful betrayals by friends. Many have been embarrassed or hurt when a friend told a secret (as Judas told where to find Jesus). Most children have known the disappointment when a friend broke a promise (like Peter's boast that he would stick by Jesus always). Although their experiences are minor compared to those Jesus experienced, the pain is similar enough to be meaningful to the children.

Epistle: Philippians 2:5-11. The language of this hymn is complicated for children to follow. But its central message speaks clearly to the childhood concern that "I not miss out on anything that is rightfully mine." Often this concern is presented as a demand for justice or fairness, but behind this demand is a drive to get "my share of the goodies." Therefore, the fact that Jesus refused to insist on what was rightfully his is significant. Without getting tangled in how Jesus preexisted with and in God, children can recognize that Jesus should have been treated royally and given the best of everything. Instead, he spent all his time taking care of others.

He healed people, even when it got him into trouble. He made friends with people others ignored or treated badly even when this embarrassed important people. He argued with leaders who claimed that God loved only people who did what the leaders told them to do; Jesus said that God loved everyone. Finally, when he had to choose between being killed and changing his loving ways, he chose to keep on loving. God then raised Jesus from death, made him more powerful, and gave him greater fame than any earthly king ever had.

There are two points in this passage for children. The most important is that Jesus loves each of us enough to give up what rightfully belongs to him in order to care for us. Second, we are called to follow Jesus' example and take care of others rather than worry about whether we are getting everything we deserve.

(Palm) Psalm: 118:1-2, 9-29;
(Passion) Isaiah 50:4-9a; Psalm: 31:9-16. Each of these passages parallels Jesus' Holy Week experience. As each is read, children will catch words and phrases that remind them of either the triumphal entry or the crucifixion. The Gospel or Epistle readings will, however, be the focus of the children's attention.

Watch Words

The word of the day in hymns and prayers is *Hosanna!* It is a fun word to say and sing because it is a greeting meant only for Jesus.

Be sure the children know the difference between Jesus' *Passion* and the lusty feelings the word *passion* usually describes today. Remember that *crucify* and *crucifixion* are terms children will encounter only in church. Translate big words *atonement* means at-one-with, as in Jesus helped us be *at one with* God; *salvation* is being saved from all the trouble our sinful behavior causes.

Let the Children Sing

"All Glory, Laud, and Honor" or "Hosanna, Loud Hosanna" are Palm Sunday hymns that children can sing easily, either as a children's choir or in the congregation.

Sing "This Is the Day" (*The United Methodist Hymnal*) responsively between choir (or leader) and congregation as the Call to Worship.

If you focus on the kingship of Jesus, close with "All Hail the Power of Jesus' Name." Though the ideas in the verses are difficult, the repeated chorus, "Crown him Lord of all!" can be sung by even the youngest worshiper.

"O Sing a Song of Bethlehem" calls us to sing our way from Christmas to Easter in four verses, and thus is a good Passion Sunday hymn to help children connect the baby to the man.

The Liturgical Child

1. If your worship will include a processional with children carrying palms:

• Provide each child with a palm branch, rather than one strip of palm leaf. (Try to get a mental picture of a crowd waving those stringy palm leaves and laying them on the road for Jesus' donkey to walk on! Those people used full branches.) Most local florists can provide branches for a nominal fee.

• Include the minister(s), choir(s), and others in the processional so that it isn't a "cute children's thing." Remember that Luke says it was adults who thought of this parade and led the way.

• Instead of processing into the sanctuary at the beginning of worship, before the story can be told, hold the palm processional at the end of worship. By then worshipers will have heard the story and explored its meaning, and now can be challenged to go out into the world to proclaim Jesus as their King. Ushers (perhaps children) can give a palm branch to each worshiper—beginning with the minister(s) and choir(s), then the other worshipers as they leave their pews.

• Suggest that the palms be displayed in homes all Holy Week (perhaps on the dinner table or in a vase on the TV), as a reminder that Jesus is our King.

2. For Passion Sunday, devote the entire service to a "Walk Through Holy Week with Jesus." Alternate Scripture readings with hymns, or sing hymns followed by a prayer. Some of the hymns can be choir anthems:

Triumphal Entry—Luke 19:28-40
Last Supper—Luke 22:7-23
The Betrayal and Arrest—Luke 22:47-53
Trials—Luke 22:66–23:25
Crucifixion and Burial—Luke 23:32-46, 50-56
Summary: Philippians 2:5-11 (This may be the base for a very brief meditation.)

Check the Good Friday suggestions when selecting hymns for this service.

Sermon Resources

1. Prominently display two crowns: a golden crown (perhaps from the Christmas pageant props) and a crown of thorns. In the sermon, explore two kinds of kings. The first lives in a palace, is strong enough to scare off enemies, and makes rules for the country. Paint a picture—not of an evil king, but of one who is authoritarian. Then describe the king that Jesus became by spending his life taking care of his people and finally dying for them.

2. After describing how we treat kings (we do whatever they say, we try to please them, we give them the best of everything, we bow or defer to them), explore who and what we tend to treat as "king of our life." Children often let a special adult, such as a teacher or professional sports figure/hero, become their king. In some neighborhoods, a child may become king of the block and totally run the show (this king may be an overtly evil gang leader or a benevolent natural leader to whom the other children always defer). The scriptural challenge is not to let anyone but Jesus be King in our lives. Jesus and his ways are to be more important than any other child or adult leader.

Draw a picture of one story about King Jesus in each empty square. Listen to today's Scripture readings and sermon for ideas.

When he was Born		
	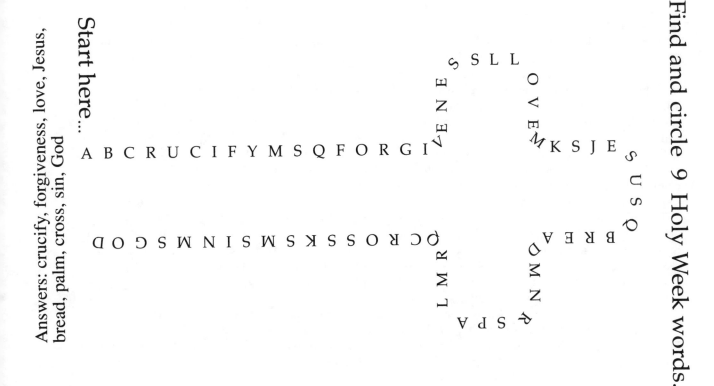	
	Blessing Children	

Find and circle 9 Holy Week words.

Start here...

A B C R U C I F Y M S Q F O R G I V E N E S S L L O V E M K S J E S U S Q B R E A D M N R S P A L M R Q C R O S S K S S M S I N M S G O D

GOOD FRIDAY

From a Child's Point of View

Gospel: John 18:1–19:42. The story is the focus of the day. It is a simple, very graphic story. Jesus was betrayed by a friend, denied by his best friend, slapped across the face by a soldier simply for answering a question, whipped, treated cruelly by soldiers who dressed him in a robe and smashed a crown of sharp thorns upon his head, and finally, crucified. Throughout it all he remained gentle, loving, and forgiving. The story needs little explanation. It speaks on its own to people of all ages.

What the story says to children is that God still loved those people, even after they did such horrible things to Jesus. (God proved that love with the resurrection.) For younger children, it is enough to hear the story of the crucifixion and to know that God's love and power is stronger than the worst things the cruelest enemies can do. Older children can begin to identify the reasons people wanted to kill Jesus. Jesus loved everyone, even those the "good" folks did not want to have around. Jesus called on everyone to share whatever they had with anyone who needed it, and many people did not want to share. Some of the older children will begin to realize that we are capable of that same selfish response to Jesus' love.

Though it is a riveting story, it also is a long one and includes several passages in which children's attention can wander and be lost. So if you read the entire text, read it in sections, interspersed with liturgy. It is also possible to omit some of the abstract trial conversations.

Epistle: Hebrews 10:16-25 or 4:14-16; 5:7-9. The concept of Jesus as the Great High Priest requires both knowledge of and appreciation for the Old Testament system of animal sacrifice. Although it is possible to present knowledge about this approach to sin and forgiveness to children, this type of sacrifice is totally foreign to them. They generally ask questions like these: "If we are expected to forgive each other 'for free,' how come God has to have a special gift to do it?" "How can killing an animal make God happy?" "Why did God need Jesus to die in order to forgive us?"

There are no answers that satisfy young minds. Appreciation of this theology will have to wait until their mental abilities develop enough to allow abstract thought.

Chapter 5:7-9 does offer one point for older children. Jesus was in trouble because he was too loving. He knew he was in trouble and that he was going to be hurt. He asked God not to let that happen, but he also kept on loving. He refused to stop loving. He lived by God's great Commandments, and for that he was killed. We are called to be as obedient as Jesus was. (Note: Good Friday is a day to celebrate *God's* love, rather than to call on worshipers to be more loving. Our best love never will be as powerful as God's love. So this point is probably best saved for another occasion.)

Old Testament: Isaiah 52:13–53:12. If this passage is introduced as one that always makes people think about Jesus, children will hear specific phrases that remind them of Jesus and his suffering. The prophetic nature of the passage is not particularly meaningful to children.

Psalm: 22. If this psalm is introduced as a psalm Jesus may have prayed on the cross, children will hear occasional phrases that remind them of what happened to Jesus.

78

Watch Words

The child's word for *scourged* is *whipped*.

Crucify and *crucifixion* are words heard only at church and mainly during the Easter season. Be sure to define them so children know what you are talking about.

Beware of "sacrifice" language such as *high priest*, *sacrifice*, *mercy*, *grace*, and *salvation*. Avoid speaking of the cross in symbolic ways (e.g., hold fast to "the cross"). Instead, tell what happened in concrete, everyday terms.

Let the Children Sing

"Were You There When They Crucified My Lord?" is the best hymn for the day because it tells the story in simple language, with music that has deep emotional quality.

This same emotional quality allows "O Sacred Head Now Wounded" to speak musically in spite of its difficult atonement vocabulary.

Avoid hymns with much symbolic language, such as "Ah, Holy Jesus," as well as "In the Cross of Christ I Glory," in which the cross is presented in symbolic terms.

The Liturgical Child

1. Begin the service with the sanctuary decorated as usual for Lent. For the call to worship, remove the flowers, purple paraments, and any other decorations. Do this in silence, during the singing of the first hymn, or while speaking informally about the solemnity of the day, telling why each item is removed. (Older children serving as acolytes may help with this.) After the crucifixion narrative is read, drape a strip of black fabric across the arms of the central cross (if it is within reach).

2. Tenebrae is a candlelight service in reverse. The service begins with all candles lit. Readers then read sections of the Passion story. After each section is read, snuff out one candle, until the room is completely dark. Experience darkness for about a minute. Then light one candle as a sign of the hope of the coming resurrection. Worshipers leave in silence.

The following readings trace the story (streamlined a bit, with children in mind).

John 18:1-14	Jesus is arrested
:15-18, 25-27	Peter's denials
:28-32, 38b-40	Jesus is tried by Pilate
19:1-6	Jesus is sentenced to death
:17-22	Jesus is crucified
:23-24	Soldiers gamble for Jesus' cloak
:25-27	Jesus cares for his mother
:28-30	Jesus dies
:38-42	Jesus' body is buried
Total darkness	
John 3:16-17	"God so loved the world . . ."

Place the tenebrae candles in a row on a long table, with a snuffer at each end. Select readers of all ages (with practice, young children can read the shorter passages). Seat the readers at the table so that the readings and candle snuffings can proceed in order from the ends of the table toward the center. The center candle should be the last to be snuffed and the one to be relighted.

Meet with the readers before the service so that all can take their places quietly on cue. Have the younger readers practice in the sanctuary so that they can be easily understood. Plan ahead to be sure that the last readers have sufficient light in order to read.

A tenebrae can be part of a longer service, or songs and prayers can be interspersed with the readings to form a Good Friday liturgy. Obviously, a tenebrae is more effective at night or in a room that is easily darkened.

Sermon Resources

This is a day for minimum preaching and maximum storytelling. Tell stories about love that "won't give up." Talk about a person going to great lengths to care for a sick pet. Describe the efforts of a child to befriend a very unlovable neighborhood outcast. Tell about parents who stand by very difficult teenage children. Then tell about Jesus, who loved us even unto death, and who rose, proving that God's love cannot be overcome.

No Worship Worksheet is provided for today because the service should be so story-oriented and dramatic that papers and pencils would be in the way.

EASTER

From a Child's Point of View

Gospel: John 20:1-18 or Luke 24:1-12. Both stories of the discovery of the empty tomb can be read to children with little explanation. The response of the children is, however, different from that of adults. For children, Easter joy has more to do with the victory of God's powerful love over the forces of evil than with resurrection from death.

It is hard for children to understand death. Most children, even those who have experienced the death of a close relative, have trouble grasping the physical finality of death. Children who grow up in Christian churches, hearing the resurrection faith that God loves us even beyond death, do not easily share the fear of death described in the New Testament. Psychologists tell us that even teenagers have little meaningful understanding of their personal mortality. So it is hard for children to get into the celebration of resurrection from death. This part of the Easter message will mean more later in their lives.

In childhood, the central message of Easter is that God refused to let the hate of Good Friday be the last word. Considering everything that had been done to Jesus, God deserved to become angry and punish the people severely. But God did not do this. Instead, God continued to love the people who had betrayed, denied, and killed Jesus. And God refused to let Jesus stay dead. Jesus rose from death to prove to us that God's love is more powerful than the worst evil and that God will continue to love us, no matter what terrible things we do. So for children, the empty tomb is God's biggest surprise, and Easter joy is our delighted response to the discovery that even though it looked as if the "bad guys" had won,

they had not. God and God's love had defeated the forces of evil and were more in control than ever.

Old Testament: Isaiah 65:17-25. The rich poetic images of Isaiah's vision of God's dreams for the world are like coded messages for which literal-minded children have no key. The Good News Bible decodes some of these images as part of its translation and therefore is easier for children to follow. Even if read from this translation, the vision is challenging for children, but if it is presented as the dream of the Easter God who has defeated and continues to defeat evil, this passage becomes a glimpse into the future toward which God is working. Children will hear in specific phrases the possibilities to anticipate.

Acts 10:34-43. (During the Easter season the Revised Common Lectionary suggests a reading from Acts as an alternative to the Old Testament reading.) Taken in context, Peter's statement in Joppa is about the fellowship of God's family, which crosses all human boundaries of nationality, race, and so on. But for Easter Sunday, it is a summary of the good news about Jesus and an opportunity for listeners to view themselves as witnesses, like Peter. Children who have celebrated the events of Holy Week are ready to respond by becoming witnesses. At the very least, they can recite the story in worship and claim it as their own. Some also can recognize the need for Christians to share the story with others.

Epistle: I Corinthians 15:19-26. This is a difficult passage for children. That we should all die because Adam and Eve ate the apple seems terribly unfair. That God should punish us for what

Adam and Eve did seems inconsistent with our insistence that God is loving. In their teen years, youths will begin to understand that what links us and our fates to Adam and Eve is that all of us disobey sometimes, in spite of our very best intentions. But this link is beyond the comprehension of most younger children. So read this passage for worshipers who are old enough to grasp the fear of death and so have the mental ability to feel linked both to Adam and Eve and to Christ.

Psalm: 118:1-2, 14-24. To children, this is a collection of short praises to the powerful God who saves us. Many of the praises require little explanation. Others, such as the verses about the rejected stone, include images that require detailed explanation. Today is not a particularly good time to explain these images, so it is better to let the psalm speak as it can to the worshipers celebrating God's Easter power.

Watch Words

Enjoy the Alleluias! *Alleluia* wraps into one word these messages: "Hurray for God!"; "God, you did a great job!"; "Thank you, God!"; "Knowing you makes us happy, God!"

Use *resurrection.* It is a good word for children to hear and to recognize as belonging to the church. But do not expect children to find much meaning in the word until their understanding of death matures.

Let the Children Sing

"Jesus Christ Is Risen Today" is probably the best Easter hymn for children. Even the youngest can join in on the Alleluias. (Challenge them to count the Alleluias for Easter fun.) Older children will pick up more of the short phrases of praise which precede the Alleluias every time they sing the song.

Children enjoy the contrasting feel of the verses and the chorus of the old gospel hymn "Up from the Grave He Arose." This hymn emphasizes the surprising nature of Easter.

Avoid hymns with lots of "resurrection" and "salvation" jargon.

The Liturgical Child

1. Children can sense Easter joy before they can explain it. So fill the sanctuary with flowers. Hang white and gold paraments. Play joyful music. Add instruments such as brass to draw special attention to the music.

2. Encourage the presence of children at sunrise services held outdoors in a garden or cemetery. Focus on telling the story, singing an Easter hymn, and praying brief prayers of praise and thanksgiving. Save sermonizing for indoor worship later in the day. The location and timing of a sunrise service adds new reality to the empty-tomb story and makes the day stand out as a very special day for our church.

If crowds at mid-morning worship services are a problem, a story-oriented sunrise service to which children are particularly invited can open seats in the later service and thus allow worship at that time to be more adult-oriented.

3. Invite worshipers to read Acts 10:37-43 as a creed in which they respond with Peter to what God has done in Jesus.

Sermon Resources

1. Like the rest of Holy Week, Easter for children is a time for storytelling and praising, rather than for critical thinking and sermonizing.

2. To focus the sermon on God's surprises, tell stories of God's surprises in the life of Jesus. Begin with God's decision to be born among us in a barn and to announce the birth to shepherds. Tell how Jesus befriended Zaccheus, a greedy tax collector. Tell about the time Jesus surprised people by proving that they had enough food for everyone in the crowd. Describe Peter's surprise and embarrassment when Jesus, his hero and God's leader, washed Peter's feet. Finally, tell of Jesus' death and the surprising way God announced his resurrection to women, rather than to important men. Create a rhetorical refrain, such as "God said, 'Surprise, I love you' " with which to conclude each story.

Happy Easter!

Today our worship is filled with Easter words. Find them in the puzzle.

Draw a butterfly  each time one of these words is said in worship.

Draw a flower  each time one of the Easter words is sung in worship.

At the end of the service, this page will be an Easter garden.

Fill in the blanks with the correct Easter words.

R — — — — —

— — E — — — —

EASTER

— — U — — —

— — R — — —

— — — R — — —

— — C — — — — —

— — T — — —

— — I — —

— O — —

— N — — — —

alive   stone   Jesus
Mary   Christ   risen
alleluia   tomb   Peter
forgiven   sunrise

SECOND SUNDAY OF EASTER

From a Child's Point of View

John 20:19-31. This passage includes two related, yet separate Easter stories.

John 20:19-23 describes Jesus' first postresurrection encounter with the disciples. His appearance tells us two things about his resurrected body. First, he appears inside a locked room; his "new" body is not like the physical body he had before death. Second, his body bears the wounds of crucifixion; his body is still the same. This is the same Jesus who was killed on Friday. Children will be curious about this.

During this encounter, Jesus reassured his disciples that he was indeed alive, and then he put them to work. The message to children is that Easter is not an ending; it is a new chapter in God's work. On Easter evening, Jesus is already looking ahead. He gives his disciples the gift of the Spirit and sends them out, saying, "As the Father sent me, so I send you."

To help the children identify what the Father sent Jesus to do, explore key stories about Jesus' ministry. Their challenge is then to find ways to do that kind of work today. Just as Jesus fed the hungry crowd, children can work to help relieve hunger. Just as Jesus befriended the friendless, children can make friends with the lonely people they meet, and so forth.

The story of Thomas reassures children that the Risen Lord is still the kind, understanding Jesus. Thomas, who was left out of the first encounter with Jesus, raises the kinds of questions any child might raise. Jesus is not offended by the questions, but honors them and offers to let Thomas touch the wounds, if that's what it takes to answer his questions. In so doing, Jesus blesses all our questions. No honest question is too silly, dis- respectful, or unworthy to be asked and answered (or at least discussed).

Acts 5:27-32. This passage gives an example of the disciples doing as Jesus instructed. They are being witnesses to what God has done through Jesus. For children, the heart of this passage is Peter's statement, "We must obey God rather than men." This is a brave stand. It calls on children to be as heroic as Peter in obeying God's laws and doing God's will, rather than going along with the crowd when the crowd is not going God's way. The "crowd" is most often other children who play together in informal settings, but it also can include their own families, school classes, or even congregation. (Children can become the conscience of their communities.)

Psalm 118:14-29 or 150. These exuberant praises are fitting psalms for Jesus' disciples after Easter. When they are read with strong, happy conviction, children understand the meaning of occasional phrases, but they respond more strongly to the mood of the psalms. Dramatic presentation is essential.

Revelation 1:4-8. This passage includes lots of imagery with Old Testament roots, which are beyond children. Two phrases, however, do stand out for children. The first is the set of phrases about God, who is "Alpha and Omega," who "was and is and is to be." These are the answers to the questions, "What was there before God?" or "Who made God?" These answers challenge children to begin thinking of God as bigger than they can imagine. Such conversations lay the foundation of children's theology and provide great security. (If we are in the care of such a power, we are safe.)

The second phrase that grabs children's attention is the description of Christians as "a kingdom of priests," or as Protestant children might say, "a kingdom of ministers." This parallels John's sending of the disciples and can be explored in much the same way.

Watch Words

The words of today's texts pose no problems for children. Avoid generalizing the messages of the texts with big words about the omnipotence of the preexistent God.

Let the Children Sing

Singing "Come Christians Join to Sing" is a good way to keep the Alleluias going the week after Easter (and throughout the Easter season).

"Rejoice, the Lord Is King," with its repeated chorus of "Lift up your heart, lift up your voice," celebrates the Lord who is King.

The Liturgical Child

1. Present John 20:19-31 with three readers. The worship leader for the day introduces the passage and recalls what happened in verses 1-18. A second reader then reads verses 19-23. A third reader picks up with verses 24-29. The first reader then concludes by reading verses 30-31. Changing readers for the different stories within the ongoing narrative helps keep the children's attention.

2. Give Acts 5:27-32 your best dramatic reading. Read the high priest's question in an authoritarian voice, looking down your nose at the disciples from one side of the lectern. Then turn slightly as you read Peter's brave, enthusiastic reply.

3. Use Psalm 150 as a call to worship before an Easter praise hymn. Readers (either a children's class, a choir, or the whole congregation) repeat the psalm in unison, pausing after verses 3, 4, and 5 for the instrument(s) mentioned in that verse to be played. In place of the trumpet, lute, and pipes, the organ could be used with the appropriate stops. Each instrumentalist plays the first line of the hymn; the congregation then sings in response to the last verse of the psalm.

4. Ask the adult choir to present Psalm 118 as a spirited choral reading for Easter people: verse 14—UNISON; verses 15-18—MEN (perhaps with solos for the shouted phrases of vss. 15-16); verses 19-20—UNISON; verses 21-23—WOMEN; and verse 24—UNISON.

5. If you sing the Gloria Patri regularly in worship, take time either just before singing it or during the sermon to explore the meaning of "As it was in the beginning, is now, and ever shall be, world without end." This is on-the-job worship education.

6. Create a benediction based on John 20:21. For example:

> Peace be with you. As the Father sent me, even so I send you . . .
>> to heal those who are sick and dying . . .
>> to befriend the friendless in Jesus' name . . .
>> to tell of God's love . . .
>> (etc., based on points of the sermon)
>
> As you go, remember that the peace of God is with you, and the power of the Holy Spirit will uphold and direct you because you are the Easter People, a kingdom of priests for God. Amen.

Sermon Resources

1. These texts and those for the following Sundays suggest a sermon series about Easter People. Explore who the Easter People are, what they do, and what they are like. Challenge worshipers of all ages to see themselves as Easter People. Consider giving each worshiper a small token, perhaps a plastic or metal cross to carry in a pocket each day during the coming weeks, as a reminder that each of them is one of the Easter People. Ask the choir to sing Avery and Marsh's song, "Every Day Is Easter Day," today and several times during the series.

From today's texts we learn that Easter People experience God's peace (John), praise God (Psalms), obey God first (Acts), and are sent to serve (Revelation and John).

2. Tell stories about people who chose to obey God rather than people. Include stories about well-known people such as Martin Luther King, Jr. Also, describe activities in your congregation that show you to be Easter People: volunteer work (serving as a kingdom of priests); mission projects (carried out by youth groups); and specific events which give a peace-filled feeling (perhaps a congregational weekend retreat in which children participate).

The New Testament was first written in Greek. Use the key below to translate this Greek verse into English.

καθὼς   ὁ   πατὴρ
___ ___ ___

ἀπέσταλκέ   με,
___ ___

κἀγὼ   πέμπω   ὑμᾶς.
___ ___ ___

John 20: 21b

Translator's key

καθὼς = as   ὁ = the
κἀγὼ = I also   πατήρ = father
με = me   ἀπέσταλκέ = sent
ὑμᾶς = you   πέμπω = send

Listen carefully to the reading of John 20:19-31. Draw a picture of Jesus meeting his disciples on Easter evening. Make their faces and bodies show their feelings.

Second Sunday of Easter / © 1994 by Abingdon Press.

THIRD SUNDAY OF EASTER

From a Child's Point of View

Resurrection means new life. Today's texts include the stories of two people who received new chances at life from the resurrected Jesus; a psalm about how God saves or heals us; and a poetic image of Jesus, "the (resurrected) Lamb."

John 21:1-19. The message of this interesting fishing story is that although Peter denied knowing Jesus three times, Jesus gave him another chance. Children need to know that God and Jesus give many second chances to those who love God but sometimes "chicken out" or make mistakes.

In order to understand the story, children need to be reminded of Peter's triple denial and how Peter felt about it.

Acts 9:1-6 (7-20). The story of Paul's conversion on the Damascus road is another interesting story that children can follow without explanation *if* it is read with dramatic flair.

The story makes two points to children. First, Paul's conversion is another Easter surprise—almost a joke played by God. God's strategy for ending the persecution of the early church was to turn the leader of the death squad into a Christian missionary! This is not a strategy many Christians would have suggested—even in jest. Some had trouble believing it when it happened. In turning Saul into Paul, God alerts us to look for new life in strange places and people. If God could turn Saul around, there's no guessing what other Easter surprises might be in store for us. Read the story to celebrate God's incredible power and sense of humor.

Second, the story promises forgiveness. If God is willing to forgive Saul, who killed Christians, and put him to work in the Easter kingdom, then perhaps there is a chance for us. To children who are frequently in trouble or feel they never measure up to what is expected of them, this is a very hopeful story.

Psalm 30. If this psalm is introduced as the prayer of a person who has been saved from something terrible, and children are urged to listen for clues to what that "terrible thing" might have been (maybe enemies or serious illness), they will hear a few of the clue phrases and catch the message of even more of the praise phrases. The psalm can also be presented as a prayer that Peter or Paul might have prayed after being given a new chance by Jesus.

Revelation 5:11-14. This passage is a coded message written during a time when a person who carried a piece of paper with Jesus' name on it could be fed to the lions. Children cannot understand the atonement theology which makes the lamb a good symbol for Jesus. But they can be told that "Lamb" is a code word for Jesus and that "one who sits on the throne" is a code for God. With this information, they can enjoy the challenge of decoding John's Easter message (God and Jesus are worthy of praise by everyone in the world).

Watch Words

Do not let the word *Lamb* lead you to use other "slain lamb" language in worship today. Children can understand *Lamb* only as a code word for Jesus.

THIRD SUNDAY OF EASTER

In talking about the second chances that Peter and Saul received, speak of *forgiveness* and of being *changed* rather than of *salvation* or *conversion*. (For most children today, *conversion* is a football term, or what you do with metric system measurements.) So unless your congregation uses the word regularly and specifically defines it, avoid using it today.

Let the Children Sing

"Come, Christians, Join to Sing" continues to be a good Easter-season choice.

"Blessing and Honor and Glory and Power" can be fun to sing because it uses the Revelation code for simply worded praises to God. Point out before singing that this would be a good hymn to sing if Christians were being persecuted by those who did not know the code.

The Liturgical Child

1. There is great dialogue in John 21. Read it as it would have been spoken. Shout out the exchange between the fishermen in the boat and Jesus on shore. Decide how you think John would have said, "It is the Lord!" and speak the line accordingly. As you read verses 15-19, show Peter's embarrassment, hesitation, and self-disgust in your voice, and then let Jesus' forgiving love be apparent. Such a reading will make the whole text (1-19) a story that children can enjoy and appreciate.

2. Before reading John 21, remind the congregation of Peter's three denials and alert them to listen for Jesus' three responses. As you read each question, answer, and command sequence, hold up one, then two, and finally three fingers as clues.

3. Pray about apparently hopeless situations in which new life (or an Easter "turn around") is needed. In addition to noting community and worldwide issues, pray for people at school and at work with whom it is really hard to get along, for peace on school buses, and for problems between brothers and sisters who must share rooms and do chores together.

4. Create a litany of confession and petition in which the worship leader describes a variety of hopeless situations on personal, community, and international levels. To each case, the congregation responds, "Lord, forgive us, and help us find your Easter surprise here." (Only the response needs to be printed in the bulletin.) For example:

Worship Leader: Lord, each of us knows some people who get on our nerves. Something about the way they act just drives us a little crazy. We would like to find a way to be friends with these people, or at least be kind to them, but they bring out the worst in us. We say cruel words almost without thinking. We treat them in ways that surprise us. We'd like to do better.

Congregation: Lord, forgive us, and help us find an Easter surprise.

Sermon Resources

1. *The Great Gilly Hopkins,* by Katherine Paterson, is an award-winning children's novel about a ten-year-old terror with one-in-a-long-line of foster parents. (The book is available in the children's section of most public libraries and generally available in bookstores.) Read part of or summarize the whole story's Easter-like changes. Then retell the stories of Saul's change of direction, Peter's forgiveness, and Jesus' resurrection. Gilly, Peter, Saul, and Jesus are all Easter people.

2. Ask the worshipers to produce the Easter tokens they were given last week. (Have the ushers ready to pass out tokens to those who do not have them.) Challenge worshipers to think about the week ahead and identify the difficult people and situations they will encounter. Then instruct them to carry their tokens with them again this week as a reminder that all hopeless situations and people are possible Easter surprises. Suggest that reaching into a pocket to hold the token can help us continue to work with God in frustrating situations.

Shade in the spaces with a *
inside to find . . .

a word that describes Easter People.

Draw a picture of a person who needs
an Easter surprise.

Write a prayer for this person.

what Jesus says to Easter People.

Answer: forgiven; follow me

FOURTH SUNDAY OF EASTER

From a Child's Point of View

John 10:22-30 and Psalm 23. These passages are based on the image of God or Jesus as a good shepherd. It was a great image in Jesus' day, and it can be meaningful today *if* we know a little bit about shepherds. Most urban children do not. To them, a shepherd is as likely to be a large, sometimes fierce dog as a person who cares for sheep.

Psalm 23 is based on the care that a shepherd must provide for totally defenseless sheep in a hostile environment. Not only must they be protected from wild animals, but they must be rescued from problems they got into but cannot get out of. For example, sheep can become tangled in thorn bushes or lost from the flock. When they wade into a fast-moving stream to drink, their wool can get so heavily soaked that they lose their footing, fall, and drown. It is the shepherd's job to protect the sheep from attacking animals, keep them together in safe pastures, and find still, shallow water so they can drink safely. Good shepherds will risk their lives for their sheep. As Easter People, we know that God in Jesus does the same for us.

To understand John's passage, children must know that shepherds often kept all the sheep of their village in one fold (fenced yard). When it was time to separate the flocks, all the shepherds called their sheep, each using a unique call. The sheep of each flock recognized their shepherd's call and left the sheepfold only with that shepherd.

Easter People recognize Jesus' call. So when they hear the call to love one another and to love God, they follow. Other people (like the Temple authorities) stand around and say it is smarter to keep what you have than to share, or that some

people really are not worth loving. Those people do not recognize Jesus' voice. Jesus promises that God is able to care for all who do follow.

The good-shepherd image offers children security. God knows them personally and is taking care of them.

Revelation 7:9-17. This is a continuation of last Sunday's coded message to Christians under persecution. Every child (and Roman soldier) knows that if you wash something in blood, it turns red, not white. That's what makes the phrase "people in the robes made white by being washed in the blood of the Lamb" such a great code. To crack this code at its full depth requires appreciation for animal-sacrifice theology, which is beyond the thinking of children. So simply present the phrase as a code for all Christians. To enjoy the clever humor, imagine with the children a soldier who tried to make sense of the passage but did not have the key to the code.

Having cracked the code, children will be ready to explore God's promises to the people in the white robes in verses 15b-17 and the rest of Revelation. In children's terms, the promise is that God loves and takes care of each of us. Some terrible things may happen to us or to the people we love. We may need to make some brave stands that might make others angry with us (or, if we live in especially dangerous times, kill us). But in the end, we will find that God was with us all the way.

Acts 9:36-43. Children easily understand what happened as they hear this story read. Unfortunately, they generally hear it as an example of the truths stated in today's other readings. And that leads to hard-to-answer questions such as, "If

God takes care of us and can do Easter surprises, why didn't God keep my Gramps from dying? Did God love Dorcas more than Gramps?" Hearing that God had different plans for Dorcas and for Gramps and that Dorcas eventually also died "for good" is not particularly satisfying. So this story might be best saved to read with other texts.

Watch Words

Use only the "shepherd" words (*rod, staff, sheep-fold, still waters*) with which the children are familiar, or explain the words as part of worship.

Avoid using "lamb" imagery such as the *blood of the lamb, slain lamb,* or *cleansing blood,* beyond the simple code word *Lamb.* These "atonement" terms are beyond the mental development of the children.

Clearly describe Jesus as the *Good Shepherd* and as the *Lamb.* Help children see that these are two ways to describe Jesus, rather than two contradictory statements.

Let the Children Sing

To keep the Alleluias going, sing one of the Easter hymns with an Alleluia chorus.

Sing "The Lord's My Shepherd," Psalm 23, taking time to point out that it is Scripture set to music; or as a second choice, use the hymn "Savior Like a Shepherd Lead Us." Children have trouble with the complex theological language of "He Leadeth Me" and "The King of Love My Shepherd Is."

The Liturgical Child

1. Psalm 23 is so well known and loved that congregations tend to read it in unison with more feeling than most unison readings arouse. It is often somewhat familiar to older children and therefore is easier for them to read with the congregation. If pew Bibles are not available, print the psalm in the worship bulletin to enable group reading.

2. Use Psalm 23 as an outline for the congregation's prayers of petition, for example:

Verses 1-2	Pray for the hungry and homeless.
Verse 3a	Pray for people who need to be restored—criminals in prison, addicts, people who have been cut out by those around them.
Verse 3b	Ask for guidance to do the right things at home, at school, at work, in our town, and in our world. Note specific issues in which God's guidance is needed now.
Verse 4	Pray for those who are facing death or illness.
Verse 5a	Pray for all who are living in war between nations, races, or in families.
Verses 5b-6	Offer prayers of thanksgiving and praise, citing examples of God's loving care.

Both the Scripture and the prayers can be voiced by one worship leader; or one leader can read the psalm phrases, to which a second replies with the prayers; or the worship leader can read the psalm phrases, the congregation responding with either printed or spontaneous prayers.

Sermon Resources

1. Easter People know an important secret: Though at times it appears they are losing, God and the Easter People will be the big winners in the end. To explore John's coded reminder of this secret in Revelation, recall a popular children's movie in which the main character is constantly in terrible trouble and seems certain to lose or die, but escapes at the last moment. Compare that story to the situation of the early Christians who were being imprisoned, tortured, and even killed. Just as the movie character might have given up when things seemed worst, it would have been easy for early Christians to forget the Easter secret and give up. John wrote to remind them of the secret, to encourage them to "hang in there," and to give them hope. John's message is a good reminder for us, too.

2. Mention the Easter token again. Challenge worshipers to use it this week to remind themselves of God's love and care for them and others. Suggest that the token might comfort them if they get into seemingly hopeless situations, and remind them to watch for others in hopeless situations who need our prayers and supportive help.

Draw a picture of a shepherd taking care of sheep. Show these things:

lost sheep   hungry bear
thorny bush   stream

Draw a picture of someone (maybe you) taking care of another person.

Unscramble the letters in each word to find an Easter message from Jesus.

"YM PESHE ERAH YM COVIE, DAN I WONK

"_ _ _ _ _ _ _ _ _ _ _ _ _ _ , _ _ _ I

MEHT, NAD ETHY WLOFLO EM."

_ _ _ _ , _ _ _ _ _ _ _ _ _ _ _ _ _ ."

_ _ _ _ , _ _ _ _ _ _ _ _ _ _ _ _ _ ."

Answer: My sheep hear my voice, and I know them, and they follow me.   (John 10:27)

Fourth Sunday of Easter / © 1994 by Abingdon Press.

FIFTH SUNDAY OF EASTER

From a Child's Point of View

John 13:31-35. Knowledge of the context is key to appreciating this text fully. The disciples and Jesus were gathered in the upper room to celebrate Passover. Judas had just left to betray Jesus. Knowing this, Jesus announced his death and gave the remaining disciples a new commandment. They were to love one another as God/Jesus had loved them (all the way to the cross).

John's intricate, abstract words in verses 31-33 will make little sense to children. But the new command in verses 34-35 is plain. And when it is set in context, children can understand that the kind of love Jesus is talking about is not a happy feeling, but a way of treating people. Loving as Jesus loved means putting ourselves on the line for others. Jesus insists that Christians will be recognized by the loving way they treat others.

Acts 11:1-18. The story of Peter and Cornelius is an example of the love Jesus commanded. Children need to be told before the story is read that Peter's people, the Jews, hated Cornelius's people, the Gentiles. They would not eat with them and claimed that God did not intend for people to eat some of the foods the Gentiles ate. It helps to compare Peter's feelings about the Gentiles with feelings held against some groups today (maybe migrant workers, homeless people, or certain kids at school). Children then appreciate how hard it was for Peter to visit (and presumably eat) in Cornelius' home, and then to baptize him and his Gentile friends. The point of the story on the Fifth Sunday of Easter is that Easter people are called to treat with love all the people they meet (even the ones they do not like or want to be around).

Revelation 21:1-6. The Revelation code images in this text, such as "a city dressed as a bride coming down from heaven" and "water from the fountain of life" are too much for children to translate. However, the message from "the one who sits on the throne" is simple. A time is coming when God will live with people and take such care of them that there will be no more tears, and every need will be met.

Psalm 148. This happy praise psalm is read also on the First Sunday After Christmas each year. Find comments on children's understanding of Psalm 148 in the section for those Sundays.

Watch Words

In speaking of God's loving care, avoid *providence*. Those children who recognize the word probably would identify it as the capital of Rhode Island. So talk in specific terms about God's loving care.

For children, *Gentiles* are a group of people Jews and the first Christians, who were Jewish, did not like. Jews did not want to live near the Gentiles, would not eat with them, and would not let them come into the main worship room of a synagogue.

Let the Children Sing

To commit yourselves to keeping Jesus' new command, sing "They'll Know We Are Christians by Our Love" or "Lord, I Want to Be a Christian."

"All Creatures of Our God and King" parallels the praises of Psalm 148 and invites worshipers to keep the Easter Alleluias going. "Come, Christians, Join to Sing" is another Easter season hymn with lots of Alleluias.

The Liturgical Child

1. In introducing Revelation 21:1-6, remind worshipers of the identity of "the one who sits on the throne" in the Revelation code, and alert them to listen carefully to everything "the one who sits on the throne" says. Raise one hand, with your index finger pointed up (the teaching pose in early Christian art), while reading each of the messages. This will help children hear the straightforward message of the passage without tripping on all the poetic images that surround the message from "the one who sits on the throne."

2. See the First Sunday After Christmas of Year A of this series for directions on reading Psalm 148 responsively.

3. To create a litany prayer of confession, one person or group recites, "Jesus commanded, 'Love one another even as I have loved you,' " to which a second person or group replies with prayers that confess the ways we fail to love as Jesus commanded. Include confessions of our failures to love within families, among friends, and especially in relating to people we do not like. Confess communal as well as personal failures to love. In the assurance of pardon, remind worshipers that Jesus loves and forgives us always.

4. If you celebrate communion today, point out that Jesus invites all people to eat and drink together at this table. As part of the "Invitation to the Table," name some of the groups that even children know are looked down on in your community as brothers and sisters who are welcome at this table.

Sermon Resources

1. Begin to explore God's promises in Revelation 21 by listing things that make us cry. Babies cry when they are wet, hungry, lonely, hurt, angry, and any other time they do not have what they want or need. Young children cry less frequently than babies: when they are hurt (but they can be brave about small hurts); when they become really angry (throw a temper tantrum); and when they see something sad. Teenagers are more likely to cry because of hurt feelings. Grown-ups cry when very sad things happen to them or to people they love. We all tend to cry at funerals and when good friends move away. Teenagers and grown-ups cry at movies. Some people even cry when they are very, very happy (but these are not the tears we are thinking about today). Describing all these tear-producing situations can set the stage for thinking about ways to love those who are in tears and for recalling God's promise that one day there will be no more tears.

2. Ask how many people still have their Easter tokens. Recall previously made points about what it means to be Easter People. Then present Jesus' new command as the identifying mark of the Easter People. Scouts, sports teams, and even schools have badges and uniforms that identify their members. Christians do not have a badge or uniform. They are to act with such love that people around them will recognize them as Christians. Suggest that the worshipers carry their tokens with them this week as a hidden reminder that their actions should be so loving that others will know they are Easter People.

3. Michele Maria Surat's book *Angel Child, Dragon Child* is both a children's modern parallel of the story of Peter and Cornelius and an example of the love Jesus commanded. It describes the misery of a young Vietnamese refugee girl, Ut, who tries to adapt to her new country while missing her mother who had to stay behind. When the school principal insists that she and Raymond, who has been bullying her, together write the story of her life, the door to understanding opens. Raymond is then instrumental in starting a carnival to raise money for Ut's mother. The book, available in most children's libraries, can be read by an adult in five minutes. Retell it as a sermon illustration.

4. Find other Worship Worksheet activities for Psalm 148 on the First Sunday After Christmas in Years A and B.

As children leave the sanctuary, take time to read and talk briefly about the calls to praise they have written on their Worship Worksheets. When you pay attention to their work, it tells children you value their presence in worship and that a Worship Worksheet is one way they participate in worship.

Psalm 148 calls on all kinds of animals and plants, and even weather to praise God.

Praise the Lord from the earth, you sea monsters and all deeps, fire and hail, snow and frost, stormy wind fulfilling his command!

Write new verses calling groups of people you know to praise God.

Praise the Lord _____

_____

Praise the Lord _____

_____

Because it is the Fifth Sunday of Easter, cross out every fifth letter below to find Jesus' message.

```
L O V E
K O N E
A R N O
T H P E R E V L
E N A S B I H A
V O E L O V S E
D Y O R
U J O H
R N 1 3
3  4 4
```

"

_____ _____ _____ _____

_____ _____ _____ ."

Answer: Love one another even as I have loved you. John 13: 34

Fifth Sunday of Easter / © 1994 by Abingdon Press.

SIXTH SUNDAY OF EASTER

From a Child's Point of View

John 14:23-29. This is a rich text, providing several themes that are important to children. All the themes are more powerful if the text is set in its context: the Last Supper.

First is the question of how to show our love for Jesus. Loyalty among friends is very important to children. Best friends prove their devotion by being together, wearing matching clothes, or joining the same teams. Children express their devotion to their heroes by collecting baseball cards, memorizing sports statistics, and wearing shirts that bear those persons' names. So the question, "How can we show our love for Jesus?" has some urgency. Jesus' answer is clear. We are to show our love not by what we wear or by memorizing all the facts about Jesus, but by following Jesus' teachings. (The GNB's "obey my teachings" makes more sense to children than the NRSV's "keep my word.")

Second, Jesus promises those who love him and obey his teachings that God will be with them always. Again, this speaks to children's insistence that friends be loyal. Jesus promises them friendship that they can count on always. Nothing can come between them and God. Just as God was with the disciples through Jesus during his life on earth, so God will be with them (and us) in the Holy Spirit after Jesus is gone. God/Jesus/Holy Spirit will be so close, they will be inside us.

Finally, Jesus promises his disciples (whose world is about to be torn apart by Jesus' crucifixion) that his presence with them will result in peace and that peace will become a mark of the church. The other texts celebrate this peace (Ps. 67), describe how people spread it (Acts and John 5), and look forward to the day when the peace will be complete (Revelation).

Psalm 67. This harvest psalm acknowledges that God gives the peace, that nations are to share it, that peace and justice are related gifts from God, and that a good harvest is a peaceful blessing from God. This is a psalm for children to enjoy rather than to understand. The New Jerusalem Bible offers a particularly clear, beautiful translation.

Revelation 21:10; 21:22–22:5. This passage is John's coded glimpse of the city of peace that will finally come. Some older children can crack enough of the code to discover that the presence of God and Jesus in the city will be so great that there will be no need for a church—the whole city will be a church. Hardly any children can decipher the significance of the life-giving river flowing from the throne of God. A few children will understand that people of all nations will be welcomed and will share their wealth. (The GNB's "wealth" or NJB's "treasures" brought to the city are clearer than NRSV's "glory.") Many children will simply enjoy the fact that the Bible includes such cleverly coded messages and perhaps learn the code words they will be able to understand later.

Acts 16:9-15. Paul and Lydia are Easter people. In response to a vision, Paul travels to a new place to tell people about Jesus. In response to what she hears about Jesus, Lydia is baptized and offers her large, comfortable house as a home for Paul and a meeting place for the first Christians in her town. Though what Lydia did does not seem as exciting as what Paul did, they are equally important. We, like Paul and Lydia, are to respond to God's Easter message and do what we can to spread God's peace.

Alternate Gospel: John 5:1-9. Paul preaches, Lydia provides a home, and Jesus heals. Children understand the hopeless situation of the man by the pool and appreciate the help Jesus gave him. The challenge to them is to recognize people around them who need help and to help them.

Watch Words

Use the word *peace* in such a way that children realize it includes justice and inclusiveness, not just absence of war.

Also describe *peace* as feeling very good inside because you know that what you are doing is right. Compare that feeling with the excited feeling of going someplace special (e.g., an amusement park), or the feeling of getting something you do not deserve (e.g., winning a game by cheating).

Let the Children Sing

"Let All the World in Every Corner Sing" is a simple praise hymn which reflects Psalm 67.

"Savior Again to Thy Dear Name We Pray" includes many of the themes of these texts in simple concrete language children can understand as they sing.

"Dona Nobis Pacem," a prayer for peace learned by many children at camp, would be effective sung as a round by several choirs of different ages, or as a congregational hymn.

"I've Got the Joy, Joy, Joy, Joy Down in My Heart" is another camp song that Christians of all ages can sing together or that a choir can present as an anthem. Be sure to include the line, "I've got the peace that passes understanding down in the depths of my heart."

The Liturgical Child

1. Ask a group of older children to pantomime the action as Acts 16 is read. You will need Paul, a Macedonian, and several women, including Lydia. Paul's vision is staged at one side of the chancel. He then crosses to the other side to meet the women and is escorted farther in that direction by Lydia. The Macedonian might say, "Come over to Macedonia and help us." Simple costumes help, and one good practice is essential.

2. To read Psalm 67 as a litany, teach the congregation the response in verses 3 and 5. The worship leader then reads the other verses, pausing at appropriate times for the congregational response. (Consider printing the response in the worship bulletin.)

3. Pass the Peace at the close of the service. The worship leaders (perhaps with the help of ushers or prepared children) move down the aisles and shake hands with the person at the end of each row, saying, "The peace of God be with you." The worshiper responds, "and also with you," and turns to pass the wish to his or her neighbor, who then passes it on down the row.

4. Pray for situations in which God's peace is needed. Pray for peace in families, peace on schoolbuses, peace among friends, peace among folks who do not get along easily, peace among different racial and ethnic groups in your community, and peace in the world. Consider asking several children in advance to identify such situations in their schools and your community.

Sermon Resources

1. Inquire about the Easter tokens. Suggest that this week worshipers carry the tokens as a reminder that God's peace is with them and that they, as the Easter People, are called to work for peace.

2. Urge the children to work on the Worship Worksheet as they listen to the sermon for ideas. Invite them to share their favorite letter drawing and prayer with you as they leave the sanctuary.

Turn each letter in the word PEACE into a picture of a person "working for peace."
Then write a prayer beside each picture.
One has been done for you.

P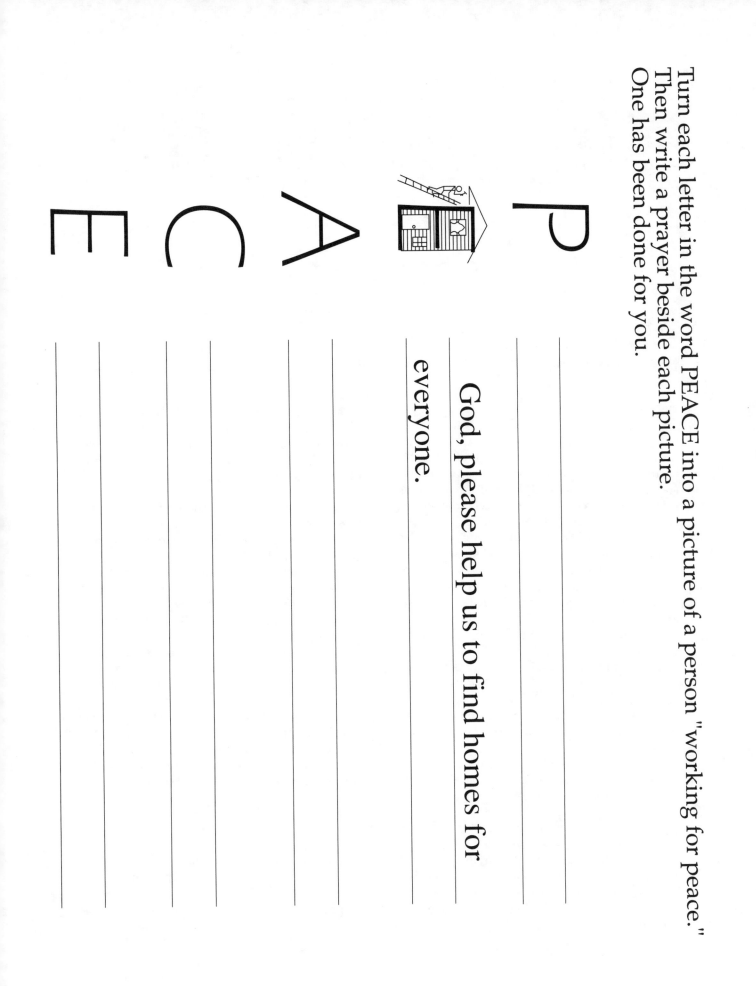

God, please help us to find homes for everyone.

A

C

E

ASCENSION OF THE LORD

Note: These texts may be used also on the Seventh Sunday of Easter to expose children to the story of the Ascension.

From a Child's Point of View

Acts 1:1-11. The Ascension story is of interest to children for two reasons. First, it answers the literal-minded questions, "What did Jesus do after Easter?" and "Where is Jesus now?" The answer is that for forty days Jesus helped his disciples understand what had happened on Good Friday and Easter. Then he returned to God. Second, the Ascension is the story of Jesus passing the baton of responsibility to his disciples. As he returned to God, Jesus instructed the disciples to pick up and continue his work. They were to be Jesus' witnesses, and they were to expect God to send the Holy Spirit to help them with the task. The "two men in white" emphasize this change when they ask why the disciples are staring into the sky. There is work to be done. So on Ascension Day, we complete our celebration of what Jesus did and get ready to go to work as his witnesses today.

Older children are especially receptive to the challenge to be witnesses. Their parallel of the phrase "in Jerusalem, Judea, and Samaria and to the ends of the earth" is "at home, at school, in [your town], and to all the world."

These eleven verses are packed with a summary of the forty days after Easter, the promise of the Holy Spirit, a discussion between Jesus and the disciples about the messianic kingdom, and the Ascension story. The Good News Bible is by far the easiest translation with which to keep up with all this action. Even so, you may need to reread verses 8-11 in order that children focus attention on the Ascension.

Luke 24:44-53. This is the easier of today's Ascension accounts for children. Reading it just before or after the Acts account will help children clarify what happened. The message is the same. The disciples (and we) are to take up Jesus' work after receiving the Holy Spirit.

Psalm 47 or 93. The inclusion of these psalms with the Ascension texts is hard to explain to children. The psalms are all pomp-and-circumstance for the triumphant "king of the world." The Ascension accounts focus on the "servant King" who calls on his followers to take up his ministry. Adults can see the significance of this pairing of servant King and triumphant King, but few children can.

On its own, however, either psalm is a great reminder that God/Jesus is King of the universe, the greatest power that ever was or ever will be.

Ephesians 1:15-23. This passage is for grown-ups. The sentence structure is too complex and the words too abstract for children. Children will hear Paul's basic message about Christ in the more concrete story of the Ascension.

Watch Words

Ascension and *ascend* are not children's words. Use them today to describe only this event.

Beware of using vocabulary about the triumphant king. Words such as *dominion, exalted,* and *subdued people* are foreign to children. Otherwise familiar words like *triumphant, victorious, conquering*, and *glorious* become meaningless when combined in long lists of adjectives or when used repetitively in varying combinations.

Take time to give the legal definition of *witness* so that children know what Jesus is asking his disciples to do.

Let the Children Sing

Most of the hymns designated for Ascension Day are filled with triumphal language and theological jargon which are beyond children's understanding. The children will more readily celebrate Jesus' Ascension by singing "Come, Christians, Join to Sing," or even "Christ the Lord Is Risen Today." Sing the latter hymn one more time to conclude the entire Easter season.

"Open My Eyes That I May See" is a good hymn with which to accept Christ's call to become his witnesses.

The Liturgical Child

1. Conclude your celebration of Easter by retracing the forty days of Easter. Reread several of the Easter lessons, matching them with different movements within your worship. Example:

John 20:1-10 (empty tomb)
Hymn: "Christ the Lord Is Risen Today"
John 20:24-29 (Thomas's encounter with the Risen Christ)
Prayers of Confession and Assurance of Pardon: Pray about ways we fail to live the Easter faith. If you used the Easter tokens, pray a one-sentence prayer about our failures, as highlighted by each use of the tokens. Jesus' response to Thomas becomes our Assurance of Pardon.

John 20:15-19 (Christ calls Peter to "feed my sheep")
Prayers of Petition
Acts 1:1-11 (the Ascension)
Sermon
Psalm 47 or hymn of praise to Christ

2. Create an Ascension litany celebrating Christ's work and committing yourselves to take up that work as his witnesses. The congregation responds after each statement:

> Christ, we will be your witnesses and carry on your work at home, in (your town), and in all the world.

Leader: Jesus, though you were God and Lord of the universe, you were not ashamed to live among us and love us. You even died for us.

Leader: Jesus, you kept an eye out for people who needed healing. You touched lepers, put healing clay on blind eyes, told the lame to stand up and walk, and went looking for the woman who touched your robe, believing you could heal her.

Leader: You made friends with people whom everyone else avoided. You invited yourself to dinner with Zaccheus, the tax-collecting cheat. You included rough fishermen and political troublemakers among your disciples.

Leader: You taught us to forgive and love even our enemies. And you showed us how to do it as you forgave the people who betrayed you, denied you, and killed you.

Leader: When we remember what you said and did, we know you were showing us how good the world could be. Give us the courage and wisdom to follow you.

3. Be aware of end-of-school events, such as special parties or trips, and concerns, such as grades, and the relief that summer is coming. Talk with children about their summer hopes (fun trips and release from homework) and summer fears (new camps, unwelcome baby-sitters or day-care set-ups; or tough kids on the loose in their neighborhoods). Pray about all these events and concerns on the appropriate Sundays.

4. Begin the benediction with a paraphrase of the question asked by the two men in white, "Why are you standing here?" Then send the congregation out to be Christ's witnesses and promise the presence of the Holy Spirit.

Sermon Resources

1. Tell stories about Christian witnesses. Include stories about people or groups in your church. In telling what was done, help the listeners understand these efforts as responses to Christ's Ascension request that we become witnesses.

Cross out the extra letter in each word of Jesus' message.

"YOUR SHALTL BEN OMY WAITNESSES"

Acts 1:8

Name or draw 1 place where witnesses are needed. Listen to the sermon for ideas.

Name or draw 1 way your church could be the needed witnesses.

Write a prayer about this need.

Ascension of the Lord / © 1994 by Abingdon Press.

SEVENTH SUNDAY OF EASTER

Note: The Ascension of the Lord texts may be substituted for the Seventh Sunday of Easter texts. This is advisable if children (and most older worshipers) will have no other opportunity to worship around the Ascension stories.

From a Child's Point of View

John 17:20-26. Children are quickly lost in the repetitive phrases and pronouns of the Great High Priestly Prayer. It helps to introduce this part of the prayer to them as Jesus' prayer for everyone in the church, including us, and to encourage them to listen to the prayer as being Jesus' hopes for us and all God's people.

In children's words, Jesus' hope is that we will be as close to God as he is. This is not an impossible wish. Jesus knows it can come true. He also knows that if we are that close to God, we will attract others to God. People will see God's love in us and in the way we treat others.

Revelation 22:12-14, 16-17, 20-21. If you have been decoding the Revelation texts, today's verses provide older children a review of Revelation code words and introduce a new one. "The bride" is a code word for the Church universal. Everything "the bride" is and does, the church (including us) is and does. According to this vision, one important job of the church is calling people to come to God.

The text also has important things to say about Jesus, the "I" of this vision. The most important to children is the reassuring promise that Jesus was there at the beginning and will be there at the end. There is no time when Jesus will not be with them, caring for them.

Acts 16:16-34. In the context of Easter and of today's lections, this is an example of a day in the life of a church member (or one in a white robe, or an Easter person) who is spreading God's love. Paul and Silas heal a mentally ill slave girl, are taken to court by her owners, are whipped and thrown into prison, are saved from prison by God (working through an earthquake), and preach to their jailer. Children are immediately impressed by the dedication of Paul and Silas and, when it is pointed out, see God's help and support.

Psalm 97. When this is introduced as a poem praising God, who rules the universe, children hear and understand a number of the phrases. For today's worship, it is a song Paul and Silas might have sung in prison and a song for Easter people everywhere, especially those who are in trouble for spreading God's Word.

Watch Words

For children, *hope* generally is related to wishing for good things that may or may not happen (e.g., receiving a desired birthday gift or winning a championship). So talk today about what we can *depend upon* or what we can *trust* God to do and be, rather than on what we *hope*.

For children, *unity* as *being one with God* and *unity* as *being one with all Christians* are different experiences. They need to hear specific examples of each. An understanding of how the two are linked will come later.

Let the Children Sing

Conclude the Easter season with "Come, Christians, Join to Sing," with all the Alleluias, or

"Rejoice, Ye Pure in Heart," with its repeated chorus of praise.

If "O Come, O Come, Emmanuel" was sung during Advent, sing it today to celebrate the Easter fulfillment of the Advent promises. Children enjoy the contrast between the sad, wishful verses and the happy chorus. Young readers may not be able to read the verses, but can join in on the chorus. The choir might sing the verses, with the congregation responding on the chorus.

The Liturgical Child

1. Instruct worshipers to close their eyes while you remind them, in your own words, of John's vision of Jesus (Rev. 1:12-16). Then, read dramatically what Christ says in today's Revelation lection. For maximum impact, Christ's words might be read loudly from a remote microphone.

2. Invite worshipers to read the psalm responsively. The two groups may be congregation and choir, two halves of the congregation, or two groups (classes or choirs) of older children who have prepared it. The New Revised Standard Version offers the easiest reading for children.

ALL:	Verse 1
Group 1:	Verse 2a
Group 2:	Verse 2b
Group 1:	Verse 3
Group 2:	Verse 4
Group 1:	Verse 5
Group 2:	Verse 6a
Group 1:	Verse 6b
Group 2:	Verse 7
Group 1:	Verse 8-9
Group 2:	Verse 10
Group 1:	Verse 11a
Group 2:	Verse 11b
ALL:	Verse 12

3. After the Acts lection is read and before Psalm 97 is read, suggest that Psalm 97 is a hymn that Paul and Silas might have sung that night in prison. Instruct worshipers to hold their hands crossed at the wrists in front of them. Wrists should not rest in laps but be held uncomfortably in the air as if chained together. Invite worshipers to imagine how it felt to sing the psalm in that situation.

4. Create a responsive prayer of petitions with the congregation responding "Come, Lord Jesus"

to each of the leader's descriptions of situations in which God's power and love are needed. For example:

> God, you call us to live in unity with one another. But we see more people who are ignoring one another or fighting than are getting along. So we pray for the children who call one another names on the playground, for the Israelis and Palestinians who fight over the Holy Land, for the Asians and Hispanics and Whites and Blacks who hate one another. (RESPONSE)

5. Remember end-of-school-year concerns in the church's prayers on the appropriate Sundays. See Ascension of the Lord, Liturgical Child 3 for specific suggestions.

Sermon Resources

1. Speak one last time of the Easter tokens. Recall the ways you have used yours during this Easter season, then offer this suggestion for future use. Fingering the two sides of the token, suggest that one side reminds bearers that God loves them and is with them always, while the other side reminds them that they are to spread God's love to others.

2. Tell of a day in the life of today's witnessing church that parallels a day of Paul and Silas in Acts. Describe either a day in the life of your congregation or in the life of the worldwide church. Cite specific examples of Christians who are witness, putting up with persecution, and knowing God's support. Include activities with which children are familiar and in which they participate (e.g., mission projects to which they have contributed, peacemaking on the playground, and so forth). Consider focusing on a specific day in the last week.

3. Both Gospel and Epistle readings point to the fulfillment of God's Advent promises. To explore that fulfillment, combine the sermon with the decorating of a freshly leafing small tree set in a bucket. As you hang each Chrismon ornament, recall what it meant at Christmas and talk about what it means after Easter. The Alpha and Omega, the star of Jesse, the morning star, and the cross over the world are especially appropriate.

Enlarge the half of the Worship Worksheet about Acts to give more space for drawings. Display drawings on a bulletin board.

Circle these 12 words in the letters below.

Listen for the words when **Revelation 22** is read.

DRAW lines between the words that go together.

ALPHA   BEGINNING   JESUS
OMEGA   COMING   CHRIST
FIRST   SPIRIT   DAVID
LAST   BRIDE   END

```
A P H A B D N O
C O M I N G A R M
N J L A S T V S E
B E G I N N I N G
R S M N K J D E A
I U F I R S T N T
D S P I R I T D T
E J S C H R I S T
```

Listen carefully when Acts 16:16-34 is read.

Draw a picture for each part of the story.

Paul gets into trouble	God saves Paul in prison	Paul and the jailor
		The End

PENTECOST

From a Child's Point of View

Acts 2:1-21. This passage tells of the giving of the Holy Spirit and is the key story for Pentecost Sunday. Because children will have trouble following the text, they will depend on you to retell and interpret the story. Two points are of particular interest to them. First, the coming of the Spirit with wind and fire invites their imaginations to work on "what it was really like." (See Sermon Resources for suggestions for exploring the feel of the wind, fire, and Holy Spirit.)

Second, the miraculous ability of the disciples to speak foreign languages on that day, in order to tell the good news to travelers from around the world, points out that God intends that we be united. Peter cites Joel's list of all the people (sons and daughters, old men, and even slaves) who will receive God's Holy Spirit as further proof that we are to be united.

Genesis 11:1-9. This is the story of the Tower of Babel, understood by the church as God's response to sinful human pride when we try to make ourselves equal to God. It is read today as a contrast to the Pentecost story, in which people of all languages are drawn together by the Holy Spirit. But children will catch none of this as they hear the passage. The story line, with all its details about brick and bituminous mortar, is hard for them to follow. And God's words sound almost as if God were intimidated by human capabilities and that God therefore erected an obstacle (differing languages) to keep us under control. So read the story from the Bible and then retell it in order to present its intended points clearly.

OR Romans 8:14-17. (The Revised Common Lectionary suggests that either Romans or Genesis be read this Sunday.) This is another passage that is hard for children to "hear" as it is read, but one which offers ideas that are meaningful to them. Its first truth is that the Holy Spirit is not scary, nor does it make us afraid of God. Wind, flames, and a Holy Ghost can sound spooky to children. If your tradition uses the term Holy Ghost, this is a good time to "define out" the Halloween connotations and explore God's presence as a positive, desirable experience. The second truth is that because God's Spirit lives within us all, we are all brothers and sisters, sharing Christ's glory and suffering in God's family.

John 14:8-17 (25-27). This is a sophisticated Greek discourse, put into Jesus' mouth by John. The repetitive statements in verses 8-11 will lose many children; they are likely to hear only occasional phrases thereafter. But this description of the work of the Holy Spirit is helpful for children because it shows that:

1. The Holy Spirit lives deep inside each of us.

2. The Holy Spirit helps us to know God's love and will, and reminds us about Jesus. The Holy Spirit is speaking when we know that God does not want us to do something (maybe to call someone mean names) or when we feel God calling us to action (perhaps to defend someone who is being teased, or to make friends with someone who is lonely). The Holy Spirit reminds us that God made us special and loves us—even on days when everyone else is treating us like junk.

3. Because the Holy Spirit lives in us, we can experience peace inside—even when it is not peaceful around us.

Psalm 104:24-34, 35b. This passage celebrates God's creation of the sea animals. The poet credits God's Spirit with both creating and caring for these animals. Before reading this lighthearted praise poem, alert children to the presence of a sea monster named Leviathan.

Watch Words

Use the word *Pentecost* often to build familiarity with the name of this less-well-known holy day.

Choose your Holy Spirit language carefully. *Holy Spirit* or *God's Spirit* are probably the best terms for children. *Holy Ghost* sounds like a possibly friendly Halloween spook. *Comforter, counselor,* and *helper* are more helpful as descriptions than as names. *Breath of God,* if examined in relationship to the wind symbol, can become a meaningful way to explain and understand how God lives within us. Either stick with one term or use as many terms as possible, challenging the children to collect them, and explaining them as you go.

Let the Children Sing

Sing "I'm Gonna Sing When the Spirit Says Sing" and offer original verses related to the worship theme. Or sing "They'll Know We Are Christians by Our Love."

Try "Breathe on Me, Breath of God," with its repeated phrase at the beginning of each verse (if you have explored the "breath of God").

To continue the praise of Psalm 104, sing "All Things Bright and Beautiful," "This Is My Father's World," or "I Sing the Almighty Power of God."

The Liturgical Child

1. Decorate the sanctuary with flame-red paraments. Invite worshipers in advance to wear something red in honor of Pentecost. Use red flowers in the worship center. Print the bulletin on red paper or in red ink. To emphasize the gift of the Holy Spirit to all, drape around the shoulders of each worshiper a red crepe-paper stole decorated with Pentecost symbols to wear during worship. (An older children's class may make the stoles by gluing cut-out symbols on either end of 36-inch red streamers; the class can help distribute them after the reading of Acts 2.) In the wor-ship center, place a birthday cake for the church, decorated with red icing and twenty red candles. Serve it with red punch after worship.

2. Point out *Holy Spirit/Holy Ghost* in weekly responses such as the Gloria Patri and Doxology as you come to them. Note its significance in each song.

3. Invite the congregation to sing the one verse of "Spirit of Living God" as a response to spoken prayers for the church and the world. It may be sung once at the end, or several times as a response to specific prayers within the whole prayer.

4. After the benediction, ask children or ushers to give each worshiper a red flower as a reminder of the presence of the Holy Spirit in our life.

Sermon Resources

1. To explore the significance of the fact that people of all nationalities heard the good news in their own language, paraphrase Acts 2:5-12, replacing New Testament countries with more familiar current ones. For example, "Are not all these who are speaking Mexicans? How can they speak to each of us in our own language? Germans and French and Japanese, people from Zaire and Argentina."

2. Explore the Pentecost wind and fire symbols so that children "get the feel" of God's presence. Recall experiences with "strong rushing winds." A stiff breeze in our face usually feels fresh and good. We feel strong as we walk into it. An autumn wind blows away the dead leaves of summer to make way for new growth next spring. Children often play in the wind with pinwheels, kites, and streamers (and often with the scarves we wish were on their heads). Thus the wind of the Spirit can easily be perceived as a cleansing, invigorating, welcome presence.

Children who camp have the edge on appreciating fire as a symbol of God's presence. Just as a flame ignites a bright lantern (the lantern is a brighter light than a softly glowing candle), God's Spirit ignites wishy-washy, easily frightened people into brave folks who will stand up to tell the world the good news. Just as a campfire or fireplace is a source of warmth and comfort on cold nights, God's Spirit comforts us when people are treating us coldly. Just as a flame may be used to sterilize a needle when we remove a splinter, God's Spirit works within us to clean out bad attitudes, ideas, and ways.

Listen to Acts 2:1-21. Write the answers to the questions below in the Pentecost Puzzle spaces.

1. P _ _ _ _
2. _ E _ _ _
3. _ _ N _
4. _ _ T _
5. _ _ E _ _ _ _
6. _ C _ _ _
7. _ O _
8. _ S _ _ _ _
9. _ _ T

1. The spirit gave the people _____ .
2. What was seen over people's heads?
3. What was heard and felt?
4. Who gave the first Pentecost sermon?
5. In what city did this happen?
6. Pentecost is the birthday of the _____ .
7+8 What did God give on Pentecost?
7+9 What is another name for this gift?

Answers: 1. power 2. flames 3. wind 4. Peter
5. Jerusalem 6. church 7. Holy 8. Spirit 9. Ghost

Draw or write about a time when you felt the Holy Spirit very close to you.

Pentecost / © 1994 by Abingdon Press.

TRINITY SUNDAY

From a Child's Point of View

The doctrine of the Trinity is very abstract and complex. Scholars have argued about it for centuries. Many adults have difficulty understanding it. Often on Trinity Sunday, worship takes an educational bent as pastors strive to help their congregations grasp this basic but illusive doctrine.

Three of today's texts that deal with the Trinity are way beyond the understanding of children. But that does not mean there is no way for children to participate in the worship of the Triune God. If the worship leaders are aware of children's understanding of the Trinity, some of the liturgy and the sermon can meet the children where they are, invite them to worship God as they now experience God, and challenge them to stretch their understanding.

All that we can reasonably expect of children is that they know the names of the three persons of the Trinity and sense that these three persons are somehow intimately related to one another. Children relate personally to God (who created the world and cares for them) and to Jesus (who lived among us, showed us how to live, and loved us enough to die for us). They voice questions about the relationship between God and Jesus, but few answers can truly satisfy their literalistic thinking.

Most children are less familiar or comfortable with the Holy Spirit. Older children can begin to interpret the warm community feelings within the congregation and their personal experiences of God's loving care as the work of the Holy Spirit. During their adolescence, as they acquire the ability for abstract thought and a sense of closeness to God as a prime desire, the Holy Spirit will become both understandable and significant.

So talking of the Holy Spirit with children is a matter of planting a few seeds which, though they seem insignificant now, will blossom later.

Children can share fully in praising God, who created and cares for the world. They can confess and be pardoned by God/Jesus who loves and forgives them. They can lay their concerns before God, who cares deeply about each person in this world and calls us to do likewise. They can be led to think about what they already know about God and then stretch that knowledge a little. In the process, they may sense God's presence with them and their faith community.

Psalm 8. This is the one text for the day that is truly child-accessible. It is a response to the greatness of God the Creator. Children can respond to this greatness without dealing with the other texts. They can follow the poet's line of prayer, from praising God to wondering why God pays any attention at all to people, to meditating on the important place in the natural order to which we have been assigned by God.

Watch Words

Trinity and *Triune* are unfamiliar. Although children are not ready to define the words, they can hear and accept them as "words we use at church in talking about God."

As you speak of God, be careful to choose words that in no way limit God. Especially watch pronouns that imply that God is only male. God is greater than either male or female. If you cannot bring yourself to speak of God as Mother as well as Father, avoid both terms and talk of the many ways God loves us and cares for us. (It is hard work to edit exclusively masculine language out of our talk about God, but it is good theology, and it is important to an increasingly large number of women and their daughters. Trinity Sunday offers a good opportunity to work consciously on this task.)

Let the Children Sing

"Now Thank We All Our God" is probably the best general praise hymn for the day. "Holy, Holy, Holy," with its difficult vocabulary balanced by the repeated opening phrase, is a good second choice.

Consider three hymns, one for each person of the Trinity. To God the Creator, sing "For the Beauty of the Earth" or "This Is My Father's World." (To stretch your understanding of God, sing this song with female pronouns, e.g., "This Is My Mother's World . . . her hands the wonders wrought.") Sing "Jesus Loves Me," "Tell Me the Stories of Jesus," or "Come Christians, Join to Sing" for the Son. And try "Breathe on Me, Breath of God" for the Holy Spirit, especially if you sang it last week as you celebrated the coming of the Holy Spirit at Pentecost.

The Liturgical Child

1. Point out the Trinitarian statements in the responses you sing or say every week in worship (e.g., the Gloria Patri and Doxology).
2. Create a child-accessible confession such as the following, based on the three persons of the Trinity.

> God, because we cannot see you, it is easy for us to ignore you or act as if you do not exist. Forgive us.

> Creator God, when we look at the trees and rocks and animals, we often see only things for us to use. We "forget on purpose" that you made them and that we are to take care of them. Forgive us.

> Jesus, we think so much about what we want and what we are doing that we forget what you taught us about loving other people. Forgive us.

Holy Spirit, our feelings of happiness and anger and sadness and joy are so strong that we sometimes do not even notice your presence with us. Please forgive us. Amen.

Assurance of Pardon: God loves and forgives all who confess their sin. Just as God made and loves the trees and animals, God made and loves each one of us. Jesus loved us so much that he died for us. The Holy Spirit, God's strong, loving presence, promises to be with us always—even 'til the end of the world. Thanks be to God!

3. To help worshipers feel both the wonder and the thoughtful questions of Psalm 8, "line it out." A worship leader reads the psalm one line at a time, then the congregation repeats each line, matching the tone and emphases of the reader. A dramatic reader can help the congregation, especially the children, understand the message of the psalm as the phrases are repeated. (When books were scarce in colonial America, lining out was an every-Sunday approach to both reading the Bible and singing the hymns.)

Sermon Resources

1. Divide the sermon into three sections to explore the three persons of the Trinity. After each section, lead a prayer addressed to that person of the Trinity. Then invite the congregation to sing a hymn related to this aspect of God. (See the list of possible hymns in "Let the Children Sing.")
2. Talk about "used to thinks." Describe some ideas about God you "used to think" but have now discarded. For example, I used to think that when God talked to people, they would hear a voice inside their heads. I have since learned that God speaks through the words of other people, through what we read in the Bible, and through feelings deep inside us. Describe some childhood "used to thinks" and some of your currently changing ideas about God. Encourage worshipers to identify ways their understanding of God has grown and to expect that their current understanding will continue to grow.

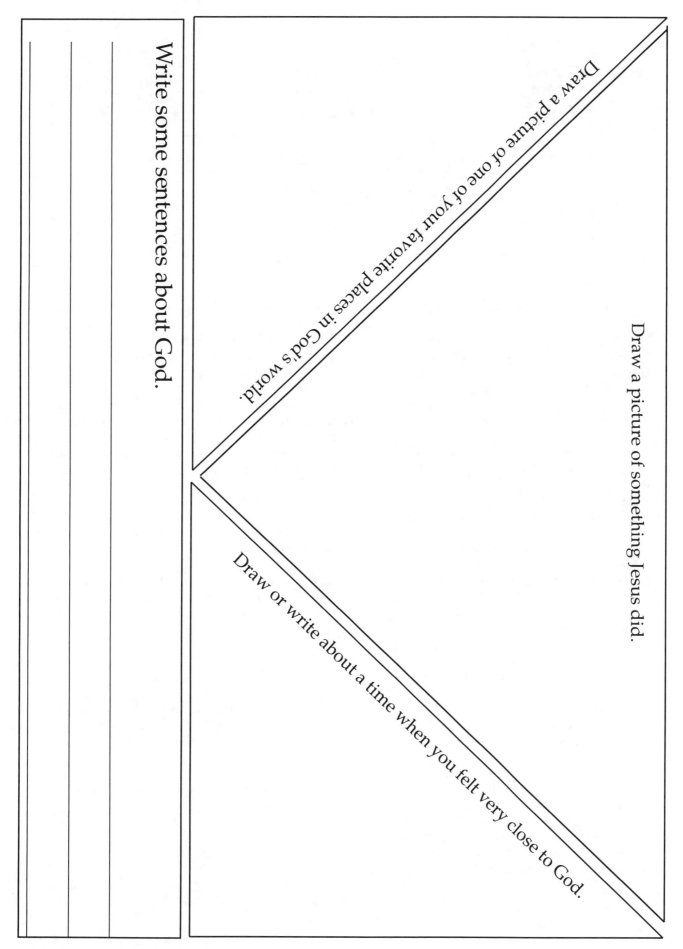

Write some sentences about God.

Draw a picture of one of your favorite places in God's world.

Draw a picture of something Jesus did.

Draw or write about a time when you felt very close to God.

Trinity Sunday / © 1994 by Abingdon Press.

PROPER FOUR

(Sunday between May 29 and June 4 inclusive, if after Trinity Sunday)

From a Child's Point of View

Old Testament: I Kings 18:20-21 (22-29), 30-39. Children enjoy this action-packed story in which God is proved to be "real" and Baal is proved to be a fake. Most children can follow the story of two sacrifices when they are well read from any translation. They, however, need help understanding the problem that led to the contest. They need to hear the situation described in verses 21 and 22 explained in simple language. (The people were trying to worship both Baal *and* God. They liked going to the Baal parties and they also went to some of the ceremonies at the Temple. Elijah said they had to make a choice.)

Though children do not choose between worshiping two different gods and cannot yet understand that sports, clothes, or popularity can be gods, they do face choices about their activities and their values. The faithful child is learning to leave slumber parties in time to go to church, to choose church school over soccer practice, and to love enemies on schoolbuses as well as at church. Elijah calls children to make "faithful" choices. They are not to be like "the people," who do whatever everyone else is doing or what seems like fun at the moment. Instead, they are to be God's faithful people every day, everywhere they are.

Gospel: Luke 7:1-10. This healing story is so tersely presented that children may misunderstand some of its details. The centurion's message about giving orders can leave children thinking that the centurion thought he could order Jesus around, rather than that Jesus could heal the slave without even being in the same room with him. That makes a big difference in the interpretation of Jesus' statement about the centurion's faith.

Jesus was impressed by the man's total trust both that Jesus *could* heal his slave and that Jesus *would* heal his slave, even though the request came from a Roman soldier. So you may need to retell the story, elaborating on the key details.

Epistle: Galatians 1:1-12. This is not a passage for children to understand intellectually, but to respond to emotionally. Paul's passion for the gospel is what impresses them. They like the fact that he became so angry at people who were spreading false ideas about Jesus that he cursed them not once but twice—in writing! In this passion Paul is the opposite of the people to whom Elijah spoke. Children are called to care as much as Paul did.

If you will be focusing on Galatians for the coming weeks, children, because they like getting mail, will be interested in the format of New Testament letters as displayed in these verses. They enjoy identifying the writer, the receivers, and the greeting in verses 1-3.

Psalm: 96. If Yahweh is introduced as a name for God used by people in Elijah's time. The New Jerusalem Bible's translation makes sense to children as a psalm that Elijah and the people might have sung after God burned up the bulls. It is also a song that the centurion or Paul could have sung. Children respond to individual short praise phrases within the psalm, rather than to the psalm as a whole.

Watch Words

Faith, the key word underlying today's texts, is a word children hear only at church. It is an

110

abstract term that adults use in many ways and have trouble defining clearly even for themselves. Children hear it, say it, and sing it before they understand it. Today, *faith* involves *choosing*. We, like Elijah's hearers, the Christians at Galatia, must make choices about what we do and whom we follow. The centurion chooses to risk Jesus' public rejection and his slave's life when he asks Jesus to heal the slave. The centurion's faith involves *trust* as well as choosing. He trusts Jesus' compassion and love. Use the word *faith* repeatedly today, but focus your comments on faithful choosing and trusting faith.

Let the Children Sing

The repeated phrase, "Sing to the Lord a new song," makes the new hymn "Earth and All Stars" a good echo of Psalm 96.

The third verse of "God Created Heaven and Earth" mentions handmade gods of wood and clay, similar to the idol Baal. To introduce this Tiwanese melody to less musically adventurous congregations, ask a children's or adult choir to sing it as an anthem. Children enjoy learning hymns from different cultures.

Sing "I Sing a Song of the Saints of God" in honor of the faithful centurion, Elijah and Paul.

Avoid "Faith of Our Fathers," which is filled with abstract ideas and dated language. Even the repeated chorus does not make much sense to children.

The Liturgical Child

1. Today's texts beg for dramatic presentation:

• Announce that you are going to share one of the great stories of God's people. Invite the children to meet you at the front. Hold the big pulpit Bible in your lap as you read or tell the story of Elijah on Mt. Carmel in your best storyteller style. Thunder Elijah's angry indignation and his knowing questions at the frustrated Baal priests; carefully describe Elijah's preparations for his sacrifice; and read with powerful awe God's response.

• Explain that Galatians is a letter Paul sent to Christians in a church he had started. Then either assume the role of Paul writing the letter as you read, or let the reading be done by someone else

who assumes Paul's role. Paul might be presented either doing his own writing or dictating to a secretary. In either case, demonstrate Paul's strong feelings in the way he says the words, paces back and forth and uses body language (if he is dictating); or writes with flourishing emphasis (if he is writing).

• Read Psalm 96 immediately after the Elijah story. Either read the whole psalm dramatically or line out the short phrases, inviting the congregation to repeat your tone, emphasis, and volume. Suggest that the people imagine themselves among those on Mt. Carmel.

2. Carefully plan today's creed or affirmation of faith. If the congregation regularly recites a given creed, present it today as a series of questions, to which the congregation replies, "Yes, we believe that!" (e.g., "Do you believe in God the Father Almighty, maker of heaven and earth?")

3. Remember to include end-of-school and beginning-of-summer concerns in the church's prayers. See Ascension of the Lord, Liturgical Child 3 for specific suggestions. Pray today for the wisdom and courage to make faithful choices at the swimming pool, at camp, and while hanging out with friends in the neighborhood.

Sermon Resources

1. Give examples of faith as choosing: choosing between basketball and church camp; between Bible school and swimming lessons; between going along with the crowd and standing up for what you know is right; and even between experimenting with alcohol, drugs, or smoking and saying No.

Give examples of faith as trusting: jumping from the edge of the swimming pool into the arms of a parent standing in the water; riding a roller coaster for the first time with a trusted friend who has ridden before and says it is fun.

2. Use the format of Paul's letter to the Galatians as the format of your sermon. Follow the form of the greeting, then speak to choices the people are called to make. Cite choices that children as well as adults face as they live faithfully. Present the letter either as what Paul might write to your congregation, or as a letter you are writing to them.

Listen carefully as **I Kings 18** is read.
Then draw a picture of the end of the contest on the mountain.

Show your picture to your pastor as you leave church today.

S H A D E   each space with an   F   in it. The word you find is

____ ____ ____ ____ ____

Draw ▷ a † on your worship bulletin by every hymn, prayer,
and reading in which you hear this word.

PROPER FIVE

*(Sunday between June 5 and 11 inclusive,
if after Trinity Sunday)*

From a Child's Point of View

I Kings 17:8-16 (17-24) and Luke 7:11-17. These two passages are very similar stories about the raising from death of the only sons of widows. Both make two important points. The first point is that God is powerful. God, working through Elijah and Jesus, can even bring dead people back to life. The second point is that God is loving and caring. God saved Elijah and the widow and her son from starvation, and God raised the only sons of two widows. In each case the raising of the son is a response to the widowed mother's plight. (At that time a woman depended upon her male relatives. A woman with neither husband nor sons lived in dire poverty.)

The widow's angry accusation of Elijah and Elijah's frustrated speech to God are difficult for children. To accept the widow's speech, one must have some understanding of the Deuteronomic explanation of suffering and the role of anger in the grieving process. To understand Elijah's frustration, one must recognize Elijah's appreciation of the widow's help and recall all that Elijah had suffered as God's prophet. The easiest way to explain all this to children is simply to say that when we are really hurting, we sometimes say mean things. Because she was so upset about her son's death, the widow lashed out at Elijah and God. God understood and kept loving her. Because his friend the widow was so upset, and because he too grieved for her son, Elijah was upset also and told God so. God understood and kept loving him.

Because these stories link God's compassion with miraculous raisings, they may raise a difficult question in two forms. Intellectually curious children may ask, "If God has the power to raise these two sons from death, why doesn't God raise everyone?" Grieving children will ask, "If God could raise those people, why doesn't God raise (my loved relative)?" The only acceptable answer to either question is, "We don't know. That is one of God's secrets." This answer needs to be given with ample assurance that God loves us and cares for us, even when we don't understand. This assurance is critical for a grieving child—for whom this discussion best takes place not in worship but one-on-one, with lots of hugs.

Psalm: 146. This psalm is a happy list of what God does to help people. The activities are concrete and everyday, so children understand most of them as they are read. Do explain unfamiliar phrases: When a prince's "breath departs," he dies; "execute justice" means to provide justice; "those who are bowed down" or "the bent" have disabilities.

Epistle: Galatians 1:11-24. Paul was trying to establish his credibility with the Galatians on their terms. To do so, he insisted that he received the good news straight from God, that he was not someone else's student. Such credibility does not mean much to children, who are constantly dependent upon the knowledge and teaching of others. They are more likely to hear in the passage a summary of Paul's change from persecutor to preacher. A particularly alert older child may ask the mechanical question, "How did God tell Paul the good news while he was in Arabia?" Unfortunately, Paul didn't tell us the answer to that one.

Watch Words

Widow may be a new term for younger children. Explain it before using it to refer to the two mothers.

In speaking of death, use the concrete terms *died* and *dead* rather than euphemisms such as *passed on*. Stick to one or two simple terms, such as *raised* or *brought back to life* to describe what happened to the sons.

In speaking of God's powerful care, avoid *providence* entirely or feature it. (Remember that *providence* is most recognized as the capital of Rhode Island.)

Let the Children Sing

"I Sing the Almighty Power of God" and "For the Beauty of the Earth" are hymns through which children can praise God's love and power.

"Immortal, Invisible, God Only Wise" is filled with impossibly big words and strangely abstract phrases describing God. Either avoid this hymn or sing it after exploring it in the sermon (see Sermon Resource 2).

The Liturgical Child

1. Read consecutively the two stories about sons being raised from the dead. Present I Kings as readers' theater, then read the Gospel story. Three readers (the Narrator, Elijah, and the Widow) take places in the chancel. The narrator stands in the middle or most prominent place. Elijah and the widow stand to either side where they can speak directly to each other and turn to speak to God. This is a task for well-rehearsed adult readers with dramatic flair. The Good News Bible offers the simplest translation.

Narrator: Our lessons today are stories about God's powerful and loving care. The first story is from I Kings 17:8-24. It is the story of Elijah and a kind widow. Hear the Word of the Lord! *(Reads I Kings 17:8-10b).*

Elijah, the Widow, and Narrator: (Read the dialogue in verses 10c through 24. Omit the "he/she saids" where it makes the reading smoother.)

Narrator: Thus ends our story from I Kings. Now hear a similar story about Jesus from Luke's Gospel. *(Reads Gospel text.)*

2. Ask a children's class to present Psalm 146 as a choral reading, highlighting its short phrases which name ways God helps people in need. Choose either the New Revised Standard Version or The Good News Bible.

ALL:	Verse 1a
Solos:	Verses 1b, 2a, and 2b
Solos (older child or class teacher): Verses 3-4	
ALL:	Verse 5
Solo:	Verses 6a, 6b, 7a, 7b, 7c, 8a, 8b, 8c, 9a, and 9b
ALL:	Verse 9c
Solos:	Verses 10a and 10b
ALL:	Verse 10c

3. In your prayers, praise God for all the wonders of summer: special summer activities such as swimming, hiking, and whatever summer sport is central for your children; and for the change of pace that comes when school ends.

Sermon Resources

1. Play with the how-great-is-God questions to explore God's great love and power:

"Who was there before God?" (Answer: No one. God always existed. You can't go back far enough to get away from God.)

"Who made God?" (Answer: No one. God always was and always will be.)

"How does God know what is happening everywhere all the time?" (Answer: We don't know how God does it, but we know God does.)

Make up more questions and answers. If you deal with such questions with an open, light-hearted attitude, children will gain a sense of security based on your certainty that God's love and power are bigger than we can imagine and sufficient to meet any need.

2. Invite worshipers to open their hymnals for ready reference while you work through some or all of the verses of "Immortal, Invisible, God Only Wise." No child will remember all the definitions or explanations. But children can sense that the words are more than we can understand because God is more than we can understand. They also can sense from you that the words and the God they describe are friendly mysteries, to be enjoyed rather than feared.

We know God as Father, Son, and Holy Spirit. So multiply your age by 3.

——— x 3= ———
your age

Now write **God loves me always** that many times.

Remember what you write. It is true!

Draw a praise picture to show God some of the people and things you are thankful for.

PROPER SIX

(Sunday between June 12 and 18 inclusive, if after Trinity Sunday)

From a Child's Point of View

Old Testament: I Kings 21:1-10 (11-14), 15-21a. This is the story of Ahab's murder of Naboth in order to get his vineyard. The message in the story is simple: God cares about us and pays attention to what we do. God will not allow Naboth's unjust death to go unnoticed, nor will God let Ahab continually get away with such terrible behavior. Younger children, who generally make moral decisions in order to avoid punishment or to claim rewards, respond especially quickly to this message. Older children may realize that not all evildoers are caught as Ahab was. Indeed, some seem to profit by their evil actions.

Gospel: Luke 7:36–8:3. This is a story (7:41-42) within a story (7:36-50), followed by a tag-along story (8:1-3).

When the verses 41-50 are read alone, they provide a counterpoint to the story of Ahab. Although God cares about what we do, we do not need to earn God's love. Jesus loved the sinful woman as much as he loved the "good" Simon. The only difference was that the woman was very sorry about what she had done, so she was a lot more appreciative of God's love than Simon was.

The good news for the children who get in fights, are frequently punished, and are constantly told that they do not do what they should, is that God loves them in spite of their deeds. God is willing to forgive, even when parents, teachers, and friends are not.

It is also a call to "good" kids/people not to think they are any better than those who do not go to church as we do, or who are not as kind as we are, or who fail to meet our standards in any area. If God loves "bad" kids/people and accepts them, they should be good enough for us. In fact, Jesus tells us a sober secret: Sometimes people who have had to be forgiven many times are more loving than those who have always been good. It takes a while for children to grasp that secret, but it is a truth that especially those who are growing up as "good" kids need to encounter.

An entire service also could be constructed around the women who traveled with Jesus and his male disciples (Luke 8:1-3). Worshipers of all ages can enjoy learning about those women and imagining how they got along.

Psalm: 5:1-8. This psalmist moves from the recognition of sin to the acceptance of both God's judgment and grace, to the petition for God's help in avoiding sin in the future. Children, however, do not follow this progression. Instead, they catch occasional phrases (especially in verses 4-6). To them, the psalm makes most sense as a prayer that might have been prayed by Ahab or the woman in Luke's story.

Epistle: Galatians 2:15-21. This passage will mean nothing to children when they hear it read. The sentences are too complex, and the vocabulary is both too abstract and too technical. But its message is very similar to Luke's message: God loves us. Jesus came to live among us and die for us to prove that God loves us. So we do not need to pile up good deeds or perfect-attendance awards to make God like us.

Watch Words

Avoid obsolete words about sin such as *transgressions* and *abominations*. Speak instead of *sin* and *doing what is wrong*. Remember that children are most likely to have heard the word *righteous* in reference to unattractive self-*righteousness*.

Rather than speaking of *vindication* or *justification*, talk of God's *forgiving love* and being friends with God.

Avoid Paul's use of *the Law* as a catch phrase for earning approval by keeping God's rules. Elementary children are at the stage of moral development in which rules and laws are seen as good ways to live, work, and play together. They make moral decisions in reference to rules and laws. Paul's image is confusing because it sounds like a put-down of all rules and laws, rather than a challenge to the Pharisee's use of God's Law.

Also tell younger children what a *vineyard* is.

Let the Children Sing

Child-accessible hymns about sin and forgiveness are hard to find. The vocabulary and images in the most familiar ones make little sense to children. It may be a good day to sing "Jesus Loves Me." (In deference to older children, who often resent the request for children to sing this song for adults, sing it together). Or sing "There's a Wideness in God's Mercy." Simple commitment hymns such as "Be Thou My Vision" or "Lord, I Want to Be a Christian" are good second choices.

The Liturgical Child

1. The story of Ahab has all the marks of a morality play. So take advantage of the children's summer schedules or a willing children's church-school class to produce a simple play. With only one good rehearsal, as few as seven children (Ahab, Jezebel, Naboth, at least one town leader, two false witnesses, and Elijah) can pantomime the story while the worship leader reads it. Simple costumes and props help. In rehearsal, help the children act with their whole bodies as well as with their faces.

2. Base a prayer of confession on the story of Ahab:

> Lord, God, Ahab and Jezebel seem absolutely terrible until we look at ourselves. When we are honest, we admit that, like Ahab, we get jealous of what others have, then mope if we cannot have it for ourselves. Like Jezebel, we twist, and

even break the rules in order to get what we want. We act as if we are somehow special and need not follow your commands. Like Ahab, we have done the wrong that others have suggested, hoping you would blame them and not us. Forgive us. Forgive us for the wrongs we do and for all the ways we deny and try to cover them up. Amen.

Assurance of Pardon: The Bible tells us that when Ahab confessed his terrible sins to God and asked for forgiveness, God forgave even him. Jesus has promised that God also will forgive us when we confess. There is nothing so sinful that it cannot be confessed to, and forgiven by, the God who loves us so much that Jesus came to live and die and rise among us.

3. Before reading Luke's story, place on the lectern a "flask of ointment" (maybe a decorative perfume bottle) and 11 cardboard coins. Explain that each coin is worth 50 denarii. Put one denarii by itself and count out the other 10 into a stack, pointing out that there are 50 denarii in one stack and 500 in the other. Urge the children to listen for each of these items in the story you will read from Luke. Point to the items as you come to them in the story.

For dramatic emphasis and clarity, present the story as a one-person play. As you read the narrative, face forward in the lectern. While reading the Pharisee's words, turn a little to one side; while reading Jesus' words, turn a little to the other side. Imagine that the woman is kneeling on the floor a little behind Jesus. Assume the roles of Jesus and Simon with your facial expression and hand movements as you read their parts.

Sermon Resources

1. Recall how Pinocchio's wooden nose grew every time he told a lie. He learned that one lie led to another and that he could not hide his sins. Compare the experiences of Ahab, Pinocchio, and ourselves in pretending that our sinful actions do not matter.

2. *Words by Heart,* by Ouida Sebestyen, is a powerful novel about an African American girl in post-Civil War Kansas, who learns to live by all the Bible verses she has memorized. She learns from her father to love and forgive a white family that causes his death. (Available in most public libraries.)

Write a prayer that the woman in Luke's story might have prayed when she went home that night.

Listen carefully to the story of Ahab when it is read from the Bible. Find 9 words from the story in the letters below. The words may go across or down.

```
L R S S I N X M K
A H A B J M U U Y
E V I N E Y A R D
L K C R Z Z A D F
I X O L E T T E R
J M V L B T D R W
A I E K E H R N Q
H N T M L I E S T
```

Words to find:

AHAB JEZEBEL

MURDER LIES

VINEYARD

SIN LETTER

COVET ELIJAH

PROPER SEVEN

(Sunday between June 19 and 25 inclusive, if after Trinity Sunday)

From a Child's Point of View

Old Testament: I Kings 19:1-4 (5-7), 8-15a. This story offers two themes of importance to children. If the focus is on Elijah's escape, the theme is that God takes care of us in difficult situations. Children need know only that Elijah had just killed all four hundred of Queen Jezebel's baal priests and that Jezebel was the meanest queen in the Bible; then they will understand why Elijah was frightened, running for his life, and ready to stop being God's prophet. With help, they can then identify the ways God took care of Elijah—feeding him on his journey, listening to his complaints, showing him God's power and quiet love, and granting his wish that someone else take over his job as prophet. They can trust that God also will be with them and care for them when they are scared and feel hopeless.

If the focus is on Elijah's encounter with God on Mount Horeb (vss. 1-4, 8-15a), the theme is "How does God speak to us?" Because children hear literally the biblical stories about God speaking, and because few have had personal experience with burning bushes or God calling in an audible voice, they often believe that God does not speak to them. They need to hear that for Elijah, God came not in a dramatic wind, fire, or earthquake, but in "the sound of a sheer silence." They should be urged to listen for God to speak to them in a variety of ways: through stories they hear, through other people, and through feelings of God being with them in difficult times.

A related, but often unnoticed, point is that even after the wind, earthquake, fire, and "sound of sheer silence," Elijah still told God exactly how frightened and unhappy he felt. Apparently he was not intimidated by God's presence, nor did God intend for him to be. We are invited to be as honest with God as Elijah was.

Psalm: 42–43. This is actually one psalm with three stanzas, each followed by the same refrain (vss. 42:5, 11; 43:5). The abstract language, poetic images, and geographic references make the psalm almost impossible for children to understand cognitively. Fortunately, the most understandable image, that of the thirsty deer, is in the first verse. If the deer catches their attention before they get lost in the more complicated images that follow, and if the psalm is read with deep feeling, children can follow its emotional sense. The refrain, especially if read from either the Good News Bible or the NIV, summarizes the psalmist's commitment to hope in a gloomy situation.

Epistle: Galatians 3:23-29. This is a very adult text. Its complex sentences deal in abstract language with an idea that is developmentally incomprehensible to children. Elementary children are at a stage of moral development in which ethical decisions are made by following or not following rules. They respond strongly to calls to follow God's rules and struggle daily with overcoming their wishes and feelings in order to follow rules. Paul's insistence that Christians are beyond the Law (or rules) baffles them. It will make little sense until their mental abilities develop enough to allow them to identify the principles behind rules. So read this passage for older worshipers.

Gospel: Luke 8:26-39. The demons make this one of the most difficult healing stories to share with children. Children want to know what demons are, why they made the man do what he did, and why the pigs ran over the cliff. They also want to know if there are still demons today? And if so, where? There are few answers that will satisfy literal thinkers.

The theory that this story is based on a prescientific understanding of mental illness is hard for children to accept because they have little understanding of mental illness. Alert older children may ask why pigs were needed.

Most children associate demons with evil beings that stalk innocent victims in horror shows, haunted houses at fairs, and scary campfire stories. Young children worry about monsters hiding in their closets or under their beds. To the fearful child, the story says that Jesus is more powerful than any monster or demon. Just as Jesus would not let the demons control this man, he will not let them "get" us.

One ambiguity that interests animal-loving children is whether the demons drove the pigs over the cliff (maybe to get even with Jesus by making the pig owners angry at him); whether the pigs were so frightened by the demons that they jumped over the cliff; or whether the pigs (being smarter than people thought) recognized the demons and, by jumping over the cliff, finished Jesus' work of destroying them.

Watch Words

Decide on one definition of *demons* for today's worship, then stick with it to avoid confusion. *Demons* may be the evil powers we all battle every day. Or they may be the worst evil beings we can imagine.

Let the Children Sing

Sing about God's loving care in difficult times: "Jesus Loves Me, This I Know," "Now Thank We All Our God," "The Lord's My Shepherd," and "Be Not Dismayed Whate're Betide" (or "God Will Take Care of You").

Sing about God speaking to us through the Holy Spirit ("Every Time I Feel the Spirit") and in creation ("This Is My Father's World").

Commit yourselves to listen to God with "Open My Eyes, That I May See" or "Take Time to Be Holy."

The Liturgical Child

1. A dramatic reading is needed to hold children's attention for Elijah's long story. Read Jezebel's threat with cold, cruel fury. Whine Elijah's frightened complaints. And read God's lines with loving patience. Describe each power display on the mountain loudly, then whisper in awe, "But the Lord was not in the _____."

2. Follow the format of Psalms 42-43. Have one or three worship leader(s) read the "verses," with the congregation repeating the refrain. (To help worshipers get into the feel of the psalm, invite them to imagine they are Elijah, running away from Queen Jezebel.)

3. Create a litany prayer of confession in which the worship leader identifies the ways God speaks to us, and the congregation replies with the repeated admission that we do not pay attention. For example:

Leader: God, we wish you would speak to us, but we ignore the messages you speak all around us. Pictures from space show us the vastness of your creative power. Tiny flowers and intricate insects speak of your care for the smallest of things. The earth and the universe are full of messages about your power and loving care.

People: But we do not pay attention. Forgive us.

Leader: You speak to us through people around us. If we listen carefully, we often hear your will in the advice of friends and leaders. If we care to, we sense your love in the love of those who love and care for us. When we watch, we can see people doing your work and join them.

People: But we do not pay attention. Forgive us.

Sermon Resources

1. To explore Elijah's experience, begin by talking about what scares people. Tell stories about being in storms or being lost (two big childhood fears) as well as stories about what adults fear. *The Diary of Anne Frank* offers excerpts about living faithfully with fear.

2. Devote the sermon to describing and calling on people to cast out specific demons that try to take over our lives and make us do terrible things. While younger children will hear only a sermon against "bad attitudes," older children will begin to identify selfishness, greed, and prejudice as demons.

God speaks to us in many ways.

Draw something larger than a house that tells you of God's power.

Draw a picture of something smaller than a softball that reminds you of God's love.

Find the letters of one word in each kite. The words are Jesus' promise to us when we are frightened.

Answer: I am with you always.

Matthew 28:20

PROPER EIGHT

(Sunday between June 26 and July 2 inclusive)

From a Child's Point of View

Today's texts cluster around the theme of discipleship.

Old Testament: II Kings 2:1-2, 6-14. This story can be told to compare Elisha's persistent faith with the excuses of the would-be disciples in the Gospel lesson. (Children are impressed by Elisha's refusal to leave Elijah, and also with his bold request of his hero.) Or it can be told with the focus on the passing of "the mantle." (If Elijah's life has been the focus for several weeks, children are pleased to hear about God's recognition of Elijah's work in the story of the fiery chariot—a neat way to die!) Whichever your focus, present this story with the same open wonder with which we tell the story of Cinderella or the Knights of the Round Table.

Psalm: 77:1-2, 11-20. Verses 11-15 form the most child-accessible section of this psalm. Children easily understand the call to remember all the powerful things God has done. If this service culminates a series on Elijah's ministry, children can use these verses to review the ways God acted powerfully through Elijah.

The water and references in verses 16-25 confuse children, who cannot make the connection between the poetic references and familiar stories.

Epistle: Galatians 5:1, 13-25. These passages will not make much sense to children as they hear them read. However, with some help, they can grasp Paul's message in verses 14-25. (The emphasis on Christian freedom in vss. 1 and 13 will be understood in later years.) Paul begins with the command to love your neighbor as you love yourself (vs. 14). Then he presents a list of what happens when people do not follow this rule (vss. 19-21), and another list of what happens when they do follow this rule (vss. 22-23). The first list, in particular, is more clear in the vocabulary of the Good News Bible or New International Version. Although some items on the list may make children giggle, they need to hear Paul's condemnation of activities that television and today's culture seem to accept. Because they often are told not to act like animals, children enjoy Paul's comparison of the people who do not love to packs of destructive animals.

Gospel: Luke 9:51-62. This passage includes two separate stories. Verses 51-55 are a lesson in what to do when someone you have tried to love refuses to love you. Children will need background information on Jewish-Samaritan relations to understand the story, but they will need no help in understanding its "reality" message. The reality is that even Jesus was turned away by some people he tried to befriend. Children need to realize that the same probably will happen to them when they try to reach out to lonely, unhappy people at school and in their neighborhoods. When this happens, they are to be as forgiving as Jesus was.

Verses 57-62 report Jesus' conversations with three would-be disciples. A child's version of these excuses: "I am not ready to be a real disciple yet. When I grow up, I'll be one. But now I'm just a kid. All I can do is learn about Jesus." Jesus' response is that *now* is the time to be a disciple. Jesus needs children to do his work on the playground, in the swimming pool, the locker room, and all those other places where adults are not as influential. So children are called to be disciples *now*.

Watch Words

In speaking of discipleship under difficult conditions, avoid terms such as *perseverance* and *forbearance*.

Before reading the Old Testament story, explain that a *mantle* is a *coat,* and urge worshipers to listen for how Elijah's mantle was used.

Avoid using *the flesh* and *the spirit* as tag words for life based on disobeying or obeying the command to love one another. Instead, speak of *obeying* and *disobeying.*

Translate into today's vernacular the unfamiliar or obsolete words that describe sexual activities.

Let the Children Sing

"Lord, I Want to Be a Christian," "Take My Life and Let It Be Consecrated," and "Breathe on Me, Breath of God" (in order of ease) are discipleship hymns children can sing.

"O Jesus, I Have Promised" will be hard for younger readers, but preadolescents often appreciate and claim for themselves this musical prayer.

Ask the children's choir or the congregation to sing "I've Got a Joy, Joy, Joy, Joy, Down in My Heart." Add verses that celebrate Paul's "fruits of the Spirit." A lighthearted congregation can enjoy even a final verse: "If the devil doesn't like it he can sit on a tack—and stay!"

Sing "Swing Low, Sweet Chariot," pointing out its base in Elijah's story. Either "I Sing a Song of the Saints of God" or "For All the Saints" can be sung to honor both Elijah and Elisha.

The Liturgical Child

1. If you have been following the Elijah readings, review them and celebrate Elijah's life with a litany. A worship leader makes a series of statements that describe what Elijah was like or recall the things Elijah did. The congregation's response to each: "I will call to mind the deeds of the Lord; I will remember your wonders of old" (Ps. 77:11).

2. To stage the three conversations in Luke 9:57-62, enlist the help of three would-be disciples (standing in a group at one side of the chancel) and Jesus (standing at the center). The worship leader (standing in the lectern) serves as narrator, introducing the passage and reading the introductory phrase for each conversation. Actors should memorize their parts, plan the emphasis and tone of their speaking, and work together to present the sequence smoothly.

3. Base a prayer of confession on Galatians 5:

Lord, when we read Paul's list of the results of living apart from you, we recognize many of them in our own lives. Each of us has done things of which we are deeply ashamed. (Pause for worshipers to offer silent confessions.) Though most of us have not practiced witchcraft, we have treated our own wants as gods. (Pause) Each of us has made enemies and waged war with them. (Pause) We know what it is to be jealous of what others have. (Pause) We are amazed at how quickly we can become really angry and lash out at others. (Pause) We often put our ambitions first, even before doing what is right and loving. (Pause) We have been part of groups that shut others out. Forgive us and help us change our ways to reflect your love. For we pray in the name of Jesus. Amen.

Assurance of Pardon: God does forgive all who repent and change their ways. We are promised that when we do love one another, we will find that love, joy, peace, patience, kindness, goodness, faithfulness, humility, and self-control fill our lives to overflowing.

Sermon Resources

Tell a story about two children in a sports camp at your state university. Put them in a group with two campers from a different area of the state who are very pushy about playing "their" plays and are very loud in their support of opposing university teams. Tell how the two disciples reach out to these difficult outsiders by helping them find a practice field, eating with them in the cafeteria, and setting up plays in their favor during practice sessions. Let the outsiders respond by showing no appreciation for help in finding a field, making rude jokes about the disciples' favorite teams and players at the cafeteria table, and stealing a play from the disciples to cause their team to lose the game. After hearing this story, worshipers of all ages will be ready to walk in the shoes of Elijah, Jesus, and his disciples; they will think about discipleship that does not give up when faced with discouraging results.

Write and draw a comicbook story
about a disciple doing hard work
at a swimming pool or on a team.

Title: _____

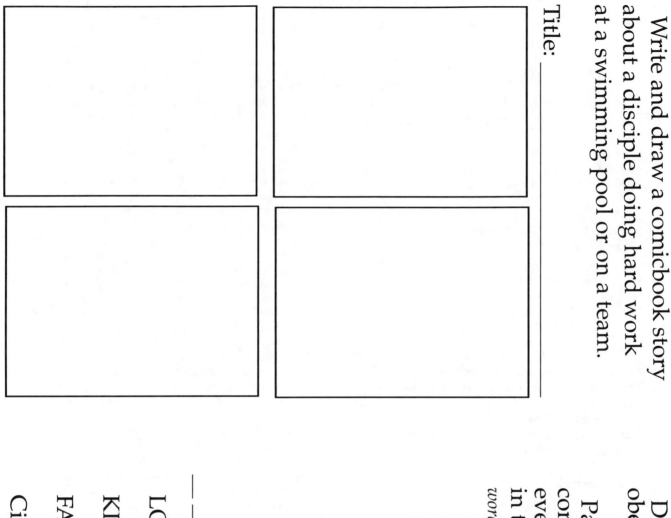

Disciples are people who love and
obey Jesus.

Paul said that people who obey Jesus'
command to love one another will have
everything listed below. Write each word
in the correct spaces. *Hint: match a letter in the
word to a letter in the word disciple.*

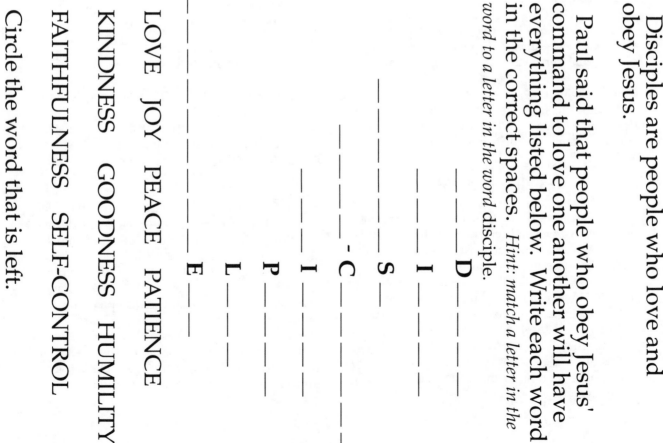

— — — D — — — —

— — — I — — — —

— — S — — —

- C — — — — — —

— — I — — —

— P — — — —

— — L — —

— — — E — —

LOVE   JOY   PEACE   PATIENCE
KINDNESS   GOODNESS   HUMILITY
FAITHFULNESS   SELF-CONTROL

Circle the word that is left.

Proper 8 / © 1994 by Abingdon Press.

PROPER NINE

(Sunday between July 3 and 9 inclusive)

From a Child's Point of View

Old Testament: II Kings 5:1-14. The story of Namaan's cure first attracts the attention of children because the heroine is a little girl. The fact that a little slave girl provided the key information about the cure and that Namaan and his wife took her suggestion seriously delights children, who often feel they have nothing important to contribute and that adults do not take their ideas seriously.

The importance of "little things" (a slave girl's information and a bath in a muddy river) is shown in two ways. First, it insists that God is at work in everyday events as well as in dramatic events. Children who grow up with the spectacular biblical stories often overlook God at work in the love of their families, the activities of their church, and the events of their own lives. This story encourages children to look for God at work in everyday events.

Second, as Namaan's servant pointed out, we should be as willing to do nonspectacular deeds as we are to do the dramatic ones. Children often undervalue their deeds of lovingkindness and playground peacemaking because they are not as dramatic as those in the Bible. They long to do heroic deeds and solve big problems in single strokes. They need to be reminded that God is working out the big plan through all our little efforts. Just as God used the information from the slave girl and cured Namaan—not with a great feat but with a bath in a muddy river—so God uses and values our efforts to love others and to share God's love with them. No loving deed is too insignificant to be noticed and used by God.

Psalm: 30. The underlying understanding of death and illness as signs of God's anger or punishment keep children from understanding all the lines of this psalm. If, however, the psalm is dramatically presented, children understand occasional lines and sense its feeling of relieved joy.

Epistle: Galatians 6:(1-6), 7-16. This passage falls into two sections. The second, verses 11-16, summarizes Paul's position on the circumcision debate, an issue children do not understand. But the first, verses 1-10, deals with consequences, a reality elementary children deal with every day, as adults encourage them to think about the consequences of their actions *before* they act and also to face up to the consequences afterward. Non-agricultural children need help with Paul's sowing and reaping images. They more readily understand the results of practicing (or not practicing) a sport or musical instrument. Paul's abstract sowing "to the flesh" or "to the Spirit" need to be illustrated with specific results that come from loving others rather than thinking only about ourselves.

Gospel: Luke 10:1-11, 16-20. This passage provides balance for last week's readings about the frustrations of being a faithful disciple. When the seventy-two were sent out, they did their work with more success than they dreamed possible. Though they may not understand the details of Jesus' instructions to the group, children will catch the drift of the story and pick up on the excitement of the seventy-two as they return successful. A dramatic reading will focus the children's attention on the disciples' excitement, rather than on the problematic promise about walking on snakes and scorpions, or on the picture of the devil falling from the sky. Children, especially older children who are defining themselves by the groups they join, are encouraged to join the excited disciples doing God's work in amazing ways.

Watch Words

Leprosy, with its social isolation, needs to be described.

Do not assume that children will understand the *reaping* and *sowing* language in Luke and Galatians.

Let the Children Sing

"I Sing a Song of the Saints of God" and "We Are the Church" (Avery and Marsh) are upbeat hymns that celebrate the church at work together. "God of Grace and God of Glory" is harder, but children can join in on the repetitive chorus.

Choosing "I Sing the Almighty Power of God" is one way to celebrate God at work in the world. "All Things Bright and Beautiful" focuses on both big and little things.

The Liturgical Child

1. The story of Namaan and Psalm 30 also are read on the Sixth Sunday After the Epiphany in Year B. See resources for that day in this series for a Prayer of Confession about our failure to do "little things" (Liturgical Child 2), directions for pantomiming the story of Namaan (Liturgical Child 1), and a Worship Worksheet with a complete-the-story activity.

2. Present Psalm 30 as Namaan's prayer. Ask someone to assume Namaan's role, reading the psalm dramatically, as if praying it on his way home.

3. Pray about "little things" in which you sense God's presence and power. Note storms, sunsets, and other weather events of the past week. Thank God for the Bible school, the church-camp experience for children, and other activities of your congregation in which you see God at work. Mention events in the community and human-interest events from abroad which indicate that God is at work among people every day. Then pray for the

will and the wisdom to do "little things." Pray for the patience to say kind words when we feel tired and crabby, for the strength to keep forgiving people we need to forgive frequently (like brothers and sisters), and for the wisdom to find little ways to help relieve hunger and end homelessness.

4. Create a praise litany citing "successes" within your congregation and within the larger church. Be sure to include some activities in which children participated. To each example, the congregation replies, "Praise God, who is doing wonderful things through us."

5. Before pronouncing the benediction, charge the congregation in the same spirit with which Jesus charged the seventy-two:

> As Jesus sent out the seventy-two disciples to teach, care for the sick, and make friends with the friendless, so I send you. Go out into (your town or area) to share God's love. Talk to those who will listen, take care of those who need help, and do your part to bring God's kingdom closer. As you go, remember that many people are waiting for you and will welcome you. Also remember that Jesus will be with you always. Amen.

Sermon Resources

1. Preach about God's work in the "little things." Tell stories about the little ways you see God at work in the life and ministry of the congregation. Describe making caring phone calls and visits, making tray favors for institutionalized people, and inviting newcomers of all ages to church. Encourage people to value the little things others are doing in God's name and to look for little things they can do to share God's love and build God's kingdom.

2. Tell stories of amazing successes in the church. For example, describe the mushrooming work of Habitat for Humanity. In less than thirty years, this house-building ministry has used volunteer labor and donations of materials and money to build thousands of houses for needy people in countries all around the world. (Read *No More Shacks* by Millard Fuller if you do not know this story.)

Or describe the effect of one Heifer Project—a flock of chicks sent by a children's church school class to a family in an underdeveloped country (eggs to eat, sell, and hatch into more chicks).

Or describe the results of work your congregation has done.

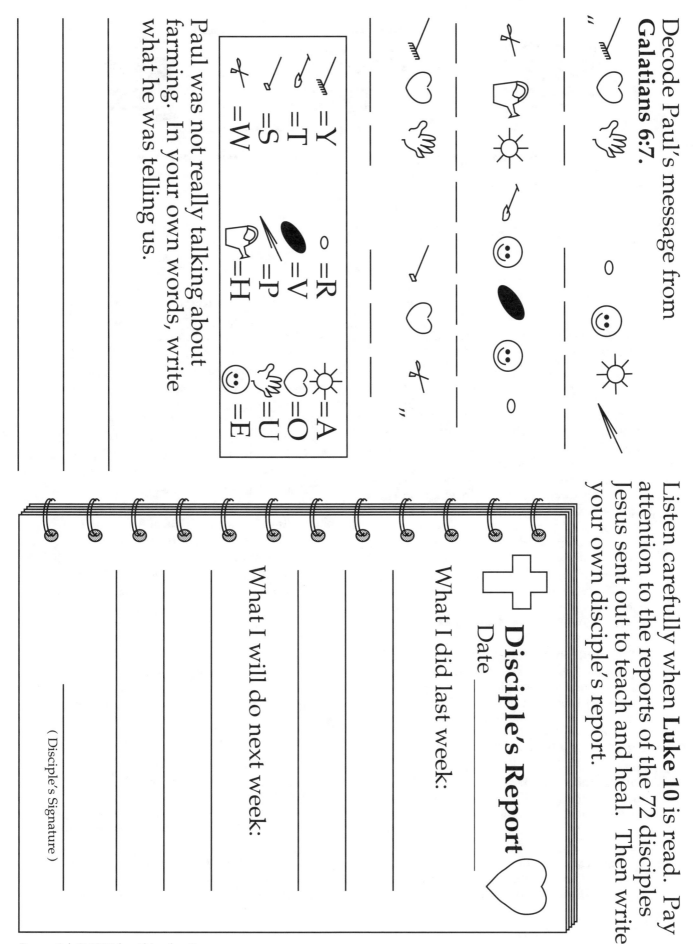

Decode Paul's message from **Galatians 6:7.**

Paul was not really talking about farming. In your own words, write what he was telling us.

Key:
= Y = T = S = W
o = R = V = P = H
= A = O = U = E

Listen carefully when **Luke 10** is read. Pay attention to the reports of the 72 disciples Jesus sent out to teach and heal. Then write your own disciple's report.

Disciple's Report

Date _____

What I did last week:

What I will do next week:

(Disciple's Signature)

PROPER TEN

(Sunday between July 10 and 16 inclusive)

From a Child's Point of View

Old Testament: Amos 7:7-17. For children, this contains two rather separate stories. Verses 7-9 focus on the plumb line and God's demanded accountability. Because few children have seen or used plumb lines, they need to learn about them before they can understand Amos's point. The check sheets or star charts with which children record their performance of assigned chores are a familiar equivalent of Amos's plumb line. The point of each is that we are responsible for what we do and for what we do not do. God cares about what we do.

Verses 10-17 are a story of Amos's courageous bravery in doing what God had sent him to do. When the story is dramatically presented so that children realize the risk Amos took in standing up to Amaziah, they are duly impressed and can hear God's call that they should be that courageous in standing up for what is right.

Psalm: 82. Successfully explaining in worship the psalmist's references to a heavenly court is nearly impossible. Most children will simply hear occasional lines that demand justice and will assume that they are addressed to all people.

Gospel: Luke 10:25-37. The parable of the good Samaritan appears in much church school curriculum and therefore is familiar to children. Without knowing about Jewish-Samaritan relationships, young children can grasp Jesus' basic message that we are to treat as neighbor any person who needs our help. As older children learn the significance of the good neighbor being a Samaritan, they can use the parable to reevaluate their responsibility to people who are not in "their group." For fifth- and sixth-graders, who have strong group loyalties, this is an important task. Retelling the parable in modern settings and making up versions of the parable that include children the same age as those in your congregation are often ways to help children get the point.

Epistle: Colossians 1:1-14. This is the greeting (vss. 1-2) and opening prayer (vss. 3-14) of Paul's letter to the church in Colossae. Paul writes in cosmic, abstract terms about the faith of the Colossians. Basically, he is thanking God that the Colossians have responded to the good news and praying that God will give them the power to live as good disciples. But children will not be able to pull this meaning from the long, complex sentences and abstract terms. Given the richness of the other texts for the day, it is advisable to speak to children through those texts rather than through this one.

Watch Words

Children take pride in being *responsible.* Therefore, speaking about *responsibility* has more impact than speaking about *accountability* or *judgment.*

The Amos text is the first of six texts that deal with the impending *exile.* This term will be new to most children and many adults. Take time to introduce it. Then use it frequently in ways that build familiarity.

Samaritan, Levite, and *priest* need not be defined in cultural terms. Offering modern parallels to each term is as, or even more, effective.

Let the Children Sing

In response to Amos's call to live up to God's standards, sing "Spirit of the Living God," "Have Thine Own Way," or "Take My Life and Let It Be Consecrated." Sing, or have a choir sing, "We Are Climbing Jacob's Ladder."

"God of Grace and God of Glory" can be sung in honor of Amos's bravery and as a prayer for disciples in similar situations today. A children's choir might sing the chorus in response to congregational singing of the verses.

"Let There Be Peace on Earth" and "Lord, I Want to Be a Christian" are two hymns with which to commit ourselves to being good neighbors.

The Liturgical Child

1. Present the Amos text with a narrator and three adult men—Amos, Amaziah, and Jereboam. The narrator may read in the lectern, but the others should have their lines memorized for delivery in place. Jereboam stands authoritatively off to one side, arms folded across his chest. He may wear a crown. Amaziah stands beside the central table as if he controls it. Amos stands forward. All three use strong arm movements to emphasize their words. Amaziah and Amos may come nose-to-nose for their angry confrontation in verses 12-17.

2. Children enjoy pantomiming the story of the good Samaritan as an older child reads it from the Bible. Simple costumes help. A middle-elementary class might prepare the whole presentation as a class project. (If you are uncomfortable with a child/donkey in the sanctuary, omit the donkey and have the Samaritan support the victim with an arm around the victim's shoulders.)

3. During the church's prayers, pray aloud for the congregation's neighbors and offer times of silence in which worshipers may pray for their own neighbors. During one silent period, bid them to pray for each member of their families. After a general prayer for the congregation, bid worshipers to pray in silence for one member of the congregation whom they know has special needs. Follow the same procedure when praying for people in your community (groups such as the homeless and individuals encountered daily), and for the people of the world (victims of natural disasters and those caught up in political events). In all cases, speak of specific groups with specific needs.

Sermon Resources

1. During summer, children are more often in unsupervised groups in which they have opportunities to stand up to others for what they know to be right. Shoplifting; petty vandalism; cruel tricks on, or exclusion of, others; forbidden feats, and so forth call for the courage of Amos when he stood up to Amaziah.

2. "It doesn't matter" is a phrase used by both children and adults to evade our responsibility. Sometimes we say it when we mean that the person hurt by what we said or did does not matter (for example, that "ol' cry baby's" tears don't matter or that the people caught in the cross-fire of a war are expendable). Sometimes we say it when we mean that the damage is of no real consequence (for example, that her broken toy doesn't matter or that the extinction of the spotted owl is no great loss). And sometimes we say it when we are trying to make our larger goal justify the damage (for example, that I had to "borrow" her pen to finish my project or that we worked outside the law for "national security"). Amos says to all, "It *does* matter." God cares about what we do and do not do. We are responsible for all our words and deeds.

3. Include items from the Worship Worksheet cross-word puzzle in speaking of the ways we measure things and measure ourselves.

4. Retell the good Samaritan story, setting it in your town and including people the children in your congregation have encountered. (If I were telling the story, a mugging would take place near the bus station. The mayor and a minister would pass by, but a homeless alcoholic would stop to help.)

5. In response to the good Samaritan parable, talk about groups and group loyalty. While celebrating the benefits of groups, point out how easy it is to ignore others beyond the group and actively hurt others with group-centeredness. Cite examples such as fans of rival soccer teams fighting, groups of close friends making fun of those they do not accept in their group, and members of children's clubhouses causing trouble in the neighborhood.

MEASURING UP TO THE STANDARDS

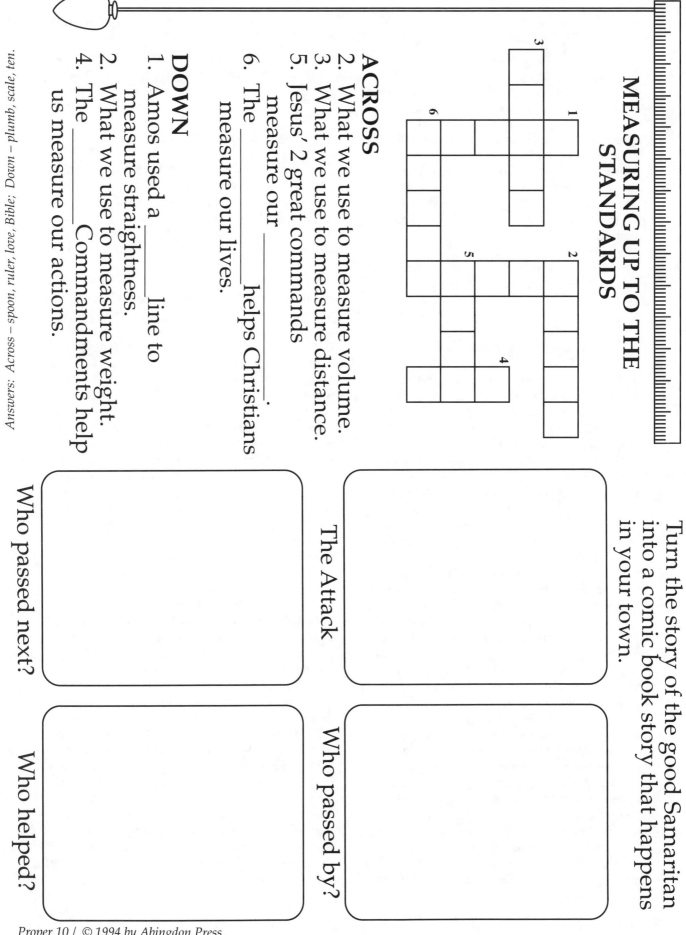

ACROSS

2. What we use to measure volume.
3. What we use to measure distance.
5. Jesus' 2 great commands measure our _____.
6. The _____ helps Christians measure our lives.

DOWN

1. Amos used a _____ line to measure straightness.
2. What we use to measure weight.
4. The _____ Commandments help us measure our actions.

Turn the story of the good Samaritan into a comic book story that happens in your town.

The Attack

Who passed by?

Who passed next?

Who helped?

PROPER ELEVEN

(Sunday between July 17 and 23 inclusive)

From a Child's Point of View

Old Testament: Amos 8:1-12. References to Old Testament worship practices, measuring units, and slavery make this text hard for children to understand. Amos's topic, however, is important to them. In children's words: Amos was speaking to people who were so greedy they couldn't wait to get out of church! They spent their time in church thinking up new ways to get their own way, to cheat and steal from those who already had less than they did. Amos insisted that God held them responsible for their behavior and would punish them severely.

Children often assume that the basket of summer fruit is a positive image and consequently are confused by Amos's negative message. They depend on the preacher to turn their attention to what is done with rotten fruit.

The Good News Bible provides a free but understandable translation of this passage.

Psalm: 52. To empathize with the strong feelings expressed in this psalm, one has to hear it in the context suggested in the subtitle, "When Doeg the Edomite came to Saul . . ." When the story of Doeg's self-serving behavior (told in I Sam. 22) and David's angry psalm response are paired, children can hear the condemnation of people who will do anything to get what they want. Childhood examples of tattling, telling secrets that will get others in trouble, cheating at games in order to win, or doing whatever the biggest or most powerful kid wants in order to stay in his or her favor illustrate Doeg's life-style. (David's anger shines through especially clearly in the New Jerusalem Bible.)

Epistle: Colossians 1:15-28. This complex passage is Paul's explanation of what it means when we say that Jesus is Christ. A child's paraphrase of Paul's points:

Christ is God made visible.
Christ was there during and before creation.
Christ's main job is making friends between God and people.
Christ was raised from death.
Christ is in charge of the church.
Christ lives and works in each of us.
(Paul is an example of this.)

Gospel: Luke 10:38-42. This is the story of Martha's complaint against her sister Mary. Most children, having fresh experiences with such sibling arguments, empathize with the sisters immediately. But the story is not really about sibling arguments. It is about choices. Each sister made a choice about what to do when Jesus arrived. No one forced Martha to go into the kitchen. So Martha had no right to complain about Mary. In the language used in parent-training courses, Martha needed to accept the "natural consequences" of her choice. Similarly, children who plead for piano lessons must then accept the reality that while they are practicing, someone else might be watching television.

Jesus also insisted that Mary had made the better choice. So children need to consider their choices carefully, because some are better than others. Just as Jesus thought it was better to sit and talk about important things than to worry about a fancy meal, it also is better for children to help a younger brother or sister get ready for church than to spend all their time worrying about what they themselves will wear. It is also better to visit a shut-in with their Sunday school class than to accept a last-minute invitation to go to the movies with a friend.

Watch Words

Children often think that *Christ* is Jesus' last name. It is more like a title, such as Batman or William the Conqueror. It might be wise to use the full *Jesus Christ* throughout today's worship.

Follow the Good News Bible to speak of *God's making friends with us* rather than *reconciliation*.

Let the Children Sing

"Come Christians, Join to Sing" and "When Morning Gilds the Skies" praise Christ and include a repeated phrase which even nonreaders can sing. Sing of Jesus' role in the natural order with the familiar "Fairest Lord Jesus."

The Old Testament and Gospel call for discipleship hymns: "Dear Lord, Lead Me Day by Day," "Lord, I Want to Be a Christian," or "Take My Life and Let It Be Consecrated."

The Liturgical Child

1. *Prayer of Confession:*

God, you give us life and families and friends. You put us in charge of this beautiful planet and universe. You gave us the Bible to show us how to live happily, and you lived among us as Jesus to save us from our sin. We should be happy, generous people, but we are not. Too often, we think only about ourselves. We are greedy. We make long lists of what we think we must have. We are jealous. We want for ourselves every fine thing that belongs to someone else. Often, we are ready to lie, cheat, and steal to get what we want. Forgive us. Help us to look beyond our own wants to the wants and needs of others. Help us learn that sharing can bring us more happiness than grabbing. Help us to recognize all your gifts and be grateful. Amen.

2. Present I Samuel 22 and Psalm 52 as two windows on the same event. First, offer some background and read I Samuel 22 from the lectern. Next, invite worshipers to hear the psalm from the lips of an adult David, who presents it dramatically from memory, standing in the chancel. David may be in biblical dress.

3. Create a litany affirmation of faith by alternating phrases of the section of the Apostles' Creed about Jesus with the congregational response: Jesus is the Christ!

4. Create a litany that asks God's help in making wise choices. The worship leader briefly describes a variety of decisions. (Include decisions about how to treat people and how to use our time; decisions made by political leaders; decisions about cheating in games and at work, etc.) To each decision, the congregation responds, "Lord, help us choose well."

5. As the story of Mary and Martha is read, have three expressive adults pantomime it. (Adults will more fully express the feelings involved and will be proof to children that adults also engage in spats.) Pause in the readings so that Martha can show her growing frustration.

Sermon Resources

1. On a central table in the chancel, display a large basket of ripe summer fruit, but include one or two rotten pieces. Begin the sermon by taking the rotten pieces from the arrangement, describing what would happen if they remained with the good fruit, and discarding them in a handy garbage can. Then explore what Amos's basket of fruit meant.

2. If the focus is on the psalm, begin by saying, "We do not know much about Doeg, but what we do know suggests that Doeg was the kind of kid who . . . (cite examples of childhood self-serving). When he was a teenager, he probably . . . . And when he was an adult we know that he . . . . (retell the story from I Samuel 22 in your own words)."

3. Point out and link to Paul's statements about Christ all symbols for Christ in your sanctuary.

4. To explore choices and their consequences, describe "Create Your Own Adventure" books. In these books, the story is interrupted frequently for the reader to decide which of two options the characters should take. Directions send the reader to different pages to find out what happened as a result of the characters' choice. Most children (third grade and older) have read at least one such book and enjoy rereading it to try out different combinations of choices.

A daring preacher with a relaxed mid-summer congregation could begin the sermon by reading part of one of these books, letting the congregation vote on the choices by show of hands. Then the story of Mary and Martha could be presented in the same format. (The first decision is what to do when Jesus arrives, followed by Martha's decision about how to respond to Mary's choice.) This sets the stage for an analysis of how we make and live with our choices.

Shade in each space with a * in it to find a word that fits these grabby fingers.

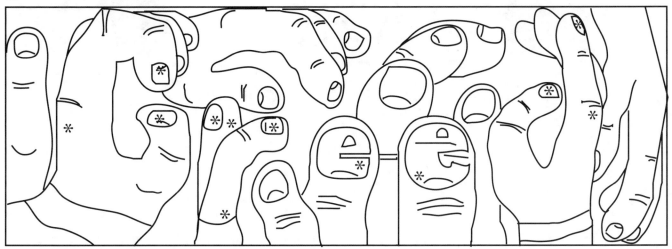

Write a prayer using this word.

_____

_____

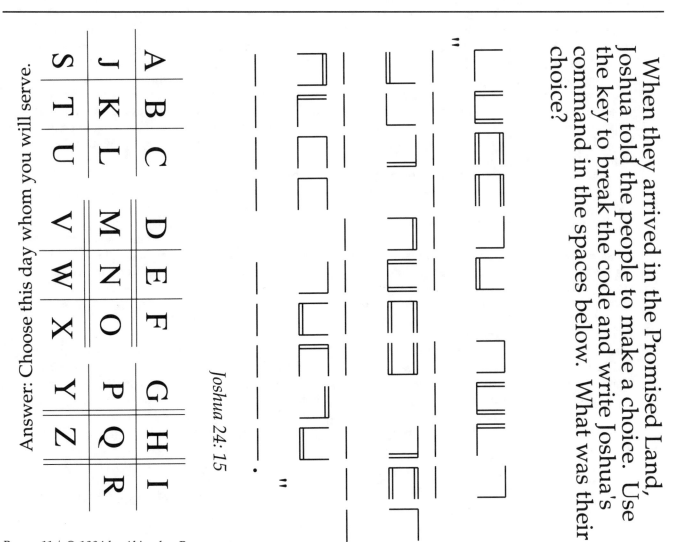

When they arrived in the Promised Land, Joshua told the people to make a choice. Use the key to break the code and write Joshua's command in the spaces below. What was their choice?

Joshua 24: 15

Answer: Choose this day whom you will serve.

A	B	C	D	E	F	G	H	I
J	K	L	M	N	O	P	Q	R
S	T	U	V	W	X	Y	Z	

PROPER TWELVE

(Sunday between July 24 and 30 inclusive)

From a Child's Point of View

Old Testament: Hosea 1:2-10. This passage is for adults. Children not only do not get the point, but are offended by the story. Because they hear literally, their first concern is for the children who are given such awful names at God's direction. They imagine the children being called on by a teacher or being called home by a parent and wonder how those children would be teased because of their names. They wonder how God could do something so mean to make a point to adults who were misbehaving. Furthermore, even worldly wise children who understand the technicalities of the relationship between Hosea and Gomer cannot understand the full dimensions of a mature marriage relationship and the pain involved when it is broken. Consequently, they cannot grasp Hosea's message. Next week's focus on the relationship between a parent and a rebellious child makes much the same point for all worshipers and is more child-accessible.

Psalm: 85. I suspect that this psalm is included among today's texts as a hopeful balance to Hosea's message of judgment. Children, however, hear the questions in verse 5 and want to know who is in trouble and why. The psalm does not say, and matching the psalm to Hosea's text looks past the punishment which the disloyal people had brought on themselves, to their restoration. That leap is too big for children.

Children with vivid imaginations giggle over the word pictures in verses 10 and 11. Expect at least one young worshiper to smack an overdramatic air-kiss to another.

Epistle: Colossians 2:6-15 (16-19). This is part of a letter written to grown-ups about grown-up intellectual problems. The children of Colossae were probably as unconcerned about these issues (except when it upset their parents) as are children today. The one point that makes sense to children is that Jesus is to be the center of their lives (vss. 6-7).

Gospel: Luke 11:1-13. This passage introduces the Lord's Prayer (vss. 1-4); it also offers a rather baffling parable and then a more sensible set of teachings about God's response to our prayers.

Older children will be interested in how this version of the Lord's Prayer developed into the one used in your church today. They also will benefit from comparing several different versions of the prayer and from exploring the meaning of each phrase.

The teachings in verses 9-15 invite children to stretch their understanding of how God responds to prayer. Many children assume that God can respond only by giving us what we ask for or by speaking audibly to us. This text suggests that God has as many options as does a loving father who tries to respond to his children's needs.

Watch Words

If you choose to focus on Hosea, speak of *loyal* husbands and wives, rather than *prostitutes* or *harlots*. Do not use *faithful* today without defining it in terms of *loyalty*. A faithful pet is the best example of the faithfulness to which we are called.

Even if they pray it regularly, most children need help with the vocabulary of the Lord's Prayer. *Hallowed* needs to translate as *holy*. All the "kingdom" words—*kingdom, thy will be done, power, glory*—need to be tied together so that children can understand the whole as the prayer of the citizens of God's kingdom. Young children will not understand *daily bread* as including any food other than bread, unless they are introduced to this possibility. *Trespassing* is going into somebody's house or yard without permission; *debts* are financial bills. Children need help to connect these realities to sin and forgiveness. *Temptation* may be a big word to learn. Remember that for many children today, the only things that are *delivered* are mail, pizza, and catalog orders. So paraphrase "deliver us from evil" with something like "guard us from evil people and things."

Let the Children Sing

If the Old Testament texts lead to a focus on loyal living, sing "O Jesus I Have Promised," which includes difficult vocabulary but relationship images that children like, or "Trust and Obey." Though children have trouble with the verses, they quickly learn the chorus. A children's choir or class might sing the chorus in response to congregational singing of the verses.

Sing the Lord's Prayer:
1. Children's or youth choirs enjoy singing "The Lord's Prayer" to a West Indies tune. Many youths know this version. (It is printed in *Songs for Today*, a youth songbook by Augsburg Press, and it may be printed in other books.) A choir may sing it as an anthem; the choir and congregation may sing it responsively, the choir singing the phrases of the prayer and the congregation singing the repeated "hallowed be thy name."
2. The traditional version of the Lord's Prayer can be sung by the adult choir or by a soloist.

The Liturgical Child

1. Use the Lord's Prayer as an outline for the prayers of the congregation. The worship leader prays the Lord's Prayer aloud, pausing after each phrase for the worshipers' own related prayers.

2. Turn the Lord's Prayer into a three-part litany. Worship Leader #1 reads one phrase at a time. Worship Leader #2 adds prayers related to that phrase and the life of the congregation. Then in silence, the worshipers add their own prayers related to each phrase.

Sermon Resources

1. To explore Luke 11:9-15, describe three kinds of gifts and compare them to three ways God responds to our prayers. The first gift is the surprise we had not even considered asking for, but which delights us. God often gives us such surprise gifts. The second gift is just what we wanted. Sometimes God gives us what we want and pray for. The third gift is not at all what we wanted, but something that becomes more valuable as we live with it. God may not respond to our prayers as we wish. Often, with time, we begin to value and understand God's response. But sometimes we do not.

In describing each gift, tell about similar gifts you have received. Include at least one childhood gift. To keep the children's attention, place three wrapped gifts on the pulpit. Point to and handle each one as you discuss it.

2. Older children appreciate a sermon that works through the phrases of the Lord's Prayer. Provide them with a printed copy of the prayer with the phrases printed in separate paragraphs. Encourage children to check them off as you work through them, or to write them in their own words next to the printed text.

3. Paraphrase the Epistle text, substituting some modern ways we are tempted to make ourselves look better. Children sometimes put all their time and energy into athletics, winning Scout badges, or working for perfect grades, just to prove they are good enough. Paul insists that we are simply to be Jesus' loyal disciples.

Both halves of this week's Worksheet focus on prayer. They respond to today's Gospel text, but also could be used on another Sunday.

Prayer
Scavenger Hunt

Prayer is talking with God. There are many ways for congregations to pray together. Draw a ☆ by those you do today.

—— Everyone reads or says a prayer aloud together.

—— A choir sings a prayer.

—— All pray their own prayers in silence.

—— One person prays aloud. Others listen and pray silently.

—— Some hymns are prayers. Write the name of one hymn you pray today.

Below each line of the Lord's Prayer, write a prayer of your own for that subject.

Our Father, who art in heaven, hallowed be thy name.

_____

Thy kingdom come. Thy will be done on earth as it is in heaven.

_____

Give us this day our daily bread.

_____

And forgive us our debts as we forgive our debtors.

_____

And lead us not into temptation, but deliver us from evil:

_____

For thine is the kingdom, and the power, and the glory forever. Amen

_____

PROPER THIRTEEN

(Sunday between July 31 and August 6 inclusive)

From a Child's Point of View

Old Testament: Hosea 11:1-11. This passage compares God's relationship with the people to that of a parent with a disobedient child. If this is explained before the reading, and if the passage is read from The New Jerusalem Bible or the Good News Bible, children will catch the meaning of a few image-filled phrases. Hosea's message is that although the people deserve to be destroyed because of the way they have acted, God has chosen instead to discipline them in order to help them come back to God. God's wish is that those people would realize how much God loves them and would learn to depend upon and love God in return. And God wants the same for us.

Psalm: 107:1-9, 43. This is the first section of a psalm whose format is interesting to children. It is a song for pilgrims to sing as they walk together toward Jerusalem (not unlike the songs we sing to pass the time on long car trips). Verses 1-3 are the introduction and are followed by sections that describe how God saves people in different kinds of trouble: those lost in the desert (4-9); prisoners (10-16); the sick (17-22); sailors in storms (23-32). Each section describes the distress of one group, explains how God saves them, and then calls on those people to praise and thank God (e.g., those who are lost in the desert are thirsty and hungry; they cry to God for help and are led by God to cities; for this they are called on to thank God). The fact that such a psalm is included in the Bible, and the possibility that other verses could be made up about people whose needs are met by God are more stimulating for children than the content of the biblical verses.

Epistle: Colossians 3:1-11. This passage says to children that there is a difference between Christians and non-Christians. Christians know that God loves them because they know that Christ died for them. They also know that enjoying and sharing God's love is the most important thing in the world, and knowing this makes them act in certain ways. The most significant items for children on Paul's list of "un-Christian" activities are being greedy (note connection to Luke text), hurting others when we are angry, hating, insulting people (calling cruel names), using obscene language, and telling lies. Because of the complex sentences and difficult language, this message needs to be presented during the sermon in words the children can understand.

Gospel: Luke 12:13-21. This passage speaks as directly to materialistic children as it does to their elders. They might prefer to store Nintendo games, bicycles, dolls, and sports equipment in their barns, but they know that when they hoard things for themselves, they are acting just like the farmer in the parable. They also know that when they become obsessed with wanting some new toy or designer shirt, they are on the wrong track. Jesus' message to them is that all the things we think we must have are not really important.

Watch Words

Before reading Hosea 11, explain that *Israel* and *Ephraim* are names for God's people. Also, use *discipline*, instead of *punishment*, to emphasize the corrective nature of God's action.

Inheritance needs to be defined as *property and money left after a person dies.*

137

Let the Children Sing

To celebrate the centrality of Christ, sing "Come, Christians, Join to Sing" with all its Alleluias, or "Fairest Lord Jesus," which, though it includes some abstract symbols, also includes many concrete nature images.

For your commitment to live disciplined lives, sing "Be Thou My Vision" (if the children sing it in other church settings) or "Lord, I Want to Be a Christian."

"Have Thine Own Way, Lord," if familiar, is a hymn through which children can commit themselves to God's discipline.

Celebrate the saving God of Psalm 107 by singing "Now Thank We All Our God."

The Liturgical Child

1. Read Luke with great dramatic inflection. Take the part of each speaker by changing your tone of voice and expression, and by the use of your hands and body. As you read the parable, remember that Jesus was known as a great storyteller for his delivery, as well as his content. Let the words of the barn-building fool swagger. Decide what God's tone will be in speaking to the man. Use your hands for emphasis. Eye the congregation as Jesus would have, as he made his final point in verse 21.

2. Use Colossians 3:1-11 as the base for confession and pardon:

> *Leader:* Let us confess our sins to one another and to God.
> *People:* Lord, we say we belong to Jesus, but we do not live as if we do.
> *Leader:* We become so wrapped up in getting what we want that we will bend, or even break rules to get our way.
> *People:* Lord, we say we belong to Jesus, but we do not live as if we do.
> *Leader:* And we want so much! We see clothes, houses, cars, and all kinds of toys that we feel we must have in order to be happy.
> *People:* Lord, we say we belong to Jesus, but we do not live as if we do.
> *Leader:* Our feelings often rule us. When we are angry, we hurt others. We give in to hating people we do not like.
> *People:* Lord, we say we belong to Jesus, but we do not live as if we do.
> *Leader:* Our mouths show us at our worst. We stoop to name-calling, foul language, and lies. Even we cannot believe what sometimes comes out of our mouths.
> *People:* Lord, we say we belong to Jesus, but we do not live as if we do.
> *Leader:* But God has not left us to live with our own failures and sin. God loves us. Jesus died for us. In Jesus, we are forgiven and become new people. God is constantly at work, remaking us. So let's overcome our greed.
> *People:* Let us set our hearts on living like Christ.
> *Leader:* Let's learn to control our anger and set aside personal and community hatreds.
> *People:* Let us set our hearts on living like Christ.
> *Leader:* Let's speak kind words, offer compliments and encouragement to others, and tell the truth in all situations.
> *People:* Let us set our hearts on living like Christ.
> *All:* Amen.

Sermon Resources

1. Retell the parable of the barn-building fool, describing the acquisitive habits of a fictional family in your community. Describe both the items each member of the family thought he or she needed, and why it was so important to have those items. Walk through a hectic weekend spent shopping for and taking care of all the things the family owned. After sending the exhausted family to bed, ask the congregation to ponder what those people might have done differently, had they known that a tornado would destroy them and everything they had that night. This leads to questions about whether the family would have been better off if it had lived by that alternate plan anyway.

2. Describe "gotta haves" with which people of all ages become obsessed, and tell how those things affect us. Describe "gotta haves" which we really do not use once we have them, "gotta haves" that turn out to be bad for us (like a computer game that becomes the sole interest in our life), and "gotta haves" we enjoy but really could do without. Talk about how we, as Christians, manage the "gotta haves" in our lives.

3. Provide modern examples of discipline which, like God's discipline of Israel, are aimed at teaching important lessons. For example, tell the story of a child whose parents insisted that she earn the money to buy another bicycle when hers was stolen because she had left it in the front yard (after repeated warnings).

Travelers walking to Jerusalem made up songs about God rescuing people. Listen to Psalm 107. Then write a verse about a group that God helps. (You may be in that group!)

Describe their troubles.

There were some _____

who _____

_____ .

How did God save them?

In their sadness, they called on the Lord, and God saved them by

___ ___ ___ ___

___ ___ ___ ___

OF

GREED . "

Luke 12:15

How can they thank God?

Let them thank the Lord for such constant love and

_____

_____

_____ .

Each word in the message below is upside down and backward. Turn the words forward and right side up to find Jesus' warning about keeping our lives right side up.

" GUARD

YOURSELVES

FROM EVERY

KIND

Answer: Guard yourselves from every kind of greed.

PROPER FOURTEEN

(Sunday between August 7 and 13 inclusive)

From a Child's Point of View

Old Testament: Isaiah 1:1, 10-20. Isaiah's message is one children can understand: God is not fooled by people who worship God, but do not obey. Isaiah's references to Old Testament worship practices, however, are a problem. The easiest way to solve this problem is to point out that sacrifices, new moon festivals, and sabbaths were ways people in Isaiah's day worshiped, just as choir anthems, Christmas pageants, Easter flowers, and beautiful prayers are ways we worship today. The Good News Bible offers the clearest translation for children.

Psalm: 50:1-8, 22-23. Consider reading this entire psalm for the sake of clarity. (The jump from verse 8 to 22 is a long one.) When they hear the psalm read dramatically, children hear, in occasional lines, a message that parallels that of Isaiah.

Epistle: Hebrews 11:1-3, 8-16. This passage is an attempt to define *faith*. For children, faith is trust. Abraham and Sarah trusted God when they were called to move to an unknown land, and also when God promised them a son, though they knew they were too old to have children.

We are called to trust God as Abraham and Sarah did. Today that means trusting that God loves us and made us with a good plan in mind for us. It also means we know that God is working to make the world a loving, happy place and that we are ready to help.

Gospel: Luke 12:32-40. In its opening verses (32-34), this passage continues the theme of last week's Gospel lesson, but it involves a number of abstract images (the Kingdom, purses that do not wear out, and the location of treasures and hearts) which must be worked through if children are to understand them.

The second part of the passage focuses on the need to be constantly prepared for God's presence. Three prepared people are noted: servants prepared for their master's return from a wedding feast at any hour; a homeowner prepared for a thief whose approach is known; and a Christian prepared for God's presence. Children need help to find each of these people in the somewhat run-together passage, but they can appreciate them when found. They also need specific suggestions about what they can do in order to be prepared for God (e.g., use well the talents God has given them, be loving, worship God on their own and with others).

Watch Words

Hypocrite may be a new word. Today it describes a person who goes to church and sings about loving God and prays about serving God, but then is selfish and cruel during the week.

Faith is best paraphrased as *trust*.

Let the Children Sing

When it is pointed out, older children appreciate the connection between worship and discipleship in "Lord Speak to Me."

Conclude worship and begin living as disciples with "Go Forth for God." Though younger children have trouble with the verses, they enjoy singing the repeated first and last lines.

Faith hymns tend to be filled with abstract jargon. For children, sing "Jesus Loves Me" or "The Lord's My Shepherd."

The Liturgical Child

1. Invite different groups within your worshiping community to share in the *Prayer of Confession:*

Leader: We gather here as God's people to worship, to sing God's praises, to hear God's Word. But to be honest, we want to keep what we sing and pray and hear just between you and me. We are not ready to take it out to our workplaces, shopping malls, playgrounds, and swimming pools. So our worship must include confession. Let us pray.

Choir: Lord of the arts, we love to sing your praises. We enjoy beautiful music and find friends among choir members. But we are not so ready to praise you during the week. We are slow to speak up for you at work, hesitant to stand up for what is right among our friends, and unwilling to live up to our sung praises. Forgive us.

Ushers: Lord of loving friends, we are happy to welcome people to worship. We gladly smile and help them find a seat. But we are not always so open to others. We often ignore people who come our way. We feel no responsibility for those who need our help. Forgive us.

Preacher(s): Lord of the Word, *I/we* work hard to find beautiful words to praise you and clear words to help others understand your will. But *I/we* often fail to practice what *I/we* preach. *My/Our* actions do not live up to *my/our* words. Forgive *me/us.*

Congregation: Lord of the Church, we come to hear words that reassure us and to sing hymns that give us hope. We want to be told that we are O.K. and that God loves us. We would rather not hear your calls to take care of others and to change our ways. Forgive us.

ALL: Forgive us when our actions do not match our songs and prayers. Amen.

2. Present the psalm with two readers. The first reader takes the part of the narrator and sets the scene for the heavenly encounter with God, reading verses 1-4, 6, and 16*a*. The second reader takes the part of God, reading verses 5, 7-15, and 16*b*-23. God's outrage should be evident in the presentation. (The New Jerusalem Bible offers an especially clear translation.)

3. Before reading the Luke passage, alert the children to listen for the three prepared people. As you come to each of them in the reading, raise one, then two, and finally three fingers.

4. Create a litany prayer about being ready. The worship leader offers petitions for God's work (name mission activities of the congregation, specific community concerns, and global issues, being sure to include some activities in which children participate). After each petition, the congregation responds, "Let us prepare the way of the Lord!"

Sermon Resources

1. At the beginning of the sermon, have someone assume Isaiah's role and interrupt the service to deliver a paraphrase of Isaiah's message, substituting modern worship practices for the Old Testament ones (e.g., I have heard enough of your fancy music). "Isaiah" would then call for the activities described in verses 16-17 and warn that God is willing to forgive those who change their ways, but will see that those who do not change die. (For a less dramatic alternative, the preacher could take Isaiah's role, after inviting the congregation to imagine how Isaiah's listeners felt when they heard what he said.)

2. Talk about who and what we trust. Describe our trust in appliance-repair people, doctors, pilots, drivers of vehicles in which we ride, the friend to whom we tell a secret, the baby-sitter with whom parents leave their children, or the teacher or coach who teaches us to play a musical instrument or to excel in a sport. Recall current commercials that ask us to trust their products. Talk about the kid who dares us to try something new (perhaps swinging across a creek on a rope or taking drugs). Compare trusting people to trusting God's love and God's call to be peacemakers and loving friends.

3. To explore Luke 12:32-34, bring some props:

• Pull out your wallet or purse. Show the congregation what is in it. Describe your feelings and what you would have to do if it were lost or stolen. Then reread Jesus' message and talk about safer purses.

• Bring several of your treasures (or pictures of nontransportable treasures). Include a variety, such as a collector's item, a hobby tool, a memento of a person or trip, a picture of your family, and so on. Describe the objects' value to you and how you would respond if they were "messed with."

Then talk about how protecting our valuables can turn us into defensive worriers and keep us from loving people and letting them love us. In the process, encourage worshipers to identify some of their treasures that may be getting in their way.

Shade each space with a dot in it to find 2 words that mean almost the same thing.

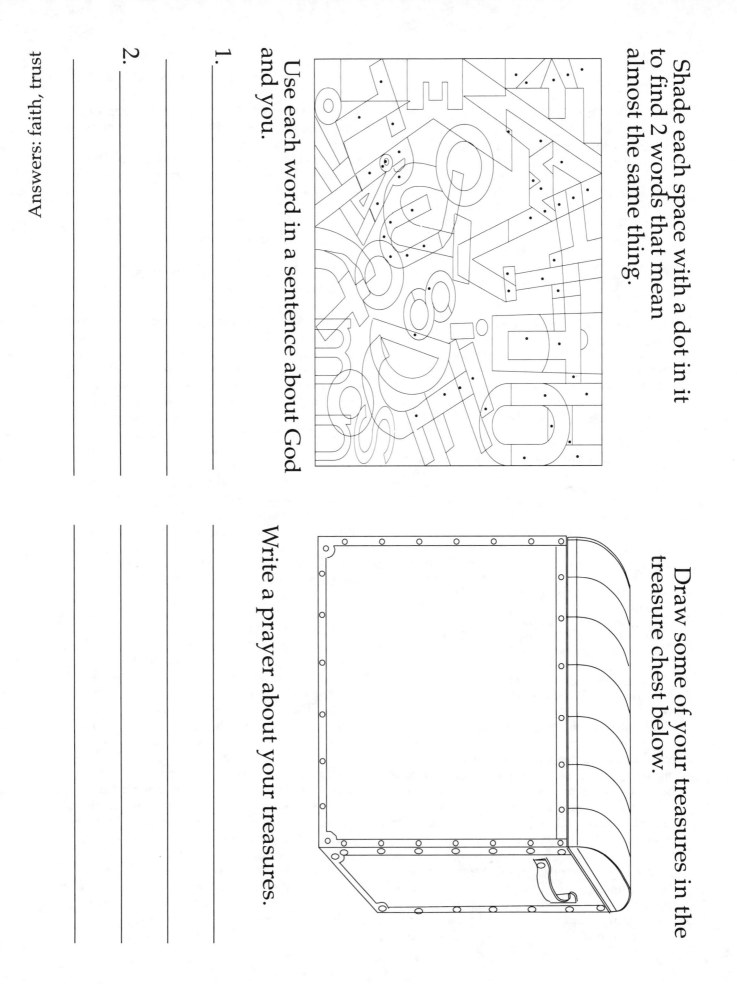

Draw some of your treasures in the treasure chest below.

Use each word in a sentence about God and you.

1. _____

2. _____

Write a prayer about your treasures.

1. _____

2. _____

Answers: faith, trust

PROPER FIFTEEN

(Sunday between August 14 and 20 inclusive)

From a Child's Point of View

Old Testament: Isaiah 51:1-7; Psalm: 80:1-2, 8-19. Both Old Testament texts speak of Israel as a grapevine. Isaiah speaks of a vine that has not met its owner's expectations and thus is destroyed. The psalmist prays for God to protect the vine/Israel, which is currently being plundered. Since most children today have little experience with vineyards or wine-making, they need help with vocabulary and an explanation of the agricultural process. Since allegorical thinking is beyond the capability of children, they have difficulty drawing the message from the vine images. The best idea is to tell them something about vineyard keeping, and then put the prophet's message into direct words about God's expectations, discipline, and continued care. Children will make the connection between the images and the message when their mental abilities mature.

Gospel: Luke 12:49-56. The part of this passage that children are most likely to hear is the section about potential division within families. Because they are so dependent on their families, the verses are frightening. They need to hear their fear recognized and hear also that adults are as frightened by these verses as they are. Only then are they ready to explore Jesus' insistence that living as God's person may bring trouble, rather than peaceful happiness. Disciples must be ready to stand up for God's ways, no matter what people—even their friends and relatives—think and say. The tendency to soft-pedal this point with children does them no favor. They know that it is risky to stand up for God's ways on playgrounds, on school buses, and in backyards. Adult failure to acknowledge this appears to children to be a startling lack of perception of the realities children confront. It is far more helpful to recognize these realities and prepare children to cope with them by interpreting them in light of Jesus' message.

Epistle: Hebrews 11:29–12:2. Verses 11:29-40 recall in general terms the stories of faith heroes and heroines. Because children are more likely to recall biblical heroes other than those mentioned by name, it may be wise to focus on verses 33-37, adding names and specific details where possible.

The summary verses (12:1-2) are filled with poetic images and generalities that mean little to children. A children's paraphrase of them could be: "Let us follow the examples of all the faith heroes and heroines who have lived before us. Let us ignore everything that gets in the way of being disciples, so that we too can become heroes and heroines. Let us remember Jesus, who did not give up because of the cross, but faced the pain and disgrace and now sits at God's right side."

Watch Words

Vineyard and *wine vat* may be new to urban children. Some younger children may even be unaware that *grapes* grow on *vines*, instead of on bushes or trees.

The *witnesses* of Hebrews 12 are more readily recognized as *heroes* and *heroines*, or as *examples*. If talking about them leads to talk of *inspiration*, take time to introduce that important term with a description of how one of your heroes or heroines *gave you the power* to live heroically.

Let the Children Sing

Choose the following hymns (listed in order of ease for children) to celebrate the faith heroes: "I Sing a Song of the Saints of God," "For All the Saints Who from Their Labors Rest" (the younger readers will settle for the Alleluias), or "God of Grace and God of Glory" (the repeated chorus can be sung by all).

A good opening praise hymn for the day is "Come Christians, Join to Sing."

The Liturgical Child

1. Instead of flowers, display a large arrangement of grapes and grapevines. If possible, make it a two-part arrangement, comparing lush domestic grapes and small, hard wild grapes. Refer to the display before reading the Old Testament lessons.

2. Introduce the Isaiah text as the work of a very clever prophet who tricked people into hearing more of God's message than they wanted to hear. Describe his disguise as a wandering singer, then assume his role, reading verses 1-6 as if they told a sad story. Then abruptly, change your tone and point your finger at the congregation as you spring the trap and make the accusations of verse 8.

3. After a sermon identifying faith heroes and heroines, invite worshipers to praise God for their own faith heroes and heroines:

> Lord God, we are indeed surrounded by people who have lived heroically faithful lives for you. The Bible is full of the stories of everyday people who lived brave, loving lives. For Moses, leading the people across the dry Red Sea; for Rahab, who hid spies; for Isaiah, who bravely told people that God was angry with them and would punish them; for Jesus, willing to die rather than stop loving us, we thank you. Each of us praises you for those people in the Bible who are important to us. (Pause)
>
> But still others have gone before us to show us the way. We remember Martin Luther, who challenged the church to keep its faith strong. We remember Christians who have died rather than give up their faith. We remember missionaries who have risked their lives to tell others of God's love. Each of us praises you for those heroes of the church who show us the way. (Pause)
>
> Each of us also praises you for people we have known personally. For parents, or children, or Sunday school teachers, or friends who have been examples to us and have inspired us to live by God's ways. Hear our thanksgiving for these people. (Pause)
>
> Even as we thank you for this cloud of heroes who surround and inspire us, we are aware of our responsibility. So we ask you for the courage, wisdom, and love to live as heroically as they did. Help us to make good decisions. Give us the power to do what we know you would have us do; for we pray in the name of Jesus. Amen.

4. Know when school starts for your children and include that in your prayers on the appropriate week. Pray about excitement and fears. In smaller churches, pray by name for children entering school for the first time this fall and those headed for college. Pray for students and teachers and bus drivers and coaches.

Sermon Resources

1. The baseball (and other sports) cards that many children and some adults collect are hero references. Find or borrow a card that describes a current sports hero, and use it as a format in creating "cards" for faith figures. Tell about some of the faith hero/ines you would include in your collection and encourage worshipers to identify and design cards for their faith hero/ines.

2. Include in the sermon a story or two about heroes in the history of your congregation. If possible, link the stories to a building, a tree, or an item seen regularly around the church. Or bring special papers or pictures from the church safe or from a member's home to give reality to the person and events described. Challenge children and adults to follow in the faithful footsteps of their congregational ancestors.

Draw or write about one place where a faith hero is needed today.

FAITH HERO NEEDED

Talk to God about ways you could be that hero.

Draw a picture of or write the name of one of your faith heroes in each frame below. Listen to the sermon for ideas.

Write a prayer about one of them.

Thank you, God, for _____
because _____

Help me to be like _____
by _____
_____
_____ .

PROPER SIXTEEN

(Sunday between August 21 and 27 inclusive)

From a Child's Point of View

Old Testament: Jeremiah 1:4-10. The story of God's call to Jeremiah speaks pointedly to children at the beginning of a school year. With help from the preacher, children can hear that just as God knew Jeremiah before he was born and had a plan for his life, God knew them before they were born and has plans for their lives. They are not to offer Jeremiah's excuse, "I'm too young," but to be willing to live as God's people wherever they are—even at school. They appreciate God's empathy for their fears, represented in both a warning and a promise. The warning is not to be afraid of *them*. *(Them* may be teachers who intimidate students; demanding courses and tests; other kids who are smarter or more athletic; or vicious bullies.) God knows that it is easy to be frightened, so we are sent out with a promise: I will be with you and protect you.

Psalm: 71:1-6. See Fourth Sunday After the Epiphany.

Gospel: Luke 13:10-17. Children are interested in the possibility of being bent over. They imagine what a person would look like terribly bent over (maybe walking with a cane that could touch the chin) and how being that bent would affect what you could do. Some may have heard the story of the hunchback of Notre Dame and have an idea of how hard life would be for such a person. Consequently, they are ready to join the crowd in being happy about what Jesus did for the woman.

Because sabbath observance is not currently an issue for most children, they slide over Jesus' criticism of the religious leaders that brought such joy to the crowd.

Epistle: Hebrews 12:18-29. This is a passage for advanced Bible students. Children and many adults will not understand it as it is read. Rather than introduce and explain the comparison between the people worshiping God at the foot of Mount Sinai and Christians worshiping God, simply state the writer's message—that we are to worship God and be happy because God is so awesome. God rules all people of all ages and has acted through Jesus Christ to build an invisible, never-ending community which we are invited to join. For children, this is mainly an invitation to celebrate God's love and power as they hear it described in the Bible (e.g., the healing in today's Gospel) and as they experience it themselves.

Watch Words

To avoid the giggles that follow mention of *wombs*, use the Good News Bible for the Old Testament lessons and psalm.

Let the Children Sing

Praise God with rejoicing hymns. "Now Thank We All Our God" and "Praise Ye the Lord, the Almighty" are two of the easiest for children to understand. Though the vocabulary of "Holy, Holy, Holy" is difficult for children, the repeated phrase describing the awesome God—"Holy, holy, holy"—sets the mood and can be sung by even nonreaders.

Choose hymns about healing carefully. Most of them equate physical and spiritual healing in ways that baffle children. The seven verses of

"When Jesus the Healer Passed Through Galilee," however, are a happy recalling of the many people (including the bent-over woman) Jesus healed. It can be sung in unison by a children's choir or the congregation. Or it can be sung responsively, with a children's choir or soloist singing the verses and an adult choir or the congregation singing the double refrain in each verse. (Find this new hymn in *The United Methodist Hymnal*.)

The next several Sundays focus on themes of repentance and commitment. Choose one of the following to sing several times during the series: "Be Thou My Vision," "Lord, I Want to Be a Christian," or "Take My Life and Let It Be Consecrated." Consider using one as a "hymn of the month" to build the children's familiarity.

The verses of "Go Forth for God" do not make much sense to children, although they enjoy the repetition of the first and last lines of each verse and can sing them (if nothing else) when they are pointed out by the worship leader.

The Liturgical Child

1. Give the simple story in Luke a dramatic reading. Take the parts of the religious leaders and Jesus. Point your finger menacingly and speak with great indignation when reading the accusations of the religious leaders. Then, with hands turned up in resignation, voice Jesus' amazed response.

2. In the mood of the people celebrating Jesus' healing ministry among them, and of the writer of Hebrews describing God's awesome activity, create a praise litany celebrating what God is doing in your congregation. In advance, ask several people to describe *briefly* one way God is at work in your congregation. Give each person a specific assignment, such as the church's Bible school, youth mission trips or camps, special church-wide events, mission work of the congregation, seasonal glories, national and international events in which you see God at work, and so forth. Include people who represent all ages and groups in the congregation. To each person's description, the congregation responds: Truly God is at work among us.

Have one practice session with speakers during which you can help them edit their statements (if needed) and prepare for a smooth presentation. In a small sanctuary, speakers may stand to speak loudly and clearly from their seats. In larger sanctuaries, they will need to be near microphones.

3. Use Jeremiah's call for a "back-to-school" Charge and Benediction. Ask all worshipers who will attend school this fall to stand, then say: Hear the word of the Lord. I knew you before I gave you life. I chose you before you were born. I send you now to school. Study and learn. Be my people in the classroom. Stand up for my ways in the lunchroom and on the playground. Be my witnesses on the bus.

Ask all who will not be students this fall to stand also, then say: Hear the word of the Lord to you. I also knew you before I gave you life. I chose you before you were born. Do not say to me, "I am only a housewife," or "I am the least important person in my office." I am sending you to that office or factory or community. Be my people. Stand up for my ways. Speak my words to those you meet.

And all of you, students, teachers, business folks, homemakers, remember God's promise to Jeremiah and to you. God says, "Do not be afraid. I will be with you to protect you. I will put my words in your mouth." So go in peace.

Sermon Resources

Most sermons are aimed at adults, with some efforts to include children. Because the beginning of school is such an intense time for children, it is worth planning a "back-to-school" sermon aimed at the children. Because adults have been where the children are now, and because the whole culture gets in a back-to-work frame of mind as summer ends and fall schedules begin, adults resonate with the situation and translate school examples to their workplaces.

Jeremiah's call is a natural text with which to remind children that God made them and has a plan for them. It is an opportunity to build self-esteem, especially for those children who do not do well in school. It is also an opportunity to send children to school to be faithful disciples and witnesses to God's love, forgiveness, and justice.

Note: Jeremiah 1:4-10 and Psalm 71:1-6 are used also on the Fourth Sunday of the Epiphany. Consult that Sunday of this book for additional ideas about using these texts and a Worship Worksheet activity on the Jeremiah text.

Cross out every other letter in this word trail to learn what God said to Jeremiah.

Start Here →

I B C A H O O S J E R Y A O R U L B A E T F G O G B A R S E M I S O A R S E M I S V W E S Y A O S U R L A I R F F B E

_ _ _ _ _ _ _ " _ _ _ _ _ _ _ _ _ _ _ _ . _ _ _ _ _ _ _ _ _ _ _ _ _ "

Jeremiah 1:5

The woman Jesus healed might have prayed:

For making me stand straight again, God, I thank you.

Think about this summer. Then write your own end-of-summer thank-you prayers for God.

For _____
God, I thank you.

For _____
God, I thank you.

For _____
God, I thank you.

For _____
God, I thank you.

PROPER SEVENTEEN

(Sunday between August 28 and September 3 inclusive)

From a Child's Point of View

Old Testament: Jeremiah 2:4-13. To understand Jeremiah's accusation, children need to be briefly reminded of the Exodus history, and they need help with the water images in verse 13. The first requires a simple sketching of how God brought the people to the Promised Land and how the people acted when they settled there. The second requires more careful attention.

The easiest way to introduce the water images to literal thinkers is with a question: "Which would you rather drink—a cup of clear water from a cold mountain stream or a cup of muddy water from a leaky well?" The choice is obvious. Jeremiah's point (for literal thinkers) is that choosing to ignore God is as dumb as choosing to drink muddy water.

The two accusations of verse 13 should be paraphrased for children: (1) My people have forgotten and ignored me; and (2) My people have chosen to worship worthless gods and spend their lives on activities that will not make them healthy and happy.

Psalm: 81:1, 10-16. The Good News Bible offers the clearest translation of this psalm for children. The psalm parallels Jeremiah's message. Once either of these is explained, the other makes sense also.

Epistle: Hebrews 13:1-8, 15-16. This is a series of minilectures about how to live. Children are frequently on the receiving end of such lectures and will recognize them. The lectures are in verses 1 (on loving); 2 (on treating strangers kindly); 3*a* (on remembering prisoners); 3*b* (on caring for those who are not well treated by others); 4 (on honoring marriage); 5-6 (on love of money); and 7 (on respecting leaders). Children can understand them, but none of the lectures are developed in a way that speaks to their lives with particular clarity and force. Verses 8 and 15-16 provide the content for doing the things mentioned in verses 1-7—that is, we do them in response to Jesus Christ.

Gospel: Luke 14:1, 7-14. This passage tells two parables about parties. The first story is for party guests. Reminders of arguments about who gets to sit by Grandma, or who has to share the piano bench at a family reunion dinner, help children understand the feelings attached to seat assignments at first-century dinner parties. With this background, children can deal with the two levels of Jesus' teachings. They appreciate the practical fact that if you take a "good place," you will be embarrassed when you are asked to move. They can also appreciate Jesus' unstated message that where you sit is not that important anyway, and we should not be upset about such matters.

The second story is for hosts—of birthday parties, spend-the-night parties, trips to football games, and afternoons at the movies. Like adults, most children treat parties as chances to invite only those they want to invite. They choose their friends and those they would like to have for friends. Older children, especially girls, already recognize the possibility of inviting people who will "invite you back." Jesus suggests that a party is a chance to extend our friendship to people without friends, and to those who do not have anything to return. Because children often are given strict limits as to the number of friends they may invite to parties or outings, this is a call for tough, self-sacrificing living. Be aware that Jesus is asking more of children than of adults in this parable.

149

Watch Words

Cisterns are *wells*, and even wells are not familiar to many children.

The problem with God's people, according to Jeremiah, is that they were *disloyal* to God.

Let the Children Sing

Sing "For the Beauty of the Earth" to recite God's wonders on a holiday weekend when people tend to be outdoors.

Repeat the discipleship hymns sung last week, to build familiarity, or choose a new one: "Lord, I Want to Be a Christian," "Be Thou My Vision," or "Go Forth for God."

The Liturgical Child

1. If it is Labor Day weekend, pray about last picnics and other end-of-summer events. Pray about settling into fall schedules with school and after-school activities. Review the prayer suggestions regarding the beginning of school in Proper #15.

2. Take the role of Jeremiah, reading his indignant message with all the passion with which he delivered it. Pay attention to the delivery of the rhetorical questions. Emphasize the different groups of leaders (vs. 8) who failed to be loyal to God. Pause before verse 12. Then say, "Be appalled," using strong inflection a person might use with a child or teenager who has done something beyond belief—"I'm appalled!" Raise one, then two fingers, to emphasize the two accusations of verse 8.

3. Create a responsive prayer of petitions about living as God's people. A worship leader describes a series of temptations, based on the chosen Scripture texts for the day. To each, the congregation responds with the following line from the Lord's Prayer: "Lead us not into temptation, but deliver us from evil." For example:

It is tempting to forget you—to be so busy with our friends that we have no time to become friends with you; to pay so much attention to what we want that we forget to think about what you want for us; to read newspapers and novels, but not the Bible. So we pray . . . (RESPONSE)

It is tempting to do what others do, say what others say, and think as others think—to go along with our friends rather than stick with what we know to be right; to fall for all the TV ads that promise us happiness if we buy the right things; to spend our time and energy following sports heroes and heroines instead of faith heroes and heroines. So we pray . . . (RESPONSE)

Sermon Resources

1. To illustrate Jeremiah's image, display two large glasses of water on either side of the pulpit. Fill one with clear water and the other with muddy water. Lift each up for the congregation to see as you ask which they would rather drink. To relate Jeremiah's point to modern living and choices, identify activities that are about as worthwhile as drinking muddy water. Children's muddy-water activities include: being so intent on winning class elections, games, and so forth that we are poor sports when we lose; thinking we must have certain toys or wear certain clothes to be happy; and spending every free minute on TV or computer games.

2. Challenge worshipers to make a list of the five people they would invite to a super birthday party—for children, it might be a bowling and pizza party; for youths, a set of concert tickets; for adults, dinner in a fine restaurant. As they work, explore Jesus' insights into how we usually compile such lists. Next, ask the worshipers to think of two people in their class at school, at their workplace, or in their neighborhood, who probably never are invited to parties. After they have had a minute to think, reread Jesus' points about who to invite, and encourage everyone to imagine including one of those two outcasts on their list. Suggest possible impact on the new guest. Imagine what difference it would make at the party.

Each letter in the word WORTHLESS is numbered. Use the numbers to fill in the missing letters below to learn what Jeremiah said about God's people.

"___ Y ___ N ___
4 5 7   1 7   4

A F ___ ___ ___ ___ ___ ING ___
        4 7 3   4 5   8

WORTHLESS
1 2 3 4 5 6 7 8 8

AND

B ___ CAM ___ **WORTHLESS**
    7   7   1 2 3 4 5 6 7 8 8

___ ___ M ___ V ___ ___ ."
4 5 7   8 7 6   7 8

Listen to the reading of Jeremiah 2 : 4 - 13 for the answer.

List 5 people to invite to a party.

1. _____
2. _____
3. _____
4. _____
5. _____

Draw a picture of what you would do at that party.

Now listen when Luke is read. What does Jesus say about parties?

Proper 17 / © 1994 by Abingdon Press.

PROPER EIGHTEEN

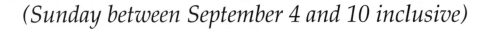

(Sunday between September 4 and 10 inclusive)

From a Child's Point of View

Old Testament: Jeremiah 18:1-11. This passage presents an image that is both familiar and challenging for children. Though they may not have seen a potter working at a wheel, most children have had many enjoyable experiences working with clay. They understand the process of reworking a piece until you get what you want. Younger children, however, will need help making the connection between potters working with clay and God working with us. The natural expectation of concrete thinkers is to visualize God reworking the shapes of our bodies. To get beyond this to Jeremiah's message, children need to hear such examples as God working selfishness into generosity, or a quick temper into a controlled one. Children also need to explore what this reworking is like. Obviously, God does not punch us down into a lump (or turn us back into babies) and start over again. God works on us by giving us teachers and examples in the lives of others. God gives us the messages of the Bible to help us know how to live. God is with us, helping us learn from events in our lives.

Although we often focus on God's shaping of our personal lives, God was speaking to Jeremiah about shaping the nations. Older children, having an interest in the larger world and focusing on groups to which they belong, are primed to hear that God shapes and reworks the lives of groups and nations.

Psalm: 139:1-6, 13-18. This is the psalmist's praise of God, who created him and knows him thoroughly. The original Jerusalem Bible translation is probably clearest to children. It emphasizes the psalmist's appreciation for the way he was made. To children, it is an opportunity to appreciate the unique talents and potentials that God has given them.

Epistle: Philemon 1-21. This passage deals with a situation totally foreign to children. They have neither an understanding of first-century slavery nor appreciation for the social stand Paul was asking of Philemon. If asked what Philemon should do, their response is, "Simple! He should do what Paul asked, because Paul was the great teacher and leader of the church." They are generally impressed with Onesimus' courage in returning to Philemon.

Gospel: Luke 14:25-33. This passage includes two concrete stories which illustrate a very "hard" lesson about discipleship. Children can understand the stories about the tower builder and the king going to war, but they will need help to interpret them and relate them to Jesus' point in verses 25-27 and 33.

Jesus was speaking to adults, not to children, when he demanded that they "hate"—that is, "be totally detached from" their families. He overstated his case to make the point that our discipleship is to take priority over *all* other loyalties and commitments, even those to family. For adults, this is difficult but possible. For children, who are dependent upon the love and care of their families, it is not even remotely comprehensible. It is also scary because of what it demands of children and what it suggests might be demanded of the parents upon whom they are so dependent. Children need to hear this verse with reassurances about Jesus' point. It helps to read it with verses 27 and 33, which insist that each of us must be a good disciple and that following Jesus is to be the most important thing in our lives.

Watch Words

The job of the *potter* and the function of the *potter's wheel* need to be described so that children can recognize the similarity between that process and their own experiences working with clay.

Let the Children Sing

The Jeremiah text all but demands the use of "Have Thine Own Way, Lord." While the concepts in verses 2-4 are beyond most children, there is no better Sunday on which to introduce the hymn.

Sing of God's creative work in us with "Now Thank We All Our God," "He Leadeth Me: O Blessed Thought" (children pick up on the chorus first), or "God Will Take Care of You" (the repeated phrase and easy chorus overshadow the obsolete vocabulary of the verses).

Sing your featured discipleship hymn or "I Sing a Song of the Saints of God," to celebrate the sainthood to which Philemon and we are called.

The Liturgical Child

1. To bring Jeremiah's experience in the potter's shop to life, arrange for a local potter to work at a potter's wheel during the reading of the Scripture. Read slowly enough so that the potter can demonstrate what Jeremiah saw, or take time just before the reading to discuss with the potter how pots are shaped and reshaped.

2. Follow the psalmist in praising the wonderful ways God has created and cares for each of us:

Lord, we want to talk to you about how you have made us and shaped our lives.

Creator God, you gave each of us a one-of-a-kind body. There are things we like about our bodies and things we wish were different. We confess that we sometimes eat and drink things that are harmful to our bodies. In the silence, let us each speak to God about our bodies. (PAUSE)

Lord of Our Lives, you gave each of us special talents and skills. Sometimes we forget to say thank you for them. Sometimes we need to talk to you about how we use these skills in order to love others. In the silence, let each of us speak to God about our talents and skills. (PAUSE)

Loving God, you placed certain qualities in each of us. It's easy for us to list those with which we struggle. But we are less ready to notice our admirable qualities—the patience and kindness and generosity you have planted in us. In the silence, let us each honestly thank God for the good qualities that we recognize in ourselves. (PAUSE)

The worship leader concludes the prayer by praying aloud Psalm 139:13-18, changing the singular pronouns to plural ones.

3. Children are fascinated by Philemon because it is the shortest book in the Bible. So invite worshipers to follow along in their Bibles as you read the entire book. Then congratulate them on having read a whole book of the Bible and encourage them to read others.

Before the reading, explain the situation that prompted this letter and encourage worshipers to imagine themselves as Philemon, opening his door to his runaway slave and reading this letter from Paul.

Sermon Resources

1. Give each worshiper an egg-sized lump of clay to work in their hands during the sermon. The physical experience of working the clay will sharpen Jeremiah's message. Having something to do with their hands also helps children listen to the sermon. The clay could be passed out by ushers or by a children's class as the sermon begins. Children's modeling dough (either homemade or purchased) is the cleanest and least expensive to use. Invite worshipers to leave their clay in a dishpan at the rear of the church or take it home with them.

2. Tell stories about starting things that cannot be finished: an unhappy eight-year-old who runs away from home without food or any idea of where to go; an overly ambitious science-fair project (perhaps dissecting a pig, which cannot be obtained); a boast about being brave enough to explore a deserted house. Proceed to ambitious discipleship stories: a commitment to set aside snack money each day for a hunger offering at church; a decision to keep on forgiving someone who continually teases you; and so on.

153

Turn this body into a picture of you. Draw around it pictures of things you do well.

Write words that describe you in the frame.

Listen carefully when Philemon is read. Then draw a picture or write a story about what you think Philemon did after he read Paul's letter.

Then...

PROPER NINETEEN

(Sunday between September 11 and 17 inclusive)

From a Child's Point of View

Today's texts deal with sin and forgiveness. The Old Testament readings describe the seriousness of sin. The Gospel speaks of God's joy over even one repentant sinner. And in the Epistle, Paul uses himself as an example of God's willingness to forgive even the most flagrant sinners.

Old Testament: Jeremiah 4:11-12, 22-28. Today's environmentally minded children easily misunderstand the natural disasters described in verses 23-26 as being the direct result of environmental sins; and they hear God's anger with people for being such poor stewards of the earth. Jeremiah, however, was describing the aftermath of a military invasion ordered by God to discipline a sinful nation. He was warning people of what would happen if they did not change their ways, much as a parent warns children that they will be punished unless they change their ways.

As a counterpoint to the Gospel and Epistle readings, Jeremiah insists that sin is very serious. God cares about what we do and will discipline us when we need it.

Psalm: 14. A children's paraphrase of "There is no God" would be "I will not be caught" or "What I do will not matter." The problem for the people described here is that they believe they can get away with anything, so they take what they want and do what they want. Only the psalmist knows that they are in for a surprise. Because children have difficulty with the poetic language of the psalm and because other readings for the day are so clear, it is advisable to focus on those other readings.

Gospel: Luke 15:1-10. This passage includes the parables of the lost sheep and the lost coin, tied together by Jesus' insistence that God rejoices over the repentance of one "lost" person. These parables frequently appear in church school curriculum and therefore may be familiar to most young worshipers. Children will enjoy hearing a familiar story read and explored in worship.

Because children think concretely, they need to work at these parables from two sides. They will not see the connection between these sides until their thinking matures. On the concrete level, children have experience with being physically lost. Psychologists tell us that the fear of being lost or abandoned is one of the deep, disturbing fears of childhood. So for them, the parables promise that God will never abandon them. Then with adult direction, they can explore Jesus' promise that they can never do anything so awful that God will not forgive them. Just as the shepherd goes after the one lost sheep, so God will come after them. Later, when children can comprehend being lost in sin, they will realize that these truths merge in the parables.

Epistle: I Timothy 1:12-17. This passage assumes knowledge of Paul's life that most children and some adults will not recall without help. So begin by briefly outlining Paul's persecution of the church, his conversion, and his missionary career.

Verses 15 and 16 are the key ones for children, who will not follow the theological language in much of the rest of the passage. Reminded of Paul's story, children can see the truth of what he is saying and can conclude that if God could still love and use Paul after he repented of his persecution of the church, then there is probably nothing they can do that God will not forgive, when they repent as Paul did. This is reassuring. It also reminds children to forgive others as willingly as God forgives them.

Watch Words

Remember that for children, *lost* describes physical abandonment. So avoid using it to describe being lost in sin. Instead, talk about *sin* and *forgiveness.*

Avoid *mercy, pardon,* and *grace,* in favor of *forgiveness.* Or choose to use one of those words and take time in the sermon to explore its meaning. Speak of God's *discipline* which corrects, rather than of God's *punishment,* which may be misunderstood by children as God's revenge.

Instead of talking about Paul's *persecution* of the church, describe how he hunted and killed Christians.

Let the Children Sing

Continue singing the chosen hymns of commitment.

To celebrate God's "good shepherd" love, sing the version of "The Lord's My Shepherd" most familiar to your children, or "Jesus Loves Me." Be sure to sing the following verse:

> Jesus loves me when I'm good,
> When I do the things I should.
> Jesus loves me when I'm bad,
> Even though it makes him sad.

Even though its first line comes from I Timothy 1:10, children will be baffled by the abstract language of "Immortal, Invisible, God Only Wise." Save it for a day when you are exploring God's greatness and have time to define and enjoy all the big words together.

The Liturgical Child

1. Paraphrase the traditional prayer of confession based on the lost-sheep image:

> Loving God, who takes care of us as a shepherd takes care of sheep, we admit that we have wandered off like lost sheep. We have ignored

your rules and teachings to follow our most selfish and mean desires. We act and speak without thinking that we might hurt others. We think only about how we feel and what we want. Forgive us. Lead us to kind actions and gentle words; for we pray in Jesus' name. Amen.

> *Assurance of Pardon:* Jesus said that God rejoices when one sinner repents. God welcomes us back home and helps us live more loving lives. We can depend on that. We are forgiven.

2. As another assurance of pardon, have worshipers read or "line out" I Timothy 1:15-16, claiming Paul's conviction of forgiveness for themselves. (In "lining out," the congregation repeats each line after the worship leader.)

3. Proper 12 in Year B of this series includes directions for a prayer of confession and assurance of pardon based on Psalm 14.

4. Before praying the Lord's Prayer, highlight the phrase, "Forgive us our debts (trespasses) as we forgive our debtors (those who trespass against us)." Briefly outline the way the focal text of the day affects the way we pray this phrase (e.g., imagine what it meant to Paul to pray this phrase after being forgiven for killing Christians).

Sermon Resources

1. If the tale of the lost sheep leads you to tell stories about lost children, remember that few lost children see themselves as the cause of their being lost. Rather, it is their parents who wander off: "I was staying nearby, looking at the toys, and then I looked up and Mom was gone!" Or they are doing something perfectly reasonable (to them) and are surprised to find themselves lost: "I was going to the bath house, like we did last night. Only it looked different in the day, and I couldn't find it."

2. In a large church, arrange for 100 children (perhaps several children's classes) to join you in the chancel. As they come forward, touch and count each one. (It should be crowded and a bit chaotic.) When all are in place, remark on how many 100 really are! Then imagine what it would be like to spend the whole day as group. Imagine what it would be like to be one shepherd, responsible for that many sheep. Send the children back to their seats, then retell the parable, beginning, "Once there was a shepherd who had 100 sheep . . . ."

Trace a path to find the lost sheep, lost coin, and lost person in this maze. Start over each time you find the thorn bush.

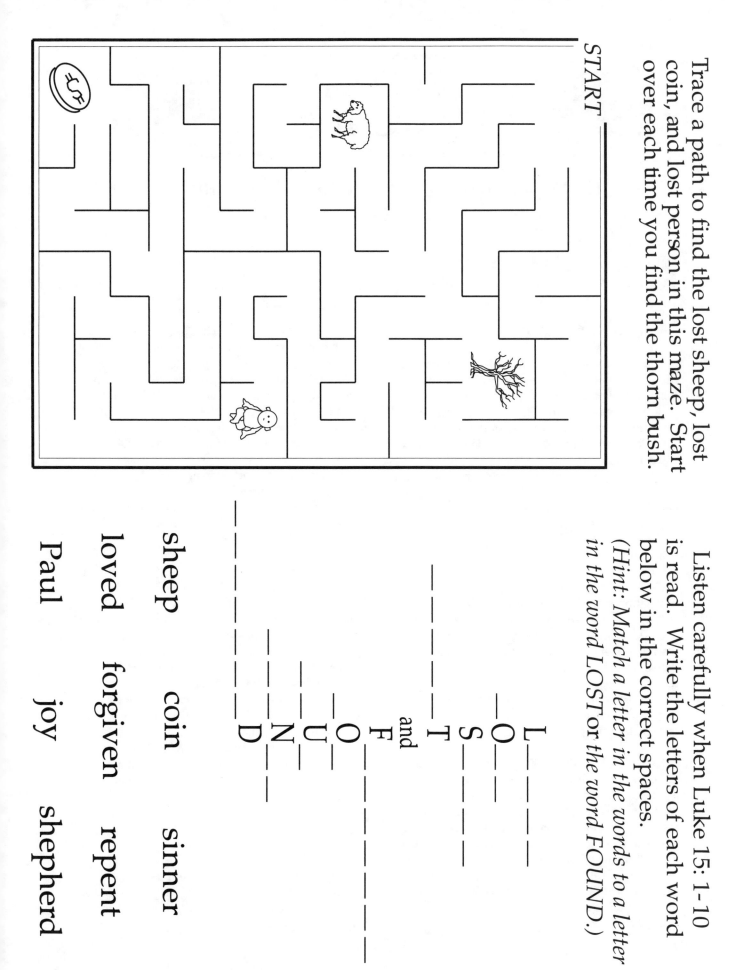

START

Listen carefully when Luke 15: 1-10 is read. Write the letters of each word below in the correct spaces. (*Hint: Match a letter in the words to a letter in the word LOST or the word FOUND.*)

L — — — —
— O — —
— S — —
— T — — — —
and
F — — — —
— O — — — — —
— U — —
— N — — — —
D — — — — — —

sheep   coin   sinner

loved   forgiven   repent

Paul   joy   shepherd

Proper 19 / © 1994 by Abingdon Press.

PROPER TWENTY

(Sunday between September 18 and 24 inclusive)

From a Child's Point of View

Old Testament: Jeremiah 8:18–9:1. When children hear Jeremiah's lament over his people's suffering in context, they easily understand why Jeremiah was so sad. The passage, however, offers no meaningful message for them.

Children who know "There Is a Balm in Gilead" catch the reference to the "balm in Gilead" and appreciate a simple explanation of what that balm is, what it means in Jeremiah's wish for his people, and what it means in the song.

Psalm: 79:1-9. Children quickly understand this psalm when it is introduced as a poet's prayer after invaders have destroyed Jerusalem. The vivid words in verses 1-4 of the Good News translation make clear just how bad it was.

In this psalm we can hear a people who had decided against God's ways and ignored God's warnings, respond positively to God's punishment. Apparently God's punishment worked. They were ready to listen. Their situation can be used to point out that sometimes God must punish people to get their attention and to urge them not to be so stubborn that drastic punishment is required.

Epistle: I Timothy 2:1-7. This passage calls on us to pray for all people everywhere. God loves all people. Jesus came for all people. Therefore, we are to treat all people well. For children, praying for all people everywhere is one specific way to show their love for God's worldwide family. By including verse 8 in this section, The New Jerusalem Bible suggests that we should pray especially for those with whom we have disagreements. This is a challenging discipline for worshipers of all ages.

Gospel: Luke 16:1-13. This passage includes a parable and four related teachings that are difficult both to understand and to apply to life. The parable (vss. 1-8*a*) describes the action and conversation of two "bad guys." Children need to be told that Jesus did not approve of what the servant did or of the master's compliment. Instead, Jesus was using their outrageous story to make four important points:

First, Christians should work as hard at doing God's work as the bad servant worked at stealing his master's money (8*b*).

Second, we should be generous in sharing our money and toys (9). People who share have many friends. And having friends makes a person happier than having money or things.

Third, if we use our money and things well (generously), God will entrust us with even more exciting and important work (10-12). Therefore, when you learn to share your small amount of money and numerous toys as a child, you will be prepared to use wisely the larger amounts of money you will have as an adult, in order to do responsible work in God's church.

Fourth, we are not to be greedy (13). Doing God's work is much more important than what we wear or what we eat or what we want for our birthday.

Children (and many adults) will not be able to grasp any of these points from the reading of the text, but will need to hear the passage explained during the sermon.

Watch Words

Balm is often heard by children as *bomb*. Some children may be familiar with *lip balm* for chapped lips. Others may need to hear *balm* compared to *first-aid cream*.

Mammon needs to be defined as all the things money can buy. Jesus is warning us against *greed*.

Let the Children Sing

"O God of Every Nation" unites the themes of Jeremiah, I Timothy, and Luke. Although the hymn includes many abstract words, they are words that are familiar. Singing this hymn frequently in worship will help children catch the meaning of more and more of the phrases. This might be a good hymn for the whole congregation to learn together.

Especially if you sang it last week in response to the potter images, sing "Have Thine Own Way, Lord," to commit yourselves to God's disciplines.

Ask a children's class, a children's choir, or the whole congregation to sing "He's Got the Whole World in His Hands," in response to I Timothy.

The Liturgical Child

1. In the spirit of the I Timothy reading, take a prayer trip around the world. Pray for people of several different countries (in geographical sequence), and their needs. Print a world map in your order of worship and/or place a globe in your worship center.

2. Before the prayer of petition, give the worshipers a brief time of silence in which to identify people with whom they have problems. Then voice corporate prayers, with pauses for individual prayers:

Lord, we pray for all the people of the world. We pray for our own country (Pause), for the leaders who are our heroes, and for the elected leaders with whom we disagree. (Pause)

We pray for (several friendly nations or groups with specific needs). (Pause)

And we pray for (unfriendly countries, terrorist groups, etc.). (Pause)

We pray for people we love and love to be with in our families (Pause), at school and work (Pause), and at church. (Pause)

We even pray for those people and groups who drive us a little nuts. (Pause)

Bring us all closer together. Help us to treat one another with loving respect, so that the world may indeed have peace. We pray in the name of Jesus, who loves us all, and who died that we might have life and love one another. Amen.

3. Focus prayers of confession on the different "I wants" and "I needs" that overly influence our lives.

4. Before the offering is collected, briefly connect it to the Gospel teaching about wealth:

When we are seven, it is hard to give up one of the quarters we are saving for a video game or piece of sports equipment. When we are seventeen, it is hard to give up the dollar we earned ourselves and would like to spend on ourselves. When we are thirty-seven, and fifty-seven, and seventy-seven, there are bills to pay, things we need to be saving for, and all those other things we want. It is never easy to share our money. But the Bible is clear. Sharing our money is a key part of being one of God's people. Jesus said to all of us, in all situations of life, and at all ages, "You cannot serve both God and wealth." So we invite you now to join in the discipline of sharing your wealth.

Sermon Resources

1. The Luke passage, with all its difficulties, suggests an open-Bible teaching sermon. Invite worshipers to follow along in pew Bibles, or have the text printed in the order of worship. Work through the parable and the four points, explaining the meaning of each one, and illustrate them with examples from childhood and adulthood. (If the text is printed in the order of worship, suggest that people underline key words and write [or draw] notes in the margins.)

2. If you focus on the use of money, remember that children also spend and save money. They have allowances, gift money, and wages from small jobs. They need to be encouraged to begin at an early age to contribute some of their own funds to the work of the church. The well-intentioned parental practice of providing all the money children contribute to the church deprives them of the joy of sending their very own money to buy a bicycle for a missionary or to pay for the new organ.

MAMMON is a fancy word for money and what money can buy. Jesus warned us not to love mammon. That is hard!

Draw pictures of mammon that you like.

OR

Write a word beginning with each letter in the word mammon to describe mammon that you like.

M

A

M

M

O

N

Write a prayer about one of them.

The First Letter to Timothy tells us to pray for everyone. Write a prayer for one person you will see today. Decorate it with pictures of what that person does and likes.

Make a prayer calendar with the name of a different person you will pray for each day this week.

Monday
Tuesday
Wednesday
Thursday
Friday
Saturday
Sunday

PROPER TWENTY-ONE

(Sunday between September 25 and October 1 inclusive)

From a Child's Point of View

Old Testament: Jeremiah 32:1-3a, 6-15. Older children are fascinated by the details of this intricate land transaction, but are unable to catch the message Jeremiah is acting out. They depend on adults to point out that buying land when a country is about to be conquered is foolish, because the land will be claimed by the conquerors. In buying the land, Jeremiah was promising the people that the conquerors would eventually leave and their nation (with its land rights) would be restored. Jeremiah's purchase is a symbol of hope.

Children who live very much in the present have trouble finding hope in the promise that things will get better—but a long time from now. Children who are self-centered, rather than community-centered, have trouble finding hope in the promise that although they are going to be conquered and killed or taken as slaves, their country will not be wiped out forever.

Psalm 91:1-6, 14-16. Children who have led safe comfortable lives hear in this psalm the promise of God's loving care and protection in the midst of all disasters. They can benefit from exploring some of the images of God as a mother bird protecting her young, as a fortress, and as a shield. Alert children whose experiences have taught them that the good are not always protected, question the reality of the psalm. Therefore, it may be wise to focus more attention on the Jeremiah passage.

Gospel: Luke 16:19-31. This is the story of the rich man and Lazarus. The rich man's sin is not that he is rich, but that he, who had the resources to relieve Lazarus' suffering, was so caught up in his own self-interest that he did not even notice Lazarus' need. This happened in spite of the fact that he (and his five brothers) had read the Law and the Prophets, in which such self-centered oblivion to the needs of others is repeatedly condemned.

Children will need help to find this point in the story, but it is a point they need to consider. Even young children can learn to be aware of the needs of those around them. They can learn to "see" when their parents are tired and busy and find ways to help them, rather than make more demands. They can "watch" for unhappy children at school and try to support them. And they can understand this awareness of the needs of others as disciples' work, set out for us by God.

Epistle: I Timothy 6:6-19. This passage contains a series of instructions and warnings about living the Christian life. The warnings are aimed at adult concerns and framed in abstract generalizations and theological jargon. Children will understand little when the passage is read. With help, they can hear the message of verses 17-19—that it is better to do good deeds than to collect neat things.

Watch Words

In a day when suicide is becoming increasingly common among children, be precise in using *hope*. For Christians, *hope* is not a vaguely optimistic feeling that life will be good, but the belief that the world was created by God, who is good, and that God is at work in the world and in us to bring about good things. We are called to share in

161

that work. Even when it looks as if evil is winning, we have God's promise that in the end, God will win.

Let the Children Sing

With help, children can sing several traditional hymns of hope. Direct their attention to verses with vocabulary and meaning that are easiest for them: the first verse of "Sing Praise to God Who Reigns Above" and the third verse of "God of Our Life." Read through the words of "O God, Our Help in Ages Past" before it is sung. Instruct worshipers to listen for its hints that we can rely on God's care in the past, present, and future. Urge even nonreaders to sing the repeated chorus of "Great Is Thy Faithfulness" and suggest that older readers listen in the verses for reasons to trust that God will be with us always.

"Be Thou My Vision" fits several of today's themes. Consider highlighting the message of a key verse before singing it.

The Liturgical Child

1. Create a confession that describes some ways we can lose hope. Pattern each confession on one format. For example:

> Lord of the Universe, we know that you created this world wonderfully, but sometimes we see only problems. We see only snakes and mosquitos, sweaty summers and freezing winters. We are overwhelmed by the way we have polluted the air and water. So we give up. Forgive us.
>
> Loving God, we know that you created each of us with unique talents and abilities. We know you have hopes and dreams for us. But it is easy for us to see only what we cannot do and things about us that we wish were different. So we give up on ourselves. Forgive us.

2. Present Jesus' story dramatically. Either have three readers (narrator, the rich man, and Abraham) read the passage, or enlist three older youths or adults (Lazarus, the rich man, and Abraham) to pantomime the action while you read. Plan with the actors a central location for the beginning of the story—a place to one side for "heaven," and a place to the other side for "hell." Simple costumes would help the children recognize the characters.

3. Invite worshipers to pray for members of their families, people they encounter every day, and people with special needs in the larger world. Begin each of the three sections with a corporate prayer, followed by silence for individual prayers.

4. If this is Worldwide Communion Sunday, use breads from around the world (San Francisco sourdough, Russian pumpernickel, pita bread from the Middle East, etc.) for the sacrament. The breads may be precut into bite-size pieces and mixed together in baskets to pass among the worshipers. Or the worshipers may break bread from one of the loaves. Present the sacrament as a symbol of hope. God promises that even though nations and races fight constantly, one day we will eat happily together at God's Table. God also promises that the rich and poor will eat together at God's Table.

Sermon Resources

1. Decorate the sanctuary with symbols of hope as sermon illustrations—the Alpha and Omega in paraments (God was at the beginning and will be at the end of all things), a rainbow banner (God will not destroy the world), Easter lilies and butterfly banners (from sleeping bulbs and cocoons come new life), even a clay pot into which rolled deeds can be placed.

2. Situations that make a child feel hopeless: being stuck with a teacher he senses does not like or appreciate him; serious conflict at home; living with an abusive or alcoholic parent; being unable to make friends in a new school; being told repeatedly that she is "just like" a problem parent or older sibling; being constantly unfavorably compared with a parent or older sibling ("Why can't you be like . . . ?").

3. Introduce Time Out as a game that families can use to become aware of one another's needs and find ways out of unhappy situations. The game starts with one family member calling "time out" when he or she feels that people are bickering or that a blow-up is imminent. When "time out" is called, they all stop what they are doing. Each person then can speak one sentence to express what he or she feels and wants at the moment. Then the group agrees on what to do to get the work at hand done and to meet everyone's needs as much as possible.

Shade the spaces with •s in them to find an important word.

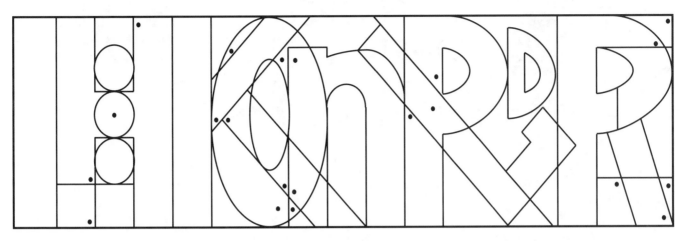

Circle each picture when you hear this word there.

SONG

Holy Bible

Sermon

Prayer

PAY ATTENTION

The rich man saw Lazarus every day, but he did not pay attention to him. Make a list of people and things you want to pay attention to this week.

Talk to God about each one during worship today.

Proper 21 / © 1994 by Abingdon Press.

PROPER TWENTY-TWO

(Sunday between October 2 and 8 inclusive)

From a Child's Point of View

Old Testament: Lamentations 1:1-6; Lamentations 3:19-26 (the suggested psalm). When children hear these poems read dramatically and are told that they were written by people whose hometown, Jerusalem, had been destroyed in war and that they had been forcibly moved to the conqueror's country, they empathize with the feelings expressed and are impressed by the quiet confidence of chapter 3. The New Jerusalem Bible offers children the most straightforward translation of the many poetic images.

Psalm: 137 (the alternate psalm). With some adult help, children understand the realities and feelings expressed in verses 1-6. They are, however, even more offended than adults by the wishes that someone would smash their captors' babies against rocks. Teenagers and adults can understand being hurt and angry enough to wish something that awful. Children, unless they have personally experienced war or witnessed physical violence against their own family, want to tell those angry people to be nicer. So for the children, it may be better to read only the first six verses of this psalm or the first-choice Lamentations poem.

Epistle: II Timothy 1:1-14. This passage contains encouragement from an older preacher to a young man who is overly cautious about doing God's work. If invited to "read over Timothy's shoulder," children can hear Paul call them to use the gifts (talents, personal qualities, leadership positions among other children) which God gave them. They are to be brave and courageous in standing up for God's ways. They are to be willing to be teased or bullied for doing God's work.

And while doing this, they are to remember that God loves and cares for them.

Gospel: Luke 17:5-10. This passage includes two separate teachings. The first is not to underestimate what we can do. Children often feel they can do nothing that will make a very big difference. They also feel overwhelmed when trying to do what is asked of them. Jesus claims that if they act faithfully, they will be surprised at what they can do.

The second teaching is that doing God's work (being fair and generous) is not something for which we should expect much attention and thanks. It is simply our job, as God's people.

Watch Words

Lamentations is a plural form of *lament*. A lament is a sad poem or song. Many modern love songs, especially in country music, are *laments* about a boy or girlfriend who has left the singer for another person.

Disciple is a word/idea behind today's New Testament texts. A *disciple* is a person who does what Jesus taught.

Faith (like a mustard seed) does not require special knowledge, nor is it a magic possession. *Faith* is being willing to do God's will (even when you are not sure how it will work out).

Let the Children Sing

Hymns for Worldwide Communion Sunday: "Blest Be the Tie That Binds" (hold hands while singing); "In Christ There Is No East or West" (see esp. verse 2); and "I Come with Joy" (communion celebrated with simple language as a meal focused on the unity and friendship Christ brings).

Share the confidence of the Lamentations poets: "Great Is Thy Faithfulness" (repeated chorus for young readers); or "Morning Has Broken" (based on Lam. 3:22-23).

Sing Hymns of Discipleship: "They'll Know We Are Christians by Our Love"; "Take My Life and Let It Be Consecrated"; "I Sing a Song of the Saints of God"; "Lord, You Give the Great Commission" (see Sermon Resources); "God of Grace and God of Glory" (words in the verses are hard, but children can sing the repeated chorus if alerted to it); "Let There Be Peace on Earth" (especially if it is Worldwide Communion Sunday).

The Liturgical Child

1. Present the Lamentations texts in their acrostic format. (The New Jerusalem Bible preserves the format most clearly.) Select one reader for each letter's verse, including readers of different ages. As the liturgist introduces the Lamentations collection of sad alphabet psalms, written after Jerusalem was destroyed and her people carried off to live in Babylon, the readers walk slowly and sadly to the chancel and position themselves as would a group of exiles at the end of a hard day. Readers freeze in position, moving only when the liturgist calls their letter and they step out to recite their verse with great feeling. The readers may wear simple biblical tunics, or matching clothes such as jeans and white shirts. (Consider combining the two Lamentations readings into one continuous presentation.)

2. Children respond well to "On the Willows," the sung version of Psalm 139:1-4 from the musical *Godspell*. The emotions behind the psalm shine through in the music.

3. If it is Worldwide Communion Sunday, present the Table as the place where disciples gather. Use a variety of breads (see directions in Proper 21) to remind worshipers of disciples around the world who do God's work. Pray for those disciples, using the directions in Proper 20 (Liturgical Child 1). Pray especially for disciples who are taking risks to do God's work today. If you use them, read the Old Testament laments on behalf of all those who come to the Lord's Table today as refugees.

4. Base the charge and benediction on the II Timothy exhortations:

Just as Paul encouraged Timothy, so I encourage you to use the gifts God has given you—not cautiously, but with courage and power and self-control. Do not be shy about standing up for God's ways. Be ready to suffer for doing God's work. And remember that God loves you, has given each of you important work to do, and is with you always. Amen.

Sermon Resources

1. Paraphrase II Timothy for children as follows:

From Paul, an older preacher, to Timothy, whom I love very much, and whom God loves: I thank God for you every day. I remember everything we did together and look forward to being with you again. I remember how much you love God, just as your mother and grandmother loved God.

Because I remember all this, I also remind you that you have a job to do. God has given you the gifts to be a fine leader, and the church has elected you to be its leader. So do not give up. God does not want you to be too cautious about using your gifts. Instead, God fills you with power, and love, and self-control. So use those gifts!

Do not be ashamed to stand up for God's ways. If people tease you, call you names, or even push you around, you can take it. Look at me—I am in prison for doing God's work, but I do not mind. I know God will take care of me, even in prison, and I know that God will take care of you.

So remember everything you have learned about God's love and plan for the world. Follow my brave example. And most of all, remember that God's Holy Spirit lives in you and gives you power to do amazing work for God.

2. Use the new hymn, "Lord, You Give the Great Commission," as an outline for a discipleship sermon. Suggest that worshipers keep their hymnals open so that you can refer to specific phrases. The verses are an interesting combination of abstract and very everyday vocabulary. Consider rehearsing the chorus so that children can join in easily as the hymn is sung following the sermon.

Today is Worldwide Communion Sunday. Christians in every country on earth are celebrating communion. Find the names of 13 of those countries in the letters below.

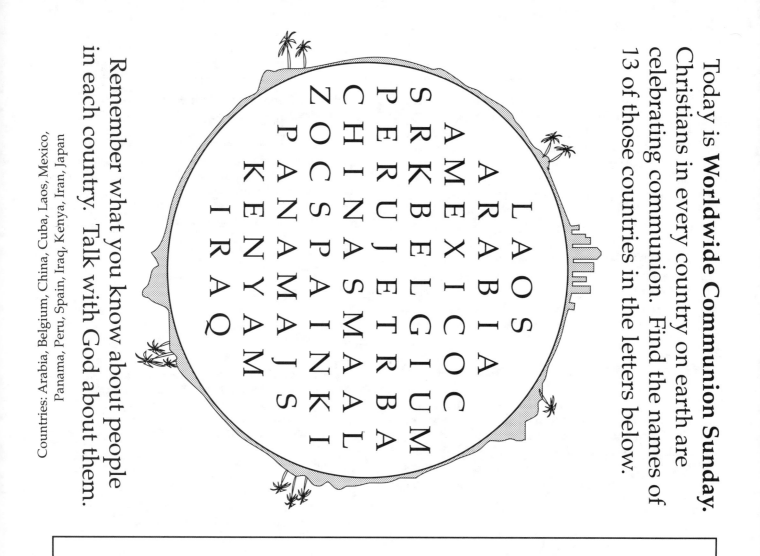

```
L A O S
A R A B I A
A M E X I C O C
S R K B E L G I U M
P E R U J E T R B A
C H I N A S M A A L
Z O C S P A I N K I
P A N A M A J S
K E N Y A M
I R A Q
```

Remember what you know about people in each country. Talk with God about them.

Countries: Arabia, Belgium, China, Cuba, Laos, Mexico, Panama, Peru, Spain, Iraq, Kenya, Iran, Japan

---

Write your name in capital letters across the page. Turn each letter of your name into a picture of you being a disciple.

Example: My name is CAROLYN. I turned the A into a picture of me drawing this page for you.

PROPER TWENTY-THREE

(Sunday between October 9 and 15 inclusive)

From a Child's Point of View

Old Testament: Jeremiah 29:1, 4-7. Exile means being stuck where you do not want to be. The Jews to whom Jeremiah spoke were stuck in Babylon, where their conquerors forced them to live. Children are often exiled: stuck in school classes they do not like; assigned to one reading group while their friends or those they want for friends are assigned to another; moved to a new town or neighborhood from an old one they loved; moved from their room or their home in the fallout from divorce, remarriage, or when older grandparents move in; and so forth. Jeremiah's encouragement to make the best of bad situations speaks pointedly to all who live in exile. Help children get Jeremiah's message by paraphrasing it to fit their exile situations. For example, make friends among your new classmates, pray for your teachers and the people with whom you are stuck, join in on what others are doing, and so forth.

Gospel: Luke 17:11-19. This story of ten lepers is often told to children to remind them of the importance of saying "Thank you." But the story is not about manners. It is about an appreciative attitude toward life. Nine lepers took their gifts (their cures) and ran. The tenth leper stopped to think about the significance of the gift he had been given and to respond to that gift. He probably responded the same way when someone gave him food, when a sick friend shared space in a dry cave, or when he saw a beautiful sunset. This attitude was a big part of the faith that made him "whole." This is similar to the attitude Jeremiah was urging upon the exiled Jews. (All this, of course, is between the lines. Children will need direction to dig out this meaning and apply it to their lives.)

Psalm: 66:1-12. This is a psalm for trusting exiles and healed lepers. Children easily understand the general praises expressed in verses 1-9 and enjoy the repeated use of the word *Awesome* to describe what God has done.

Verses 10-12 offer a concise description of the way faithful people deal with "exile" and other adversity, but children understand it only if each example is explained. For instance, they need to hear how silver is refined and to what the poetic image of "people riding over our heads" refers. Children, who regularly cope with discipline under parents and coaches, are perhaps more ready than adults to accept the idea that God would have us experience hard situations for our own good.

Epistle: II Timothy 2:8-15. This passage follows a very complex line of thinking that quickly loses the attention of children. But Paul's basic point—that he is willing to be imprisoned in order to do God's work (preaching, in his case)—is attractive, especially to idealistic older children. The picturesque claim (vs. 9) that they can chain Paul, but they cannot chain God's word makes powerful sense to these literal thinkers.

With help, in the hymn (vss. 11-13), older children can begin to understand the call to keep their commitments to Jesus. The first theological affirmation (vs. 11) is one they simply will need to grow into as their thinking matures. But the rest of the hymn can be understood as:

If we do God's work no matter what,
we shall be partners with God;

If we pretend we do not know God's teachings
    or what God wants us to do,
    God will pretend not to know us.
But even when we do not live right,
    God keeps on loving and caring for the world.

Watch Words

Either use *exile* strictly in reference to the Babylonian exile, or in reference to all situations in which we get stuck against our will. Do not alternate between the two uses without deliberate warning.

Being *faithful* is continuing to be a disciple even when it is not easy. Jeremiah told the people in exile to be *faithful*, to make the best of a bad situation, knowing that God still loved and cared for them. Paul urged Christians to be *faithful*, to live as disciples even when it got them in trouble.

Thankful, grateful, and *appreciative* are adult words about knowing that something is wonderful and good, a gift.

Let the Children Sing

Sing your gratitude with "Now Thank We All Our God" or "For the Beauty of the Earth." Sing "Father, We Thank Thee for the Night" as a round between a children's class or choir and the congregation or adult choir.

Sing of trusting God in difficult situations with "This Is My Father's World," "God Will Take Care of You" (young children learn the repeated chorus quickly), or the hymn version of Psalm 23 that is most familiar to your congregation (point out the meaning for exiles of "though I walk through the valley").

In response to Paul's message, sing "Go Forth for God," or other discipleship hymns mentioned in Proper 22.

The Liturgical Child

1. Create a praise litany in which the worship leader describes a series of God's great deeds. To each, the congregation responds, "Praise God who has done awesome deeds!" Include such deeds as creation of the world, leading the slaves safely out of Egypt, sending the people to be captives and staying with them while they learned their lesson about trusting God, and specific deeds in the life of your congregation.

2. If focusing on gratitude, before you sing "Praise God from Whom All Blessings Flow," point out its meaning and its significance in your order of worship. Be sure to define *blessings* as something other than the prayer we say before meals.

3. Invite all worshipers to make a list of ten good things, people, events, or activities they consider gifts from God. Urge them to put their lists in the offering plate along with their money gifts, as a way to express their gratitude to God.

Sermon Resources

1. To help children understand the feelings and the temptations to give in to despair faced by the exiles Jeremiah spoke to, describe the feelings and problems of refugees who start new lives in this country after fleeing from war in their own countries.

2. Retell some of the events in the story of Pollyanna, a little girl who treats all of life as a gift and has a way of finding the good in everything and everyone. Borrow the book from a public library or rent the video to review the story.

3. The task in preaching about the tenth leper is not to berate worshipers for being ungrateful, but to help them look at their lives with appreciation, identify their blessings, and learn disciplines that cultivate gratitude. Remember that when children voice thank-you prayers, they often mention their families, special friends (some of whom may be adults), a recent trip or party, unusual but beautiful weather (especially snow), and loved activities such as sports. They resent being told what to feel thankful for (e.g., most children, at certain times, are not at all thankful for their family).

Write or draw 1 person, thing, or activity
that you like a lot in each box below.

Write a prayer telling God about
1 of the things you like.

_____

_____

_____

_____

Make up a poem about another thing
you like.

_____
what you like

_____
2 words to describe it

_____
3 ing words about it

THANK YOU, GOD.

PROPER TWENTY-FOUR

(Sunday between October 16 and 22 inclusive)

From a Child's Point of View

Old Testament: Jeremiah 31:27-34. The detailed and varied poetic images in verses 27-28 make it essential that the liturgist explain directly that Jeremiah is promising the people who were in exile in Babylon that God will one day rebuild their nation. With that background, children can hear and respond strongly to the four specific promises:

• The change in the saying about eating grapes promises that people will be held responsible only for their own actions. This is as welcome to today's children, who want to be treated according to who they are and what they do, as it was to Daniel and the other children who were carried into Babylon because their parents had disobeyed God.

• "I will be their God, and they will be my people" promises the security of God's loving closeness (GNB). Children who yearn for a secure place in a strong group, led by a leader who knows them personally, respond to this invitation to be part of God's people.

• "None of them will have to teach his fellow countryman to know the LORD, because all will know me, from the least to the greatest," paints a picture of knowledge that comes not through teachings but through relationships (GNB). Any child who is tired of having to learn about God from teachers welcomes a promise of knowing God personally, rather than learning about God secondhand.

• "I will write [my law] on their hearts" promises that instead of knowing about God or even knowing God, we will find that God lives within us (NRSV). From about the age of four or five, children develop a growing understanding of the way we use the word *heart* to talk about our deepest, truest commitments. They learn to put a hand on their heart when they say the Pledge of Allegiance, say "cross my heart" as a kind of oath, and cut out valentine hearts for those they love. So, to think of God's will as being written on our hearts will be plausible, if not totally comprehended by even young children.

Psalm: 119:97-104. This section of Psalm 119 might be titled "The Law (or the Bible) and Me." Each verse tells about what the Bible means to "me" or how "I" use the Bible. Because the verses of the acrostic are loosely connected and not particularly meaningful to children, their best use may be as encouragement to worshipers to write their own verses about what the Bible means to them.

Epistle: II Timothy 3:14—4:5. This contains more of Paul's encouragement for Timothy. Verses 3:14-17 suggest that studying the Bible is the way to know about God and what God wants us to do. This is not a new idea for children, but one they need to hear emphasized repeatedly.

In 4:1-5, Paul encourages Timothy to do the work of preaching and teaching to which he has been called. He is specifically warned against putting off doing what is difficult. Like Timothy, children often try to put off discipleship until they are older or until it is easier. They need to be reminded that discipleship is never easy. Paul was put in prison for preaching. We do not know what problems Timothy met, but they were problems he wanted to avoid. Like Paul and Timothy, children can expect problems as they do God's work at school and among their friends. Like Paul and Timothy, children are to be strong and patient.

Gospel: Luke 18:1-8. This passage is also about persistence. Jesus uses a story about a villainous judge to make a point. Children are easily confused by this story, unless they are bluntly told that Jesus is saying that even a bad judge will give in to the persistence of an unwanted pest (the woman), so we can expect our loving and fair God to respond to our persistent prayers. They also need to be told bluntly that Jesus was *not* saying that God is like the bad judge, who only responds when someone becomes a pest.

Watch Words

A *covenant* is a set of "big" promises between two people or groups. While the promises made in a *contract* are specific, those in a *covenant* are broader and affect more of our life. For example, a boss and an employee sign a *contract* about the work the employee will do and the wages the boss will pay. But when a man and woman marry, they make a *covenant* to be a family for the rest of their lives.

Point out that the words *law, commandments, decrees, precepts,* and *ordinances* are all found in the Bible. Children may understand Psalm 119 better when they substitute *the Bible* for these words.

Call the Bible *the Bible* rather than *Scriptures, Holy Book,* or other names, unless you introduce the names as you use them.

Persistence means sticking with it, not giving up.

Let the Children Sing

Continue singing the hymns of discipleship mentioned for the last weeks.

"Wonderful Words of Life" celebrates the importance of the Bible for direction and has a chorus that children can sing and may know from church school.

If children are familiar with "Be Thou My Vision," sing it today to celebrate the covenant "written on our hearts."

The Liturgical Child

1. Invite an early-elementary children's class to present today's section of Psalm 119, with each child saying aloud one of the short verses. The children stand at the front of the sanctuary like a choir, with each child holding an open Bible, but repeating his or her verse from memory.

2. Create a responsive prayer of confession based on the Ten Commandments. After worshipers read each Commandment, a worship leader offers a prayer about the ways we fail to live with it "written on our hearts." For example:

People: You shall have no other gods before me.
Leader: But there are so many important things we must do, God, and so many we want to do. There are clothes and homes and toys and trips and jobs and awards that we want so badly. Sometimes we write so many wants and dreams on our hearts that they become our gods, instead of You. Forgive us, and write your will in big letters on our hearts.

3. Base the charge and benediction on Paul's charge to Timothy:

In the presence of God and Christ Jesus, I urge you, just as Paul urged Timothy, to do the work to which God calls you. Be a disciple even when it is inconvenient and risky. Do God's work even when it seems that what you do does not matter. Live by God's rules, even when everyone else is following the rules of me-first and greed. Don't give up. I know you can do this, because you remember that Jesus promised his disciples, "I will be with you always." So go in peace. Amen.

Sermon Resources

1. Help children understand Jeremiah's saying about eating sour grapes by describing more familiar eating experiences, such as the response to drinking sour milk, the way a tongue and mouth pucker when biting into a really sour dill pickle, or the burning mouth and tears that follow hot mustard or spicy chili.

2. Illustrate Jeremiah's point about a "covenant written on the heart" by describing the difference between doing a science project that fascinates you and one that is required but does not interest you, or practicing the piano because you really like a song and want to play it beautifully, instead of because your folks tell you to.

Cross out every fourth letter on this word trail to find one of God's promises.

Start Here . . . . .

I W I A L L P R U T M X Y L A W W I I T E O R I N T H I E H O R T H E A W R S T S . M A N E D W R S W E D W R S

Hint: Listen when Jeremiah 31: 33 is read.

Each of the 176 verses of **Psalm 119** tells us something about the Bible. Today we read verses 97 - 104. Most of these verses begin with "I" and tell
* one thing I learn from the Bible or
* one way I am helped by the Bible.

Write 2 sentences that tell what YOU learn from the Bible and why YOU think the Bible is important.

Proper 24 / © 1994 by Abingdon Press.

PROPER TWENTY-FIVE

(Sunday between October 23 and 29 inclusive)

From a Child's Point of View

Old Testament: Joel 2:23-32. This passage includes two rather distinct sections. The first (vss. 23-27) is Joel's prediction of the end of the locust plague that has eaten the country into a famine. Good weather and good crops are promised for the coming year. With a little explaining, children can understand the images. But today's nonagricultural children do not appreciate the significance of Joel's promised relief.

The second section (vss. 28-32) is part of Joel's vision of the Day of the Lord. One of the benefits of that day is that God's Spirit will enable great dreams and visions. From this, children learn that God's Holy Spirit is the source of our best dreams for ourselves and for the world. In fact, one job of the Holy Spirit is dream-making. So our dreams are to be taken seriously as gifts from God.

Epistle: II Timothy 4:6-8, 16-18. These are the observations of Paul, who, realizing that he soon will be executed, is looking back over his ministry. He expresses satisfaction that he has done his best, forgives those who did not stand up for him when he was arrested, and credits God for the power to use his long imprisonment as an opportunity to tell the good news to the Gentiles. It is hard for children, at the beginning of their lives, to appreciate Paul's statements, but they can see, as an example, his forgiveness of those who failed him. Adults would like them to comprehend the satisfaction of having done their best, but few children will appreciate that until they have more personal experience with having done both their best and less than their best.

Gospel: Luke 18:9-14. This passage describes the prayers of a proud Pharisee and a repentant tax collector. Children respond quickly to Jesus' caricatures and grasp his point that God is not impressed by show-offs, but by people who are honest—even about their faults. Young children accept the terms *Pharisee* and *tax collector* as labels for the two men, without asking about the significance of the words. The understanding of older children is enriched by definitions of these labels.

Psalm: 65. This is a prayer of praise and thanks that could be prayed by Paul, the tax collector, and by all those who trust the promises of Joel. It is a prayer of humble contentment with what God provides. Children will catch occasional phrases and the overall mood, if the psalm is read well. (The Good News Bible translates Old Testament agricultural images into terms today's children can understand.)

Watch Words

Define *dreams* and *visions* as ideas about what could be. They are not weird experiences in which we see things that are not there, nor do they enable us to see into the future in a magic way.

Paul's *race* and *crown-of-righteousness* images are difficult to translate and do not communicate to children what Paul wants to say. So use them for the adults and speak to children through other passages and images.

Let the Children Sing

Sing of dreaming God's dreams with "Be Thou My Vision" or "Open My Eyes That I May See."

Before singing the latter, rephrase the repeated "illumine me" to emphasize the recognition of dreams.

"Jesus Loves Me, This I Know" is a song the tax collector and Paul might have sung. Sing it with the same reliance on God that they had.

"Have Thine Own Way, Lord" is a song of submission to God's will for our lives. Children will benefit especially from singing it if you featured a potter earlier this year.

The Liturgical Child

1. Pray responsively about dreams for the world:

Leader: God, who created us and this world, you have promised that you will pour out your Spirit upon us with dreams of how the world could be and visions of how to attain these dreams. So we share these dreams and ask that you help us to bring them about.

We dream of a world in which everyone has enough food to eat and a safe, warm place to live. But we see pictures of people starving all over the world. In our own town, we know that people are living in shacks and on the streets. And we hardly know how to help.

People: Lord, pour out your Spirit among us.

Leader: We dream of a healthy world. We dream of finding cures for cancer and AIDS. We dream of medical care for everyone, so that children do not die from curable diseases like measles.

People: Lord, pour out your Spirit among us.

Leader: We dream of a beautiful world that is safe for all people, plants, and animals. We worry about all our garbage and polluted rivers and poisoned air. We want to save the whales and the elephants—and ourselves. But we cannot seem to find a way to do it.

People: Lord, pour out your Spirit among us.

Leader: We dream of a world at peace. We hope for the end of racism, for the settling of old feuds between nations and tribes, for sharing between rich and poor, and even for peace in our families. But we have trouble setting aside our own selfish wants to work for the good of us all.

People: Lord, pour out your Spirit among us.

Leader: Lord, be with us and these dreams you have given us. Give us the courage to make changes in the way we do things and to demand that others also make needed changes. Give us the strength to keep dreaming and working when it looks hopeless. And keep us open to new dreams and visions and possibilities.

People: Lord, pour out your Spirit among us.

ALL: Amen!

2. Ask the adult choir to present "The Pharisee and the Publican," by Heinrich Schutz. The work features two male solos which capture wonderfully the character of the two worshipers in the story. (Do point out that *publican* is another word for tax collector.)

3. Take the parts of both the Pharisee and the tax collector as you read the Luke text. For the Pharisee, stand to one side of the lectern with haughty posture, and read the words with a rather loud, pretentious tone. For the tax collector, stand to the other side and speak with genuine sorrow, in a calm voice.

4. Prayer of confession and petition:

God of the universe, forgive us when we are so sure we are right that we stop listening to the ideas of others. Remind us that we do not know everything.

Lord, forgive us when we are too impressed with our own ideas and what we can do. Keep us from becoming braggy.

Loving Father and Mother, forgive us when we want something so much that we ignore warnings that we may want the wrong thing. Help us to control our "wants."

God of the Bible, forgive us when we think that stories about your love are meant for us and that demands for change are meant for other people. Be with us as we read the Bible, and help us hear what you are saying to us. Amen.

Sermon Resources

Tell stories about people who work to realize dreams. Recall how the "I Have a Dream" speech of Martin Luther King, Jr., gave people the courage to work for civil rights. Describe the importance of being able to "see yourself doing it" in order to succeed in sports. Tell about children in the fifth-grade Sunday school class who worked successfully on their dream for a beautiful world by writing to the board of their church, asking that the church not use styrofoam cups and plates.

Trace a path as you follow each person under, over, and around to find Jesus' message to each of them.

1. A L L W H O E L D

2. A L L W H O M B H L B M U

B I L L
E M W
A S
S E E
D V
G E L E
R L E S M E H L B E U
E R V W T L H E T E H
A E A T
T

Joel said that children would dream God's dreams for the world. Draw or write one dream for the world.

no fighting

no hungry people

1. _____

2. _____

Answers: 1. All who humble themselves will be made great. 2. All who make themselves great will be humbled.

Proper 25 / © 1994 by Abingdon Press.

PROPER TWENTY-SIX

(Sunday between October 30 and November 5 inclusive)

Note: Consider substituting the All Saints lections for those of Proper 26, especially if Sunday falls near Halloween.

From a Child's Point of View

Old Testament: Habakkuk 1:1-4; 2:1-4. This passage deals with fairness on the national/global level. Older children appreciate Habakkuk's question when it is presented in personal terms (e.g., a farmer caught in the cross-fire between warring armies; a child starving in a country where the leaders live in luxury). They quickly agree with Habakkuk that it is not fair, and they wonder why a loving God allows such things to happen.

God's answer—that in the long haul, justice will be done—seems a bit like a cop-out to children who live so much in their own present. It helps to hear a trusted adult speak with appreciation of this view and cite examples. But it will be some years before children really accept this view.

They can, however, apply God's "sign" to their present. Basically, it says that no matter what seems to get the best results at the moment, it is always better to live by God's ways.

Psalm: 119:137-144. This is a psalm to sing while waiting for God's justice to be realized. Its vocabulary is a major obstacle to a straightforward message—*judgments, testimonies, precepts, righteousness, commands, laws,* and *faithfulness* are used interchangeably. If it is suggested that all these words describe God's ways, children can begin to understand some of the praise statements. The Good News Bible translation is particularly helpful.

Epistle: II Thessalonians 1:1-4, 11-12. In this letter, Paul and his co-workers greet the Christians at Thessalonica and compliment them on their discipleship. Verses 11 and 12, especially as presented in the Good News Bible, offer two significant encouragements to children:

1. Verse 11 expresses the hope that each of us will live up to the calling (or potential) for which God created us. Underlying that hope is the belief that God has a good plan for each person. Children dream of doing something wonderful and good during their lives. Paul, in this text, tells them that he hopes those dreams will come true. He also hopes that they will be worthy of their dreams and of God's plan for their lives.

2. Verse 12 encourages readers to live so well that people will say, "If this person is a disciple of Jesus, then Jesus must be wonderful," and "You can see the loving power of Jesus in this person."

Children will need help to dig both these encouragements out of Paul's words.

Gospel: Luke 19:1-10. This story of Zacchaeus is most likely familiar to the children. They relate quickly to the short fellow who is elbowed to the back of the crowd, is resourceful enough to climb a tree in order to see Jesus, and then is singled out by Jesus for special attention. The story gives them hope that Jesus notices and cares for them, particularly if they feel overlooked or shoved to the side.

Younger children will overlook the fact that Zacchaeus was a tax-collecting cheat. Jesus' notice of the short guy is plenty to satisfy their needs. Older children appreciate the fact that not only was Zacchaeus short (an awful fate for a ten-to-twelve-year-old boy in our sports-minded culture), but he was also unpopular—and deserved to be, because he cheated! Zacchaeus was "pond

176

scum" (substitute the ultimate put-down currently used by children in your congregation)!

Jesus' treatment of Zacchaeus does two things. First, it assures children that Jesus loves them and will forgive them—even when they have acted like pond scum. Second, it challenges them to treat the Zacchaeuses they meet with the same forgiving love that Jesus lavished upon the original.

Watch Words

Avoid speaking in generalizations about *the evil, the wicked,* and *oppression,* in favor of naming specific oppressors and evil practices that children recognize.

Instead of speaking of the *salvation* that came to Zacchaeus' house, talk about the friendship and forgiveness Jesus offered, and about Zacchaeus' response.

Let the Children Sing

The hymns of discipleship mentioned during the last weeks continue to be good choices. "We Shall Overcome" or "They'll Know We Are Christians by Our Love" are especially appropriate and are singable by children.

Celebrate the importance of the Bible with "Wonderful Words of Life."

"I Sing a Song of the Saints of God" is one way to respond to Paul's challenges.

The Liturgical Child

1. Present Psalm 119 as an acrostic, with each verse praising the Bible read by a different reader. Readers may be of different ages or members of a children's class. Young readers do better if they memorize their verses.

2. Explore the Lord's Prayer petition, "Thy kingdom come, Thy will be done on earth as it is in heaven." Then offer a litany prayer for God's justice. (To each prayer, the congregation responds: "Thy Kingdom come, thy will be done on earth as it is in heaven.")

Lord, it is easy to pray, "Thy will be done," but so much around us seems to go against your will. We need your direction and courage and power. (RESPONSE)

You created the world filled with food, but we see pictures of hungry children every day on TV. Help us find ways to share. (RESPONSE)

God, we all need a home. But so many people do not have one. Work with us to find houses for all who live in our area. Guide those who work to resettle refugees. (RESPONSE)

Lord, guide us as a nation. Give us the wisdom to elect fair leaders. Direct those leaders to laws and policies that are just. (Describe current situations in the world and your community which cry out for God's justice). (RESPONSE)

God, make us doers of your justice. Help us to play fair at school and at work. Teach us not to make enemies, but to make friends. Give us the courage to stand up for your ways among our friends. And remind us of that way when we are tempted "to forget." (RESPONSE)

We pray in Jesus' name. Amen.

3. Ask the children's choir or a children's class to sing a song about Zacchaeus as an anthem for the worship service. (Most children's groups have a much-loved Zacchaeus song in their repertory.)

4. Base the charge preceding the benediction on II Thessalonians 1:11-12:

May God make you worthy of the life to which you are called. May God give you the power to do the good deeds you want to do. May Jesus look good because of what you do. And, may you look good because of what God does through you.

5. Even if you do not celebrate All Saints, praise the God who is so powerful that we need not fear any other force in the universe. Pray for fun and safety while celebrating Halloween. And pray for the wisdom to remain our loving selves while wearing masks and costumes.

Sermon Resources

1. If you are celebrating Reformation Sunday, tell the story of Martin Luther, who learned the same lesson Zacchaeus did. Both learned that God/Jesus loved them in spite of their sinfulness.

2. Introduce the Zacchaeus Game. Every player takes the role of Jesus, watching for people who are lonely, "up a tree," or just plain having a bad day. When such a "Zacchaeus" is found, the player does something nice for him or her. Sometimes the player does not ever know if the kindness makes a difference. But sometimes the player can see the person respond—almost as readily as Zacchaeus responded to Jesus' request to be his dinner guest.

Listen when Luke 19: 1-10 is read. Draw a picture of what happened in that story. Draw faces that show what people were feeling.

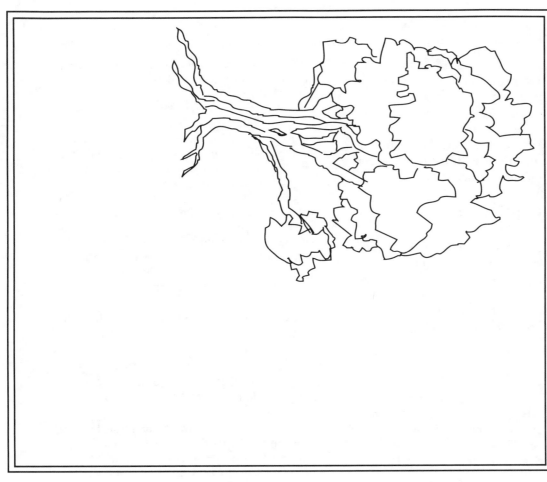

Psalm 119 is an alphabet poem about the Bible. To make up your own alphabet poem about the Bible, write a sentence that begins with each letter below. (Listen for ideas in our songs, prayers, and the sermon.)

A ll who read the Bible learn about God's love!

B _____

C _____

D _____

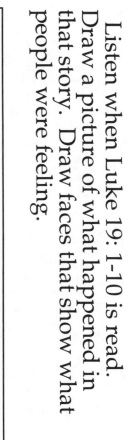

ALL SAINTS

(November 1 or First Sunday in November)

From a Child's Point of View

Old Testament: Daniel 7:1-3, 15-18. This is the beginning and end of a less-known story about Daniel, one of God's saints. Because it is less familiar, the whole story (1:1-18) probably should be read.

In the story, Daniel and three of his friends take a risk in order to show their loyalty to God by keeping Jewish dietary laws while they were captives in a foreign court. The unstated implication of the story is that because of this loyalty, they became wise, capable, respected members of the king's court. Children will hear this message quickly.

Children need to know only that one way Jews showed their loyalty to God was by not eating certain foods. Older children will be interested in some of the details of kosher cooking. But the focus is not on eating. It is on loyalty to God. Children today seldom show their loyalty by what they eat. But they can show their loyalty to God in their refusal to drink alcoholic beverages, smoke cigarettes, or experiment with drugs, all of which destroy the bodies God gave them. They can also follow God's rules about loving behavior, even when it is risky.

Psalm: 149. This psalm is a call to God's people to celebrate their identity. Verses 1-5 call worshipers to use musical instruments and dance in praising God. Verses 6-9 describe a war-like sword dance that was part of worship. The implication of these last verses is that God wants the people to conquer and enslave other nations. Because such religious nationalism was reinterpreted by Jesus, it might be wise to omit these verses. They tend to confuse children.

Epistle: Ephesians 1:11-23. This passage shows Paul at his most complicated. Children will not be able to keep up with the abstract language and compound/complex sentences. Read this for the grown-ups.

There are several ideas within the passage which speak to children: (1) Saints are people chosen by God; (2) God's Spirit (the Holy Spirit) gives us the ability to learn about God; (3) Christ is the ruler of the universe; (4) the church is made up of saints and belongs to Christ.

Gospel: Luke 6:20-31. Here are two sections of the Sermon on the Plain. First is a list of "blessings" and "woes." Especially to children hearing them for the first time, they sound backward. It is important to tell children that they also sounded backward to Jesus' listeners, and to adults today. Jesus said them that way to get everyone's attention—and it worked! With this background, children will be ready to explore what Jesus meant.

Jesus is not saying that it is better to be poor and miserable than rich and happy. He is saying that if you are a sharing saint, you probably will share so much of what comes your way that you will never be rich; that if you are a caring saint, you will be too aware of people who need help to be happy all the time; and that if you are a committed saint, you will take some stands that will make you unpopular. To children, this means that saints are to find pleasure in sharing instead of "hogging stuff," in finding ways to make other people happier, and in working for God's justice.

The second section, about loving enemies, is "hard" for people of all ages. The difficulty for children is that it speaks in very concrete language about their everyday dealings with enemies. Most children have personal experience

179

with name-calling (cursing), slapping, stealing from each other, and the problems that come with lending belongings. This section gives specific instructions for the way to treat an impossible sibling today and those who make your life miserable at school tomorrow. The two keys to this text are verses 32-35 and 31. Verses 32-35 insist that being kind to friends is no big deal. (Jesus is not interested in manners or getting along, but in active peacemaking.) Most children find this rather amazing, challenging, and strangely logical and attractive. Verse 31 is the Golden Rule. Most children have learned it in a more general setting. Hearing it here as a rule particularly for dealing with enemies can give it new power.

Watch Words

Define *saint* as a person who does God's will. Include all members of your congregation as potential *saints*.

Children who see *enemies* as bad often deny that they have any enemies. They need help to identify those who treat them and are treated by them as *enemies* before they can be serious about following Jesus' directions.

Let the Children Sing

"I Sing a Song of the Saints of God" (first choice), "For All the Saints" (the Alleluias can be sung by all), and "We Are the Church" are the best All Saints hymns for children.

If your celebration includes the Lord's Supper, sing "Take Our Bread," a good Communion hymn which, through frequent use, can be learned by elementary readers.

The Liturgical Child

1. Display pictures or other reminders of the saints of your congregation in your worship center. If you have banners from church anniversaries, hang them.

2. Invite children to come to worship dressed as one of the saints. (Those who come without costumes can be recognized as saints "in real life.") Children may lead the choirs in the processional or may be invited to stand briefly at the front to identify the saints they are to the congregation. An older children's class may be asked to undertake special duties, such as collecting the offering in their costumes.

3. Introduce the reading of Daniel by naming the four heroes of the story and encouraging worshipers to listen for the risk they took with their food.

4. Turn Psalm 149:1-5 into a responsive poem by asking the congregation to respond to each phrase read by the worship leader, saying, "Praise the Lord!" Practice saying it together, as if you mean it, a few times before reading the psalm.

5. Point out and explain the phrase "Praise him above, ye heavenly hosts" in the Doxology. Identify the "heavenly host" as saints of the church who have died. State the meaning of the phrase in the context of the song.

6. Pray for saints of the past and present. Include a few saints children will recognize. Give individual worshipers time to pray for saints who have been and are important as examples to show us how to live.

Sermon Resources

1. Outline a job description for a saint in your community. Name qualifications, personal qualities, abilities/skills required, and rewards offered. Use some examples from children's experience to illustrate your points. Work to create a job description that could be claimed by a worshiper of any age.

2. Tell stories about saints. Include stories about one or two well-known saints (Daniel, Martin Luther King, Jr., Mother Teresa, or others you recognize) and some stories about less-known saints, who could be anyone in your church. Include at least one child saint at work in a local setting—making peace on the bus, participating in mission projects of the church, or caring for people.

3. If you celebrate the Lord's Supper, highlight words and phrases used in your ritual to describe the gathering around the Table of the communion of saints past, present, future, from all lands. Put the phrases into children's words. If appropriate, elaborate on the phrases during the liturgy to name specific saints of your congregation.

Today is
ALL SAINTS DAY.

Listen carefully as you worship. Then draw a picture of one saint in action.

SAINT _____

Now picture yourself as a saint. Draw yourself being a saint at home or school.

SAINT _____
(my name)

PROPER TWENTY-SEVEN

(Sunday between November 6 and 12 inclusive)

From a Child's Point of View

Old Testament: Haggai 1:15b–2:9. This is a specific message for a specific time. Haggai encourages the people and their leaders to be courageous, to work hard, and not to be afraid as they rebuild the Jerusalem Temple after the Exile. Haggai promises that God will be with the people and that the Temple will be a rich and important center. It is a somewhat interesting but remote story for children, although the point of the text can be stretched to encourage children today to be courageous, work hard, and be fearless in doing God's work, whatever that may be for them.

Psalm: 145:1-5, 17-21, or 98. Both are general praise psalms. Both are meant to be experienced rather than understood, and thus children depend on dramatic upbeat presentations that communicate the psalms' moods. Because Psalm 98 includes more calls to easily identified parts of creation and to specific musical instruments, its content is more child accessible than that of the more abstract Psalm 145.

Epistle: II Thessalonians 2:1-5, 13-17. Verses 1-5 deal with first-century concerns about the return of Christ that are beyond the experience and interest of today's children. An exploration of Paul's practical advice and encouragement for his Thessalonian friends in verses 13-17 offers more for these children. With help, they realize that Paul's advice fits them too. God loves them and has put them in a place where they could hear the stories about God and Jesus. In response, they are to remember the stories and obey Jesus' teachings. When they do, God will be with them and help them.

Gospel: Luke 20:27-38. This is the story of another tricky question: "Whose wife will a woman who has been married and widowed seven times be, when all eight of those people get to heaven?" Children do not need to hear about leviratic practices or the Sadducee's motives to understand this question. They will need help with Jesus' answer in verses 34-36, but once it has been explained, it is one they readily accept. No one knows what life beyond death is like. That is one of God's secrets. What we do know is that God will still be loving. Therefore, we can expect only that life will be good. That answer puts the question in a familiar class of questions for which there are no answers—only mysteries.

The Sadducee's question is, of course, also a trap question. But to recognize that and to deal with Jesus' point about the God of the living (vss. 37-38) requires in-depth knowledge about the Sadducees and their logic. Explore this with the grown-ups.

Watch Words

Most children hear *lyre* (e.g., praise God with the lyre) as *liar*.

Children usually associate *resurrection* with Jesus and Easter. So for clarity, speak of *life after death*, rather than *in the resurrection*.

If you speak about the *Sadducees* at any length, point out that they were *sad, you see* because they did not believe in life after death. This will not help children understand the significance of this passage; it simply helps them recognize a name they will hear again.

Let the Children Sing

"Earth and All Stars" is based on Psalm 98 and adds calls for praise to modern groups of people and situations. (If this is used as an opening hymn, precede it with a call to worship based on Psalm 98: 1, 4-9.)

Sing "Lord, You Give the Great Commission," especially if you worked on learning it as a congregation earlier this fall. This hymn also follows the prophecy and Epistle theme.

Sing "God of Grace and God of Glory," with its repeated prayer phrase, for the Jews who rebuilt Jerusalem, the Christians who endured persecution in Thessalonica, and disciples at work today. Sing "The Battle Hymn of the Republic," but only after introducing it as a song to be sung by people who work with God. Though children do not understand the big words and complicated images, they do grasp its message in the drama of the music. So provide the most stirring, majestic instrumental backup possible. (Do remember that the chorus is the basis of innumerable children's taunt songs.)

The Liturgical Child

1. See the suggestion for responsive reading of Psalm 98 on the Sixth Sunday of Easter (Year B) of this series.

2. If you focus on the Gospel reading, display new-life symbols and banners in the worship center. Suggest that flowering bulbs (Easter lilies, if possible) be the flowers of the day. Then refer to them during the sermon.

3. Read II Thessalonians 2:13-17, or the following paraphrase of the passage, as the Charge and Benediction:

> Remember that God loves you. God chose you to hear the good news and to live among God's people. Do not forget what you have learned. Live by it. And may our Lord Jesus Christ, and God our Father, and the Holy Spirit give you the courage and strength to say kind words and do loving deeds today and every day. Amen.

Sermon Resources

1. The Jews struggling to rebuild Jerusalem and the Christians in Thessalonia had similar problems, which children can understand. God was busy doing big things in both situations, and the people were hanging back. The Jews were discouraged and frightened. Deep down inside, they didn't believe they or God could do the job. They were ready to give up. (Many children are just as pessimistic about their lives and worlds.) Some of the Christians, on the other hand, believed that God could do anything, but they were doing nothing to help. All they wanted to do was watch and cheer. (Many children are willing to hear about children's church activities, but are unwilling to get involved.) To both groups, and to hesitant disciples today, God says that great things are going to happen and that their help is needed.

2. Build a sermon recounting the great things God has done and describing the human work that was involved. Begin with biblical events (Haggai and the beginning of the church), but include other events from church history and from the recent history of your congregation. Conclude each story with a phrase such as, "Who did it? God did it! How did God do it? God worked through people!"

3. Devote the sermon to exploring ideas about life after death (heaven). Identify some ways we describe heaven: winged angels, harps, golden streets, an entry gate manned by Saint Peter, and so on. Invite people to flip through hymns about heaven or eternal life in the hymnal. Review key ideas and word pictures in several hymns.

Then work through the Gospel text to get to the fact that we really do not know much about what happens after we die. What we do know is that God, who loves us and cares for us on earth, will keep loving and caring for us after we die. We have God's promise and Jesus' promise about that. The cocoon that becomes a butterfly and the egg that hatches into a bird help children appreciate the change that happens to us at death.

No one knows exactly what heaven is like. That is God's secret. But Christians have always drawn pictures and written poems and hymns about what heaven might be like.

Draw or write what you think heaven is like.

The squiggles below are not quite real letters. Add something to each one to make it into a letter. When you have made each squiggle into the right letter, you can read God's message to people who are not ready to be real disciples.

Oh! Like this?

"⌐⊂<⊂ ⊂◯∟|⊂⌄◦ ⌐!"

"\⌄~| , ⌠◦| =

⊂⋒ ⌡⌐⌐√◯∟ !"

Haggai 2:4

Warning: Some squiggles make more than one letter. Keep trying until you find letters that make real words.

PROPER TWENTY-EIGHT

(Sunday between November 13 and 19 inclusive)

From a Child's Point of View

Three of today's texts deal with the day of the Lord or the second coming. Because children live so much in the present, promises of what will be "one day" have little power. But the convictions that underlie the promises are important for their sense of security. The fact that God will be there and in charge at the end of the world as at the beginning, assures children that they can rely on God's power at all times. The promise that God's final plans are happy ones reflects God's creation evaluation of the world, "that's good," and leads children to expect the world to be basically good.

Old Testament: Isaiah 65:17-25. Children have trouble with the detailed poetic images with which Isaiah states God's promises. The Good News Bible helps by translating some of these images into direct statements. For example, in verse 20, "No more shall there be . . . an old person who does not live out a lifetime," translates as: "All people will live out their life span." Because of their lack of experience, children need help understanding the images about getting to enjoy what you worked for (vss. 21-22a). The promises that deal with their keenest hopes are those about no more tears and no more danger from enemies ("wolf and lamb shall feed together").

When 21-22a are linked with Paul's insistence that everyone must work (the Epistle), children respond to their fairness. They like the idea that those who build houses will get to live in them and those who plant gardens will get to eat the food that grows in them. They enjoy paraphrasing the promise that reflects their own work—for example, those who clean the house for the party will get to attend.

Psalm: Isaiah 12. If they have been hearing the exile saga this fall, and if the sweep of those events is reviewed before the reading, older children can understand this as a prayer of God's people looking back over their experiences. They hear in it the response of people who have learned their lesson. If they have not focused on Exile, they simply hear occasional phrases expressing confidence in God's loving protection.

Gospel: Luke 21:5-19. This is Jesus' answer to the question, "When will 'the end' come?" In recent years there has been an increase in people predicting the "end of time" or the "second coming." As the year 2000 approaches, there probably will be more. Children need to be prepared for these well-publicized announcements, and this passage is good preparation. Jesus says plainly that no one knows when God will act. Anyone who sets the date is to be ignored.

Jesus also forewarns his disciples (and us) that there will be times when being a Christian will get us into trouble. In those situations, we are to be strong, knowing that God is with us and will help us. Persecution, whether it be teasing or imprisonment, is part of being a follower of Jesus in a selfish world.

Epistle: II Thessalonians 3:6-13. This is a very practical teaching about life in the church. Everyone, of every age, is to be a contributing member. For children, who are unable to earn their own money, the message is that they are to take part in the work at home and at church and in the community. They are to do their part of the chores, and they are to watch for other things that need to be done and do them. That is one of the responsibilities of being a member of God's family.

185

Understanding this passage is not nearly as difficult as disciplining ourselves (no matter what our age) to do the work.

Watch Words

Remember that children take apocalyptic language literally, unless you help them do otherwise. If you frequently use terms such as *second coming, day of the Lord,* or *end of time* in this service, be sure to tell children what the term(s) mean to you in your tradition.

To understand *salvation,* children need several everyday examples of things that are *saved:* a drowning person, a dog or cat from the pound, or (in this day of recycling) an item from the garbage heap being turned into something useful (maybe an empty can decorated to hold pencils).

Let the Children Sing

Sing "Rejoice, the Lord Is King" to celebrate God's lordship over all history. The repeated chorus makes it child-accessible. (Yes, boys will grin as they sing of every bosom swelling with joy.)

Sing "Take My Life and Let It Be Consecrated" to commit your whole bodies to doing God's work.

The Liturgical Child

1. Read Isaiah 12 as a responsive call to worship, with a worship leader reading the instructions in verses 1*a* and 3-4*a* and the congregation reading verses 1*b*-2 and 4*b*-6.

2. Adapt the litany prayer below to fit the work done in your congregation. The congregational response to each prayer: "Lord, help each of us see our share of the work and do it."

There's so much to do, Lord, just to keep our building clean! There are dishes to wash after every supper, and sidewalks to sweep, and grass to mow and rake, and garbage to empty. (RESPONSE)

And who will keep the furnace working, fold the bulletins each week, buy candles for the sanctuary, and remember to order the church school books? (RESPONSE)

And then there are the demanding jobs, God. We need church school teachers who will spend time preparing and leading lessons every week. We need people who will see needs in the community and lead us out to meet them. We need people to make sure our money is spent wisely to do your work. (RESPONSE)

We need people who will spend a snowy day delivering Meals-on-Wheels, or walk all ten miles of the CROP Walk, or be a Bible school helper. (Name mission projects in which your children work.) (RESPONSE)

And God, we need alert people who quietly do the little things. We need people who will drive an older member to the doctor's office, baby-sitters who refuse to charge for church meetings, children who are leaders among younger children on the lawn after church. (RESPONSE)

Lord, there's so much to be done. It will take all of us working together to get the work done. Be with us as we work. Help us to work wisely and efficiently. And let us know your peace and happiness in all we do; for we work and pray in your name. Amen.

Sermon Resources

1. If you talk about the importance of work, describe the jobs children can do at home, at church, and in the community. Be specific. If you cannot identify some jobs that are more than busywork, put the congregation to work identifying and instituting some.

2. Tell stories about people who have predicted the end of time. One recent example is the man who announced that the world would end on September 12, 1988, based on the prophecies in the book of Daniel. Many people started to attend prayer meetings every day. Some sold their homes and gave the money away in preparation for the last day. When the world did not end, the man announced that he had made a mistake in his figuring, and set a new date.

Turn each letter of WORK into a picture of you working at home or church.

This is me washing a window on church clean-up day.

WORK

Tell God your dreams for these enemies. Remember God's promise that one day all enemies will be friends.

Isaiah promised that one day a wolf and a lamb will be able to eat together as friends. Draw or write about 2 enemies you wish could be friends.

PROPER TWENTY-NINE
CHRIST THE KING

(Sunday between November 20 and 26 inclusive)

From a Child's Point of View

Old Testament: Jeremiah 23:1-6. On Christ the King Sunday, the key to this text is Jeremiah's comparison of the nation's king and its leaders to shepherds. According to Jeremiah, the job of a king (or any leader) is to take care of the people, just as a shepherd takes care of the sheep. Children need to hear specifically how their current leaders had not been good shepherds, how God's king would care for the people, and how Jesus acted like a shepherd king.

Psalm: Luke 1:68-79. This is a hard passage for children to figure out on Christ the King Sunday. During Advent, they can focus on its story setting and share Zechariah's excitement at the birth of his special son. But today it is a subtle introduction to Jesus. Zechariah's message that one job of God's king is to forgive people (vss. 76-69) must be restated in direct language for the children. It is an important point for them to understand. In many stories about kings, the king is the one who demands obedience and gets even with those who do not obey. God's king is different. God's king forgives.

Gospel: Luke 23:33-43. Children easily follow this concise story of the crucifixion. They enjoy exploring the truth that only a thief (the one we would least expect) understood what the leaders and soldiers missed: that the real King does not save himself, but suffers to save others. The thief saw Jesus forgiving, and he declared himself Jesus' loyal subject by asking for his forgiveness. To be the King is to forgive. To be the subject of the King is to be forgiven.

Epistle: Colossians 1:11-20. This passage is a description of Christ, the cosmic ruler. Verses 15-20 are a hymn rich in poetic images that are totally foreign to children. One approach is to suggest that they not try to understand, but feel the majesty of Christ in these fancy words. (If you do this, provide a majestic reading in which the poetic words and phrases are given their full dramatic impact.) A second approach is to encourage children to listen hard for short phrases they do understand. Most will recognize several of the short phrases describing Christ.

Verses 11-14 come *before* the poem in Colossians, but they may make more sense to children *after* they have heard and reflected on the poem. These verses focus attention not on Christ the King, but on us, Christ's subjects. It is a wish (or prayer) that we, who are fortunate to be the subjects of such a king, be given the power to serve our king well and faithfully.

Watch Words

Christ is another name for *Jesus*. Often we use *Jesus* when telling stories about Jesus' life on earth, and *Christ* when we talk about Christ as the Lord of the whole universe. (This might be a good time to clear up the common childhood misconception that Christ is Jesus' last name.)

Speak of Christ as *King* today, rather than as the *Messiah*.

Legitimate concerns are being raised by feminists and liberation theologians about using the language of *kingship* to describe Christ. These issues can be well explored with both adults and children. But to most children today, kings exist in imaginative stories. In these tales, kings are just as likely to be good and caring as they are to be autocratic and mean. Princes are even more likely to be good. Therefore, children enjoy the language and culture of kingship so much that it is worth occasionally speaking of *Christ the King*, his *rule* or *reign*, and his *power, glory,* and *majesty*. Call on people to obey as *loyal* subjects.

Let the Children Sing

Many great hymns praise Christ the King: "Rejoice, the Lord Is King," "When Morning Gilds the Skies," "From All That Dwell Below the Skies," and "Come, Christians, Join to Sing." These have repeated choruses or phrases that make them easy for nonreaders. "Let All the World in Every Corner Sing" is a less familiar hymn, but one with simple language for middle-elementary readers.

"The King of Love My Shepherd Is" (and most other shepherd hymns) may seem a natural choice for these texts. Children, however, get little farther than the first verse. The other verses are filled with abstract images and obsolete language.

Many people who know the spiritual "Do, Lord, Remember Me" do not realize that it quotes the repentant thief. Point this out before hearing it sung by a children's choir or singing it as a pledge to be subjects of King Jesus.

The Liturgical Child

1. Read the Colossian hymn (vss. 15-20) twice. First, read it from the translation of your choice. Invite worshipers to feel the richness of the big words that praise Christ the King. Then have a group of children read the following sentences, which put the praises into simple language. Each phrase is read by one child; three or more children may take turns.

When we see Christ, we are seeing God also.
Through Christ, God created everything in heaven and on earth.
Through Christ, God created everything visible and invisible.
Before anything else was created, Christ was here.

Christ holds all the world in his hands.
The church is Christ's Body, and Christ is the head of this Body.
Christ was the first to rise from the dead.
Christ is first in every way.
Christ was God, living among us as a person.
Through Christ, all of us can be God's friends.
Christ brought peace to the whole universe by his death on the cross.

2. The Lord's Prayer is a prayer of the loyal subjects of a loving king. Point out the "king" phrases: "Thy will be done on earth as it is in heaven" and "Thine is the kingdom and the power and the glory forever." To emphasize the relationship of God's kingship to each of the prayer requests, pray the prayer responsively or in unison, repeating "Thine is the kingdom, and the power, and the glory" after each phrase.

3. Paraphrase Colossians 1:11-14 for the Charge and Benediction:

Go forth with all the power of Christ the King to serve loyally and patiently wherever you are. Give thanks to God, who has called you to be among the King's people, has sent Christ to save you, and has forgiven you. And remember, Christ the King will be with you forever. You have his promise. Amen.

Sermon Resources

1. Christ the King Sunday is also the last day of the liturgical year. To celebrate Christ and review the year, drape the pulpit with a rainbow of paraments. Refer to each color as you use the seasons as an outline for exploring the Kingship of Christ.

2. Display two crowns on the pulpit or in the worship center—one a kingly crown (perhaps a wise man's crown can be found among the Christmas pageant costumes); the other, a crown of thorns. Compare the kings who would wear each crown. Then describe what would be required of followers of the king who wears a crown of thorns.

Find additional resources for celebrating the kingship of Christ in Proper 29 of Years A and B.

Create a poem about the kind of king Christ is. Listen
to our songs and prayers for words to use in your poem.

Christ, the King

2 words that
describe Christ ———————————   ———————————

2 "ing" words
that describe Christ ———————————   ———————————

Christ, my King

Use the decoder key to find a good prayer to pray on
Christ the King Sunday.

A	B	C		J	K	L		S	T	U
D	E	F		M	N	O		V	W	X
G	H	I		P	Q	R		Y	Z	

THANKSGIVING

From a Child's Point of View

Old Testament: Deuteronomy 26:1-11. This passage describes the liturgy for offering the first fruits. Thanks is offered both for the harvest and for God's action during the Exodus and in the conquering of the Promised Land. Because of its structure and its assumption of extensive knowledge of the Exodus saga, it is a hard passage for children to follow.

On Thanksgiving, this text calls worshipers of all ages to identify God's gifts to them and God's action in their world. Most church children know that they are to be thankful for their food. But we cannot assume that nonagricultural children, for whom food is constantly available in supermarkets at an affordable price, will genuinely see food as a gift, rather than as an expected part of life. They benefit from hearing stories of food production described in terms of God's activity.

Verses 5-11 describe with gratitude God's activity in the life of the Jewish nation. Worshipers are called to identify with gratitude God's activity in the life of the church today. (Remember that the church, not a nation, is today's equivalent of the Jewish nation in this passage. This is not a call to credit God for national successes.)

Psalm: 100. This psalm, with its short praises, is one children can appreciate easily. They do need to be told before the reading that this is a song for God's people, the church, and that the phrase "enter his gates with thanksgiving and his courts with praise" is an invitation to come to the Temple/sanctuary to worship God with others.

Epistle: Philippians 4:4-9. In this letter, Paul encourages us to develop a happy, thankful attitude. Paul states that one key to this attitude is to avoid being overly concerned about what is going on at the moment. That is a hard lesson, which most of us learn only after years of experience. Children, who live so much in the present, have trouble keeping the moment in perspective. So the value of this message is in introducing a truth with which children will struggle for years.

Verses 8 and 9 contain more directions for a happy life. Paul says that the kinds of activities and interests with which we fill our lives determine our happiness. Children need to hear that the activities they choose will determine how happy they are. Paul's list is abstract. Children need to paraphrase it with examples of activities that lead to happiness.

Gospel: John 6:25-35. This passage requires symbolic thinking that is beyond children's mental maturity. So John's discussion of the bread of heaven will mean little to them. But they can grasp John's point that, as important as food is, God's gift of Jesus is even more important. Food can keep us physically alive, but without God's love and forgiveness, that life is not too great. This point will need to be presented and discussed by the preacher.

Watch Words

Vocabulary presents few problems on Thanksgiving, *unless* worship leaders wax abstract and poetic to explore these fairly concrete themes.

Let the Children Sing

"Now Thank We All Our God" and "For the Beauty of the Earth" are probably the best Thanksgiving hymns for children.

"Come, Ye Thankful People, Come" and "We Gather Together to Ask the Lord's Blessing" are standard Thanksgiving fare. Unfortunately, they are filled with obsolete language. Schoolteachers used to help children dig out the messages behind the words. That happens less and less today. So either be sure church school teachers or choir directors are working with the children on these hymns, or select other more understandable hymns for children.

"All People That on Earth Do Dwell" is challenging reading for children. But with adult direction, older children appreciate its base in Psalm 100.

"We Plow the Fields and Scatter," while less familiar, is filled with simple food images for harvest worship.

The Liturgical Child

1. If you focus on God's gift of food, plan for a cornucopia instead of flowers in the worship center. Also consider banking around the worship center the food staples that have been collected for distribution in your community. The sight of Communion elements surrounded by food is powerful for worshipers of all ages.

2. See the First Sunday of Lent for an idea about presenting the Deuteronomy passage dramatically.

3. Read or sing Psalm 100 as a litany. Choose a responsive version of the psalm from your hymnal. Read responsively between either pastor and people, or two halves of the congregation. Provide leaders who will maintain the upbeat tone and pace of the praises. Or invite the congregation to sing "Rejoice, give thanks and sing" (the chorus of "Rejoice, Ye Pure in Heart") after the worship leader reads each phrase of the psalm.

4. "Give us this day our daily bread" can be the congregational Response to a litany about food:

> We praise you, God, for all the foods you have spread before us. We thank you for (name foods that are favorites in your community). (RESPONSE)

We praise you, God, for seeds that take food from the soil and water from the rain, to grow into corn and apple trees and lettuce. We thank you for the growing seasons, the spring rains, followed by summer sun and fall harvests. (RESPONSE)

We ask you to watch over farmers who plant and care for crops, and scientists who work to improve our crops. Teach us to work within your plan to produce food for the whole world. (RESPONSE)

Lord, guide and direct those who haul food from farms to hungry people, those who operate grocery stores, and political leaders who decide how much food goes to which people. Help them to be fair. (RESPONSE)

And last, God, we pray for people who are hungry. Whether they are hungry because of famines or floods or wars or poverty or unfair governments, be with them. Support them, and help us find ways to share our food with them. (RESPONSE)

We pray in Jesus' name. Amen.

Sermon Resources

1. Tell the story of the food supplied for a traditional Thanksgiving dinner, highlighting God's role in each phase of production and distribution.

2. Describe a variety of mealtime blessings. Point out some prayed by children. Describe family mealtime-blessing practices and silent blessings for meals at work and at school. Encourage families to try a mealtime blessing, if they do not use one, or to experiment with some new possibilities, if they already have blessing customs.

3. To explore Paul's message in Philippians, tell stories from your past about things that seemed dreadfully important, and over which you worried and made yourself miserable, but which turned out to be not so important (e.g., winning a championship, or receiving a certain gift on your birthday).

There is no Worship Worksheet for this service. Events of the service should hold the attention of children.

SCRIPTURE INDEX
for A, B, C

This index is provided especially for those who do not use the lectionary every week. It includes all texts explored in this series on all three years of the cycle. The letter following each page number indicates the year/volume in which that text is found. The page number is that on which the commentary on the text is found. Liturgical and sermon ideas appear on the pages immediately following.

TABLE OF LITURGICAL DATES

Year C, 1994–1995

Nov. 27	1st Sunday of Advent
Dec. 4	2nd Sunday of Advent
Dec. 11	3rd Sunday of Advent
Dec. 18	4th Sunday of Advent
Dec. 24/25	Christmas Eve/Day
Jan. 1	New Year's Eve/Day
	1st Sunday After Christmas
Jan. 6	Epiphany

(Note: January 1 may be observed as Epiphany Sunday.)

Jan. 8	Baptism of the Lord
Jan. 15	2nd Sunday After the Epiphany
Jan. 22	3rd Sunday After the Epiphany
Jan. 29	4th Sunday After the Epiphany
Feb. 5	5th Sunday After the Epiphany
Feb. 12	6th Sunday After the Epiphany
Feb. 19	7th Sunday After the Epiphany
Feb. 26	Transfiguration
March 1	Ash Wednesday
March 5	1st Sunday in Lent
March 12	2nd Sunday in Lent
March 19	3rd Sunday in Lent
March 26	4th Sunday in Lent
April 2	5th Sunday in Lent
April 9	Passion/Palm Sunday
April 13	Holy Thursday
April 14	Good Friday
April 16	Easter
April 23	2nd Sunday of Easter
April 30	3rd Sunday of Easter
May 7	4th Sunday of Easter
May 14	5th Sunday of Easter
May 21	6th Sunday of Easter
May 25	Ascension Day

(Note: May 28 may be observed as Ascension Sunday.)

May 28	7th Sunday of Easter
June 4	Day of Pentecost
June 11	Trinity Sunday
June 18	Proper 6
June 25	Proper 7
July 2	Proper 8
July 9	Proper 9
July 16	Proper 10
July 23	Proper 11
July 30	Proper 12
Aug. 6	Proper 13
Aug. 13	Proper 14
Aug. 20	Proper 15
Aug. 27	Proper 16
Sept. 3	Proper 17
Sept. 10	Proper 18
Sept. 17	Proper 19
Sept. 24	Proper 20
Oct. 1	Proper 21
Oct. 8	Proper 22
Oct. 15	Proper 23
Oct. 22	Proper 24
Oct. 29	Proper 25
Nov. 1	All Saints

(Note: November 5 may be observed as All Saints Sunday.)

Nov. 5	Proper 26
Nov. 12	Proper 27
Nov. 19	Proper 28
Nov. 23	Thanksgiving
Nov. 26	Christ the King/Proper 29

Year A, 1995–1996

Dec. 3	1st Sunday of Advent	May 19	7th Sunday of Easter
Dec. 10	2nd Sunday of Advent	May 26	Day of Pentecost
Dec. 17	3rd Sunday of Advent	June 2	Trinity Sunday
Dec. 24	4th Sunday of Advent	June 9	Proper 5
Dec. 24/25	Christmas Eve/Day	June 16	Proper 6
Dec. 31	1st Sunday After Christmas	June 23	Proper 7
Jan. 1	New Year's Eve/Day	June 30	Proper 8
Jan. 6	Epiphany	July 7	Proper 9
Jan. 7	Baptism of the Lord	July 14	Proper 10
Jan. 14	2nd Sunday After the Epiphany	July 21	Proper 11
Jan. 21	3rd Sunday After the Epiphany	July 28	Proper 12
Jan. 28	4th Sunday After the Epiphany	Aug. 4	Proper 13
Feb. 4	5th Sunday After the Epiphany	Aug. 11	Proper 14
Feb. 11	6th Sunday After the Epiphany	Aug. 18	Proper 15
Feb. 18	Transfiguration	Aug. 25	Proper 16
Feb. 21	Ash Wednesday	Sept. 1	Proper 17
Feb. 25	1st Sunday in Lent	Sept. 8	Proper 18
March 3	2nd Sunday in Lent	Sept. 15	Proper 19
March 10	3rd Sunday in Lent	Sept. 22	Proper 20
March 17	4th Sunday in Lent	Sept. 29	Proper 21
March 24	5th Sunday in Lent	Oct. 6	Proper 22
March 31	Passion/Palm Sunday	Oct. 13	Proper 23
April 4	Holy Thursday	Oct. 20	Proper 24
April 5	Good Friday	Oct. 27	Proper 25
April 7	Easter	Nov. 1	All Saints
April 14	2nd Sunday of Easter	*(Note: November 3 may be observed as*	
April 21	3rd Sunday of Easter	*All Saints Sunday.)*	
April 28	4th Sunday of Easter	Nov. 3	Proper 26
May 5	5th Sunday of Easter	Nov. 10	Proper 27
May 12	6th Sunday of Easter	Nov. 17	Proper 28
May 16	Ascension Day	Nov. 24	Christ the King/ Proper 29
(Note: May 19 may be observed as Ascension Sunday.)		Nov. 28	Thanksgiving

Year B, 1996–1997

Dec. 1	1st Sunday of Advent	May 18	Day of Pentecost
Dec. 8	2nd Sunday of Advent	May 25	Trinity Sunday
Dec. 15	3rd Sunday of Advent	June 1	Proper 4
Dec. 22	4th Sunday of Advent	June 8	Proper 5
Dec. 24/25	Christmas Eve/Day	June 15	Proper 6
Dec. 29	1st Sunday After Christmas	June 22	Proper 7
Jan. 1	New Year's Eve/Day	June 29	Proper 8
Jan. 5	2nd Sunday After Christmas	July 6	Proper 9
Jan. 6	Epiphany	July 13	Proper 10
(Note: January 5 may be observed as		July 20	Proper 11
Epiphany Sunday.)		July 27	Proper 12
Jan. 12	Baptism of the Lord	Aug. 3	Proper 13
Jan. 19	2nd Sunday After the Epiphany	Aug. 10	Proper 14
Jan. 26	3rd Sunday After the Epiphany	Aug. 17	Proper 15
Feb. 2	4th Sunday After the Epiphany	Aug. 24	Proper 16
Feb. 9	Transfiguration	Aug. 31	Proper 17
Feb. 12	Ash Wednesday	Sept. 7	Proper 18
Feb. 16	1st Sunday in Lent	Sept. 14	Proper 19
Feb. 23	2nd Sunday in Lent	Sept. 21	Proper 20
Mar. 2	3rd Sunday in Lent	Sept. 28	Proper 21
Mar. 9	4th Sunday in Lent	Oct. 5	Proper 22
Mar. 16	5th Sunday in Lent	Oct. 12	Proper 23
Mar. 23	Passion/Palm Sunday	Oct. 19	Proper 24
Mar. 30	Easter	Oct. 26	Proper 25
April 6	2nd Sunday of Easter	Nov. 1	All Saints
April 13	3rd Sunday of Easter	(Note: November 2 may be observed as	
April 20	4th Sunday of Easter	All Saints Sunday.)	
April 27	5th Sunday of Easter	Nov. 2	Proper 26
May 4	6th Sunday of Easter	Nov. 9	Proper 27
May 8	Ascension Day	Nov. 16	Proper 28
(Note: May 4 may be observed as		Nov. 23	Christ the King/ Proper 29
Ascension Sunday.)		Nov. 27	Thanksgiving
May 11	7th Sunday of Easter		